Garfield weighs in

BY JIM DAVIS

Ballantine Books • New York

A Ballantine Book
Published by The Ballantine Publishing Group
Copyright © 1982, 2002 by PAWS, Inc. All Rights Reserved.

All rights reserved under International and Pan-American Copyright Conventions. Published in the United States by The Ballantine Publishing Group, a division of Random House, Inc., New York, and simultaneously in Canada by Random House of Canada Limited, Toronto. Originally published in slightly different form by The Ballantine Publishing Group, a division of Random House, Inc., in 1982.

Ballantine is a registered trademark and the Ballantine colophon is a trademark of Random House, Inc.

"GARFIELD" and the GARFIELD characters are registered and unregistered trademarks of PAWS, Inc.

www.ballantinebooks.com

Library of Congress Catalog Card Number: 2001127156

ISBN 0-345-45205-4

Manufactured in the United States of America

First Colorized Edition: July 2002

10 9 8 7 6 5 4 3 2 1

A GARFIELD MORNING

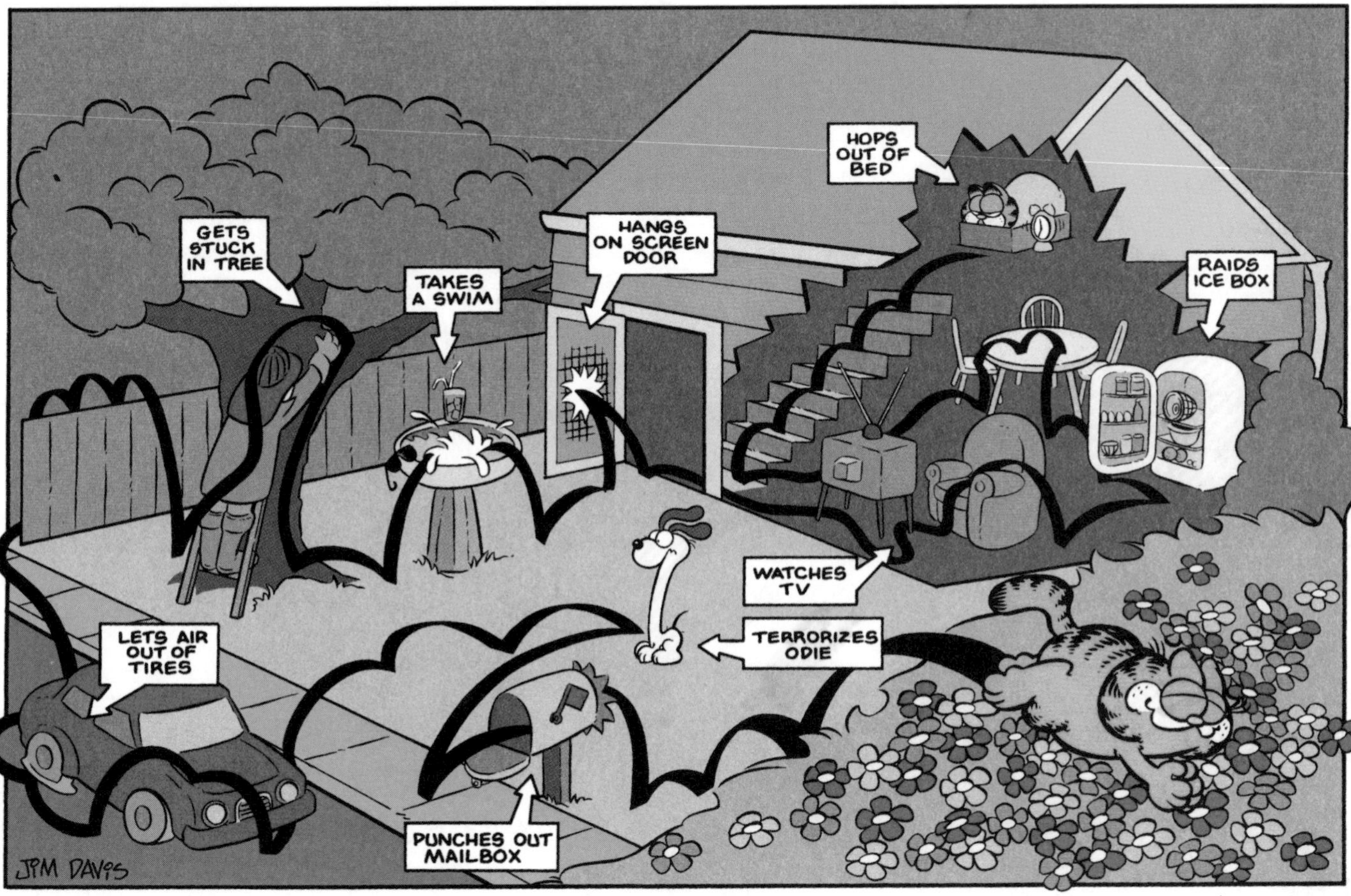
HOPS OUT OF BED
GETS STUCK IN TREE
HANGS ON SCREEN DOOR
TAKES A SWIM
RAIDS ICE BOX
WATCHES TV
TERRORIZES ODIE
LETS AIR OUT OF TIRES
PUNCHES OUT MAILBOX
JIM DAVIS

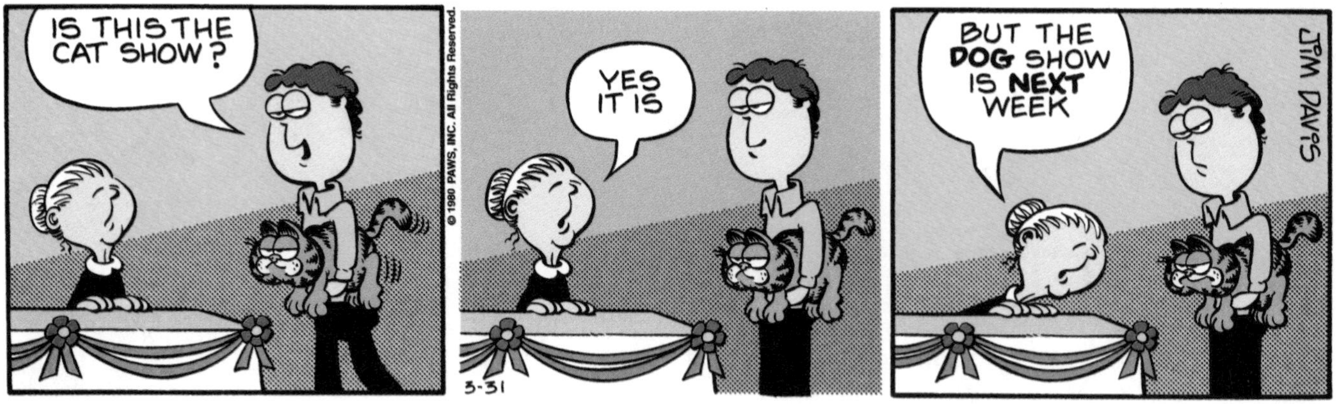
IS THIS THE CAT SHOW?
YES IT IS
BUT THE **DOG** SHOW IS **NEXT** WEEK
JIM DAVIS
3-31
© 1980 PAWS, INC. All Rights Reserved.

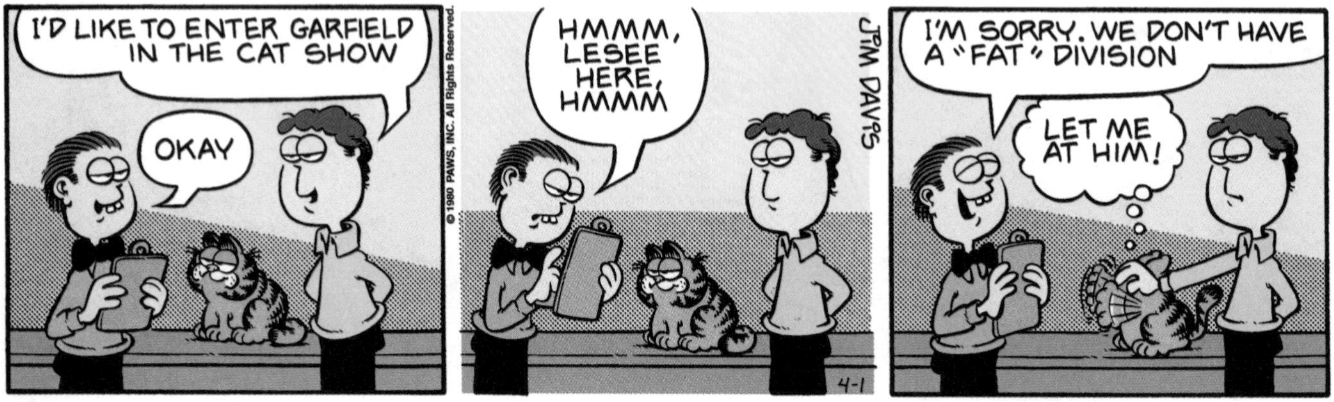
I'D LIKE TO ENTER GARFIELD IN THE CAT SHOW
OKAY
HMMM, LESEE HERE, HMMM
I'M SORRY. WE DON'T HAVE A "FAT" DIVISION
LET ME AT HIM!
JIM DAVIS
4-1
© 1980 PAWS, INC. All Rights Reserved.

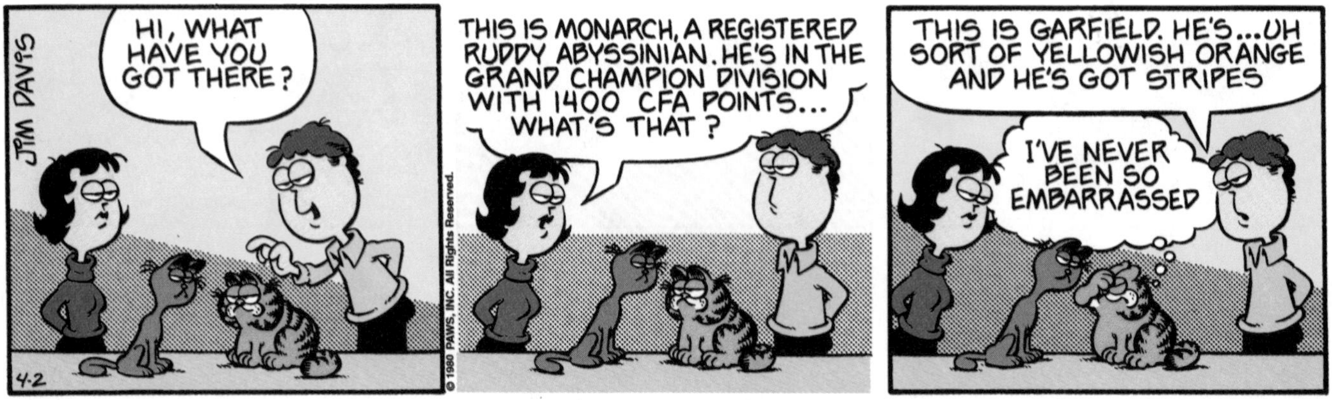
HI, WHAT HAVE YOU GOT THERE?
THIS IS MONARCH, A REGISTERED RUDDY ABYSSINIAN. HE'S IN THE GRAND CHAMPION DIVISION WITH 1400 CFA POINTS... WHAT'S THAT?
THIS IS GARFIELD. HE'S...UH SORT OF YELLOWISH ORANGE AND HE'S GOT STRIPES
I'VE NEVER BEEN SO EMBARRASSED
JIM DAVIS
4-2
© 1980 PAWS, INC. All Rights Reserved.

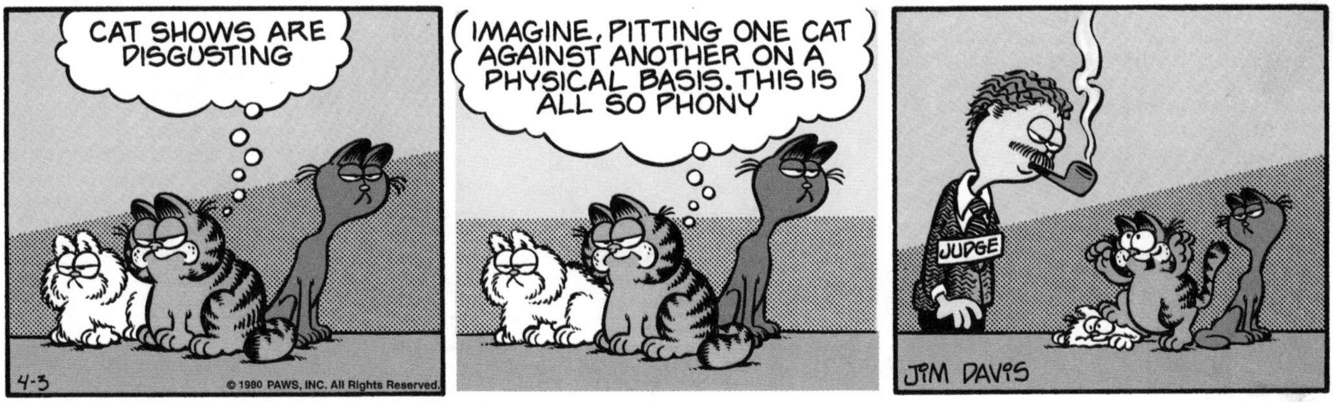
CAT SHOWS ARE DISGUSTING
IMAGINE, PITTING ONE CAT AGAINST ANOTHER ON A PHYSICAL BASIS. THIS IS ALL SO PHONY
JUDGE
4-3
© 1980 PAWS, INC. All Rights Reserved.
JIM DAVIS

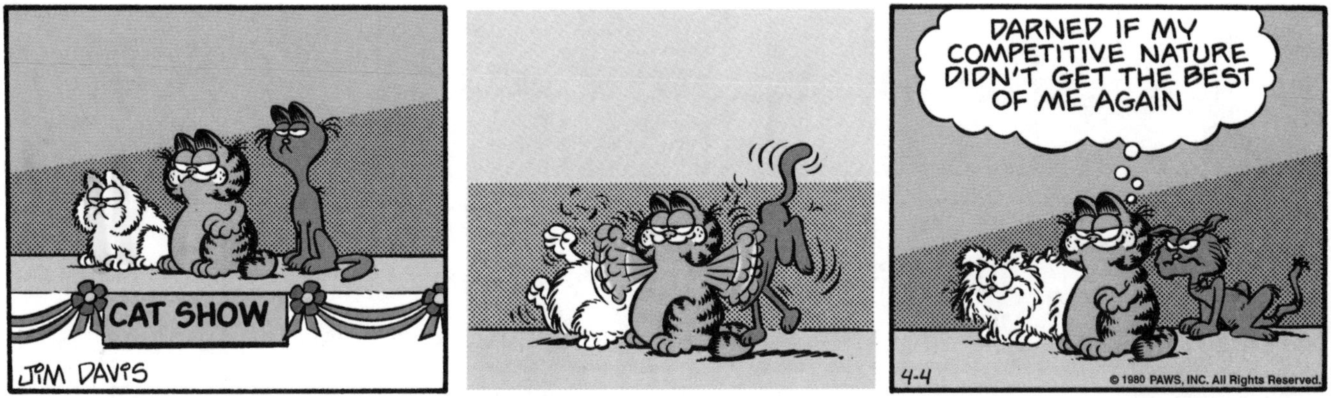
CAT SHOW
JIM DAVIS
DARNED IF MY COMPETITIVE NATURE DIDN'T GET THE BEST OF ME AGAIN
4-4
© 1980 PAWS, INC. All Rights Reserved.

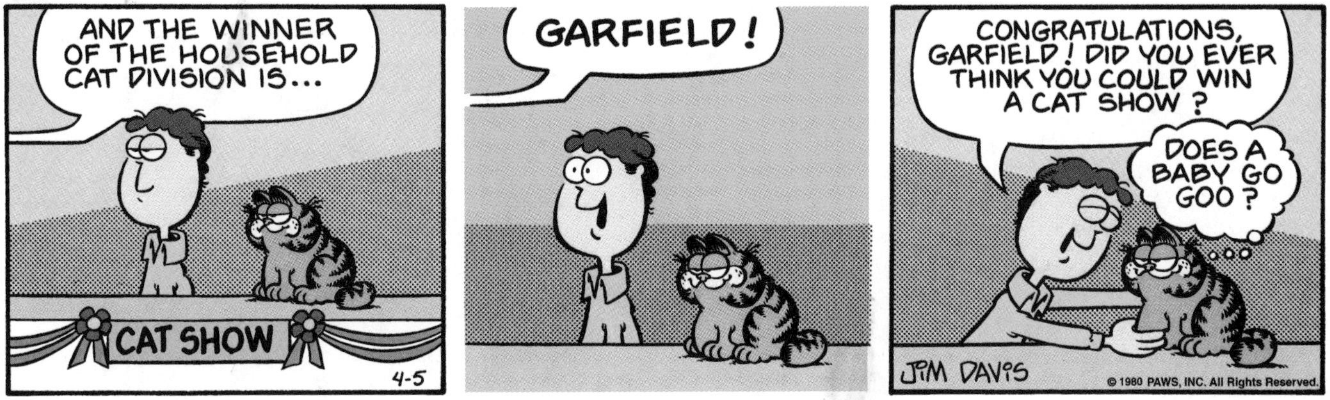
AND THE WINNER OF THE HOUSEHOLD CAT DIVISION IS...
CAT SHOW
4-5
GARFIELD!
CONGRATULATIONS, GARFIELD! DID YOU EVER THINK YOU COULD WIN A CAT SHOW?
DOES A BABY GO GOO?
JIM DAVIS
© 1980 PAWS, INC. All Rights Reserved.

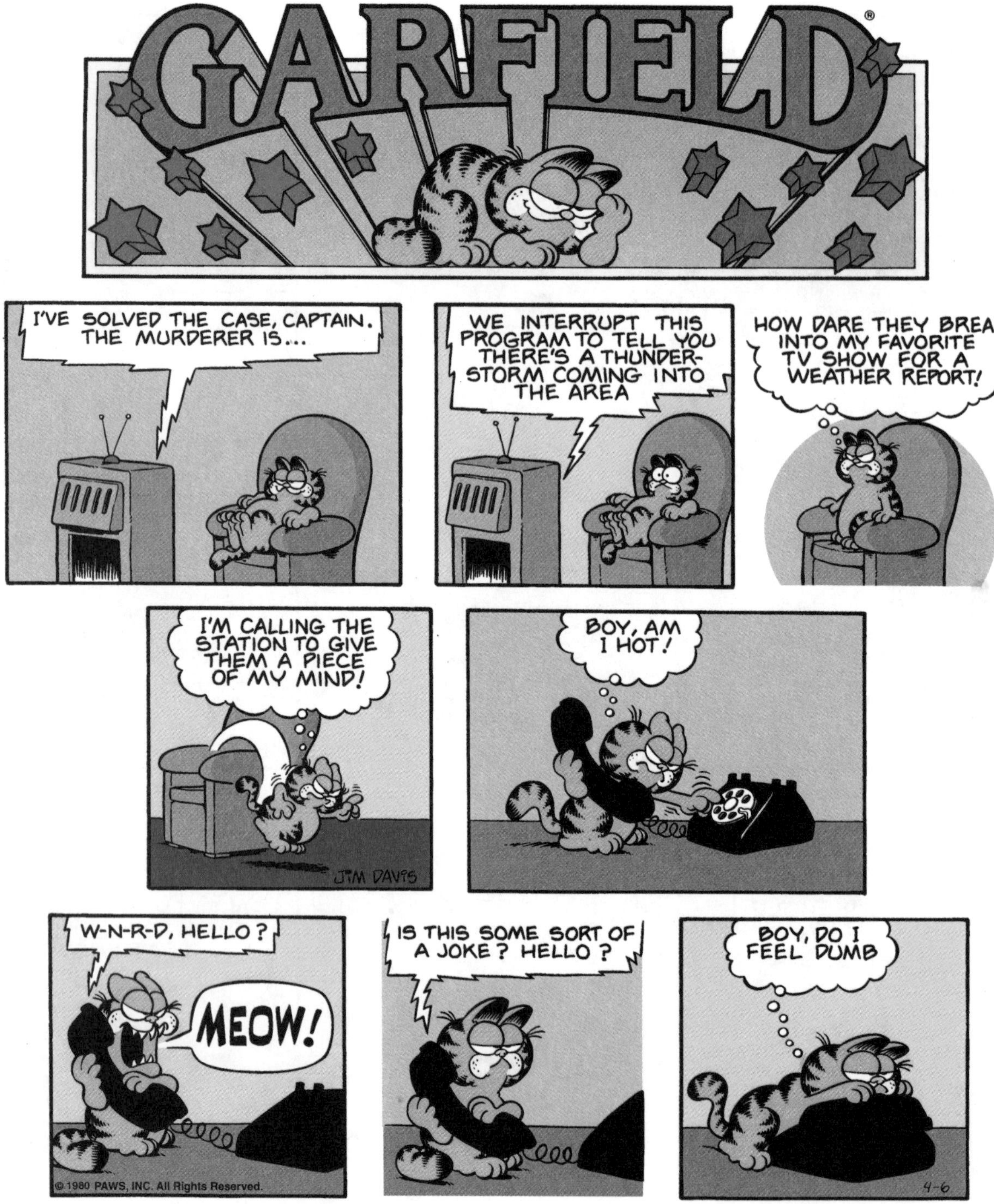
GARFIELD®
I'VE SOLVED THE CASE, CAPTAIN. THE MURDERER IS...
WE INTERRUPT THIS PROGRAM TO TELL YOU THERE'S A THUNDER-STORM COMING INTO THE AREA
HOW DARE THEY BREAK INTO MY FAVORITE TV SHOW FOR A WEATHER REPORT!
I'M CALLING THE STATION TO GIVE THEM A PIECE OF MY MIND!
JIM DAVIS
BOY, AM I HOT!
W-N-R-D, HELLO?
MEOW!
© 1980 PAWS, INC. All Rights Reserved.
IS THIS SOME SORT OF A JOKE? HELLO?
BOY, DO I FEEL DUMB
4-6

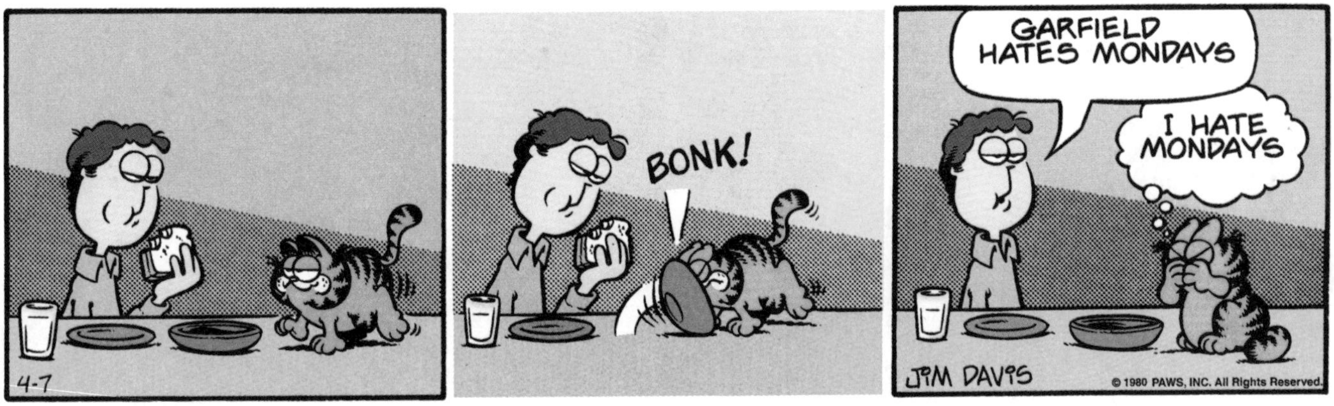
4-7
BONK!
GARFIELD HATES MONDAYS
I HATE MONDAYS
JIM DAVIS
© 1980 PAWS, INC. All Rights Reserved.

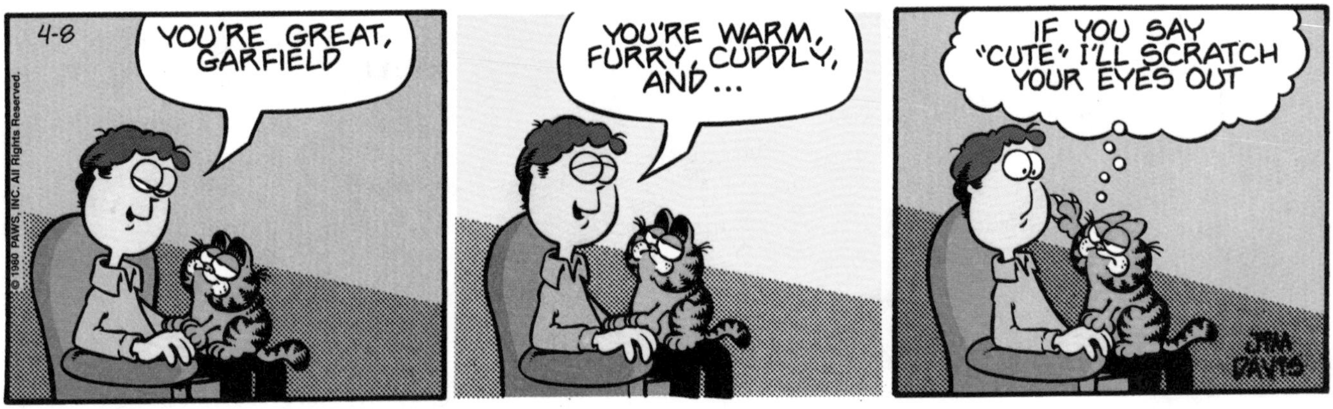
4-8
© 1980 PAWS, INC. All Rights Reserved.
YOU'RE GREAT, GARFIELD
YOU'RE WARM, FURRY, CUDDLY, AND...
IF YOU SAY "CUTE" I'LL SCRATCH YOUR EYES OUT
JIM DAVIS

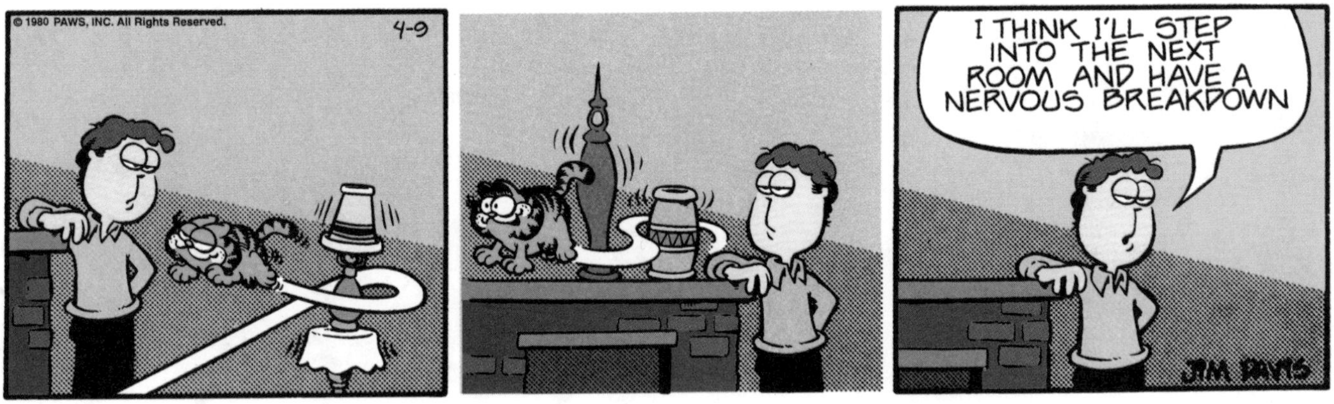
© 1980 PAWS, INC. All Rights Reserved.
4-9
I THINK I'LL STEP INTO THE NEXT ROOM AND HAVE A NERVOUS BREAKDOWN
JIM DAVIS

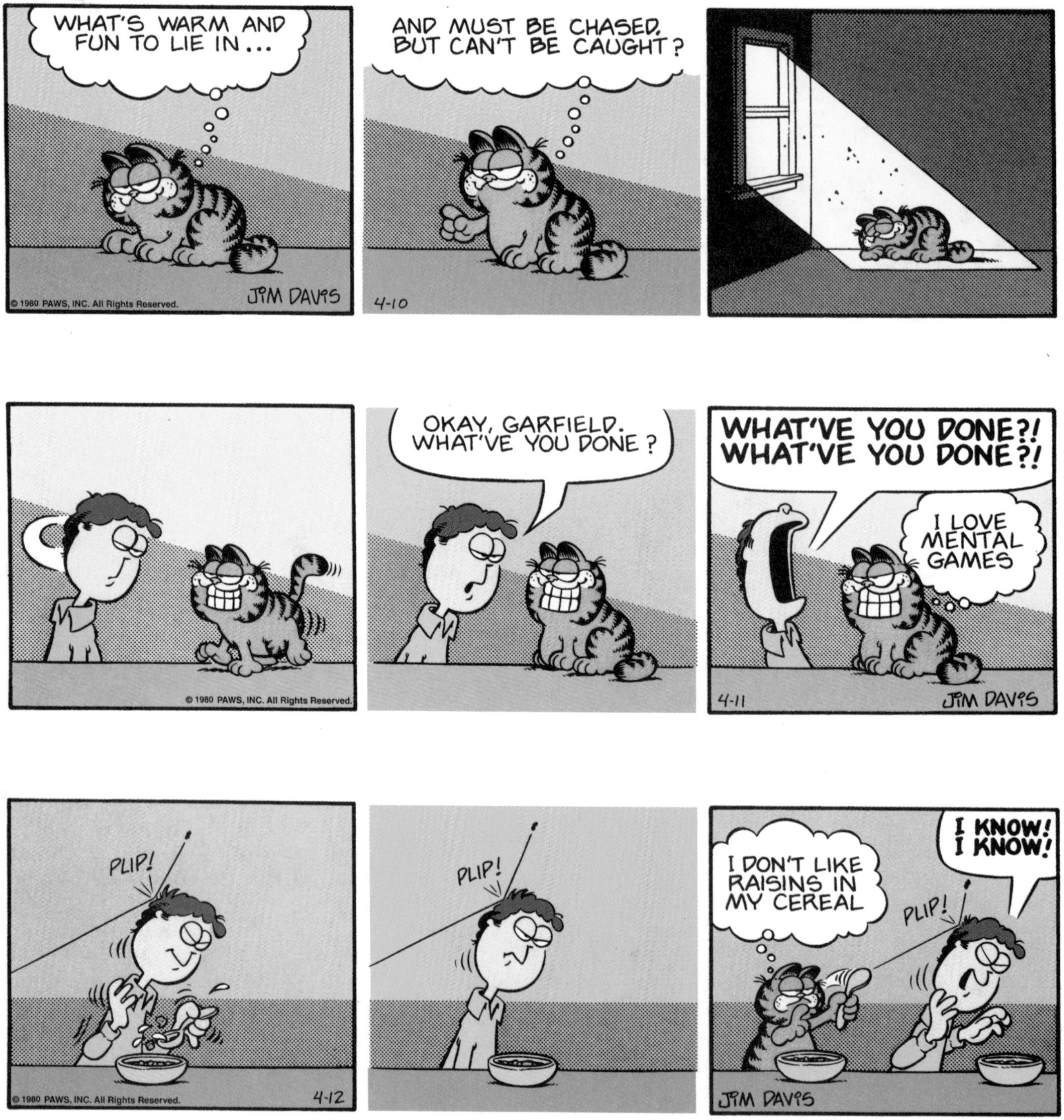
WHAT'S WARM AND FUN TO LIE IN...
© 1980 PAWS, INC. All Rights Reserved.
JIM DAVIS
AND MUST BE CHASED, BUT CAN'T BE CAUGHT?
4-10
© 1980 PAWS, INC. All Rights Reserved.
OKAY, GARFIELD. WHAT'VE YOU DONE?
WHAT'VE YOU DONE?! WHAT'VE YOU DONE?!
I LOVE MENTAL GAMES
4-11
JIM DAVIS
PLIP!
© 1980 PAWS, INC. All Rights Reserved.
4-12
PLIP!
I DON'T LIKE RAISINS IN MY CEREAL
PLIP!
I KNOW! I KNOW!
JIM DAVIS

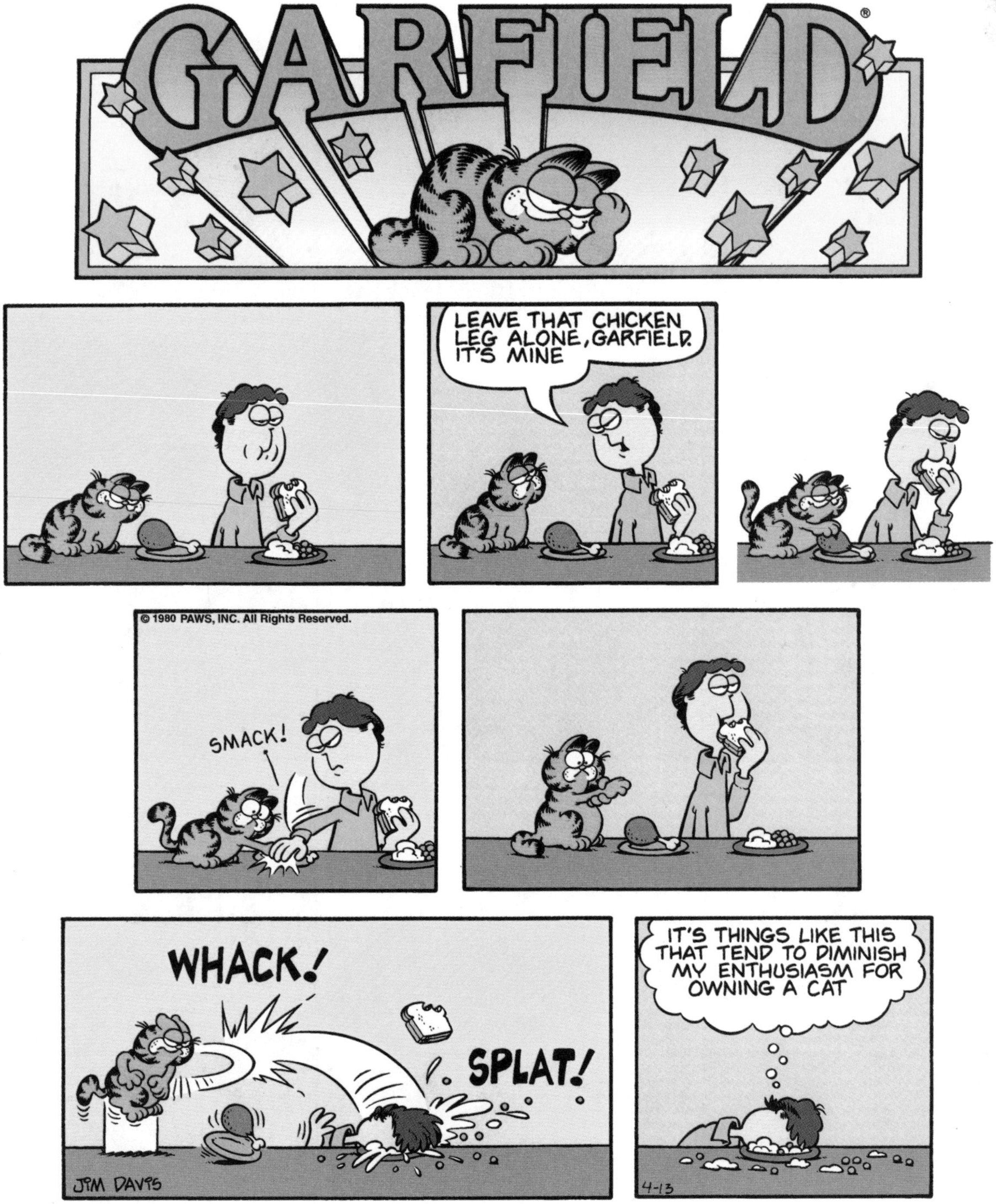
GARFIELD®
LEAVE THAT CHICKEN LEG ALONE, GARFIELD. IT'S MINE
© 1980 PAWS, INC. All Rights Reserved.
SMACK!
WHACK!
SPLAT!
JIM DAVIS
4-13
IT'S THINGS LIKE THIS THAT TEND TO DIMINISH MY ENTHUSIASM FOR OWNING A CAT

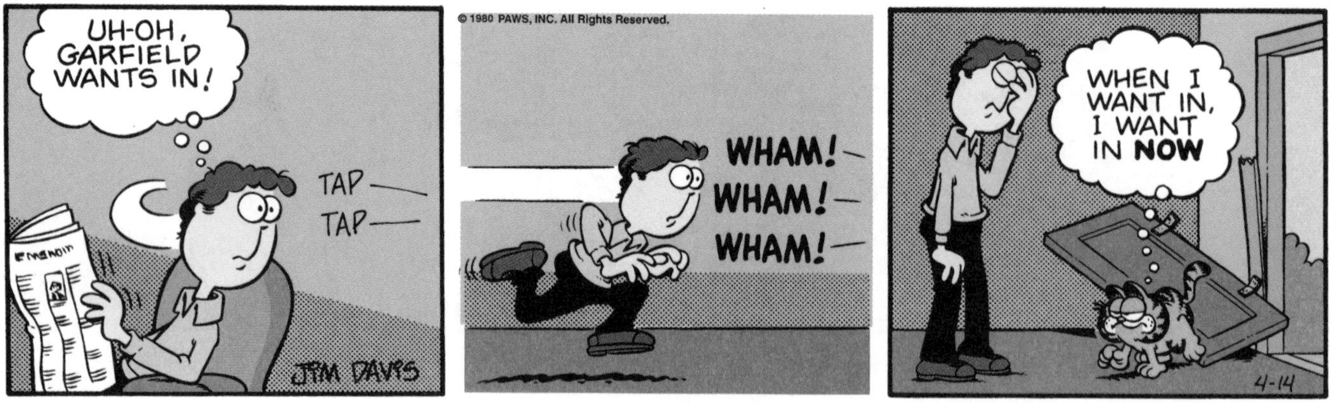
UH-OH, GARFIELD WANTS IN!
TAP
TAP
JIM DAVIS
© 1980 PAWS, INC. All Rights Reserved.
WHAM!
WHAM!
WHAM!
WHEN I WANT IN, I WANT IN **NOW**
4-14

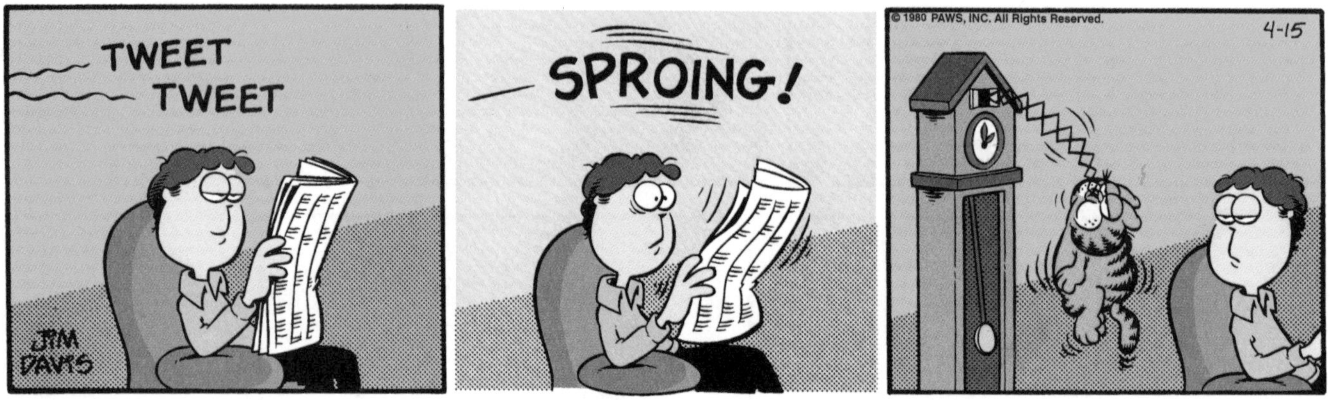
TWEET
TWEET
JIM DAVIS
SPROING!
© 1980 PAWS, INC. All Rights Reserved.
4-15

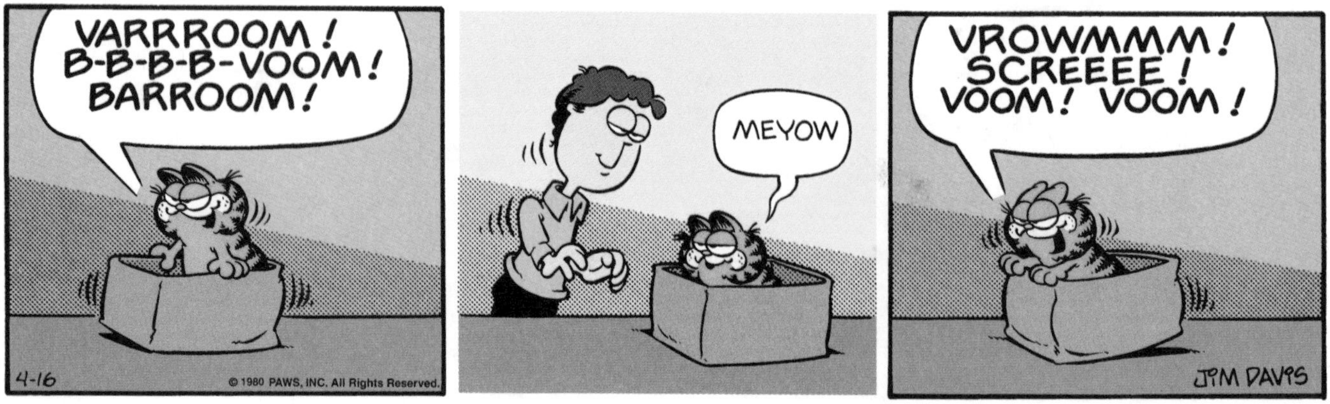
VARRROOM! B-B-B-B-VOOM! BARROOM!
4-16
© 1980 PAWS, INC. All Rights Reserved.
MEYOW
VROWMMM! SCREEEE! VOOM! VOOM!
JIM DAVIS

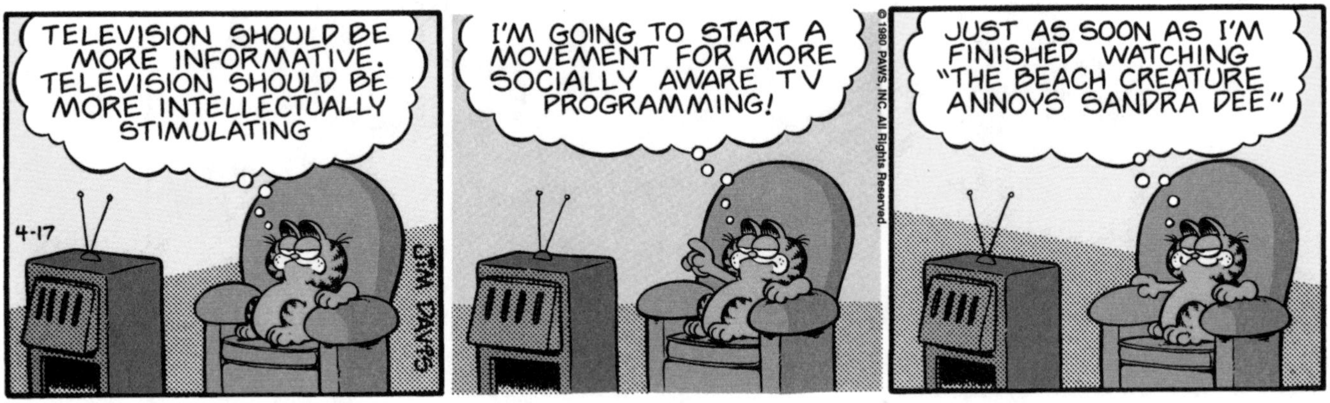
TELEVISION SHOULD BE MORE INFORMATIVE. TELEVISION SHOULD BE MORE INTELLECTUALLY STIMULATING
4-17
JIM DAVIS
I'M GOING TO START A MOVEMENT FOR MORE SOCIALLY AWARE TV PROGRAMMING!
© 1980 PAWS, INC. All Rights Reserved.
JUST AS SOON AS I'M FINISHED WATCHING "THE BEACH CREATURE ANNOYS SANDRA DEE"

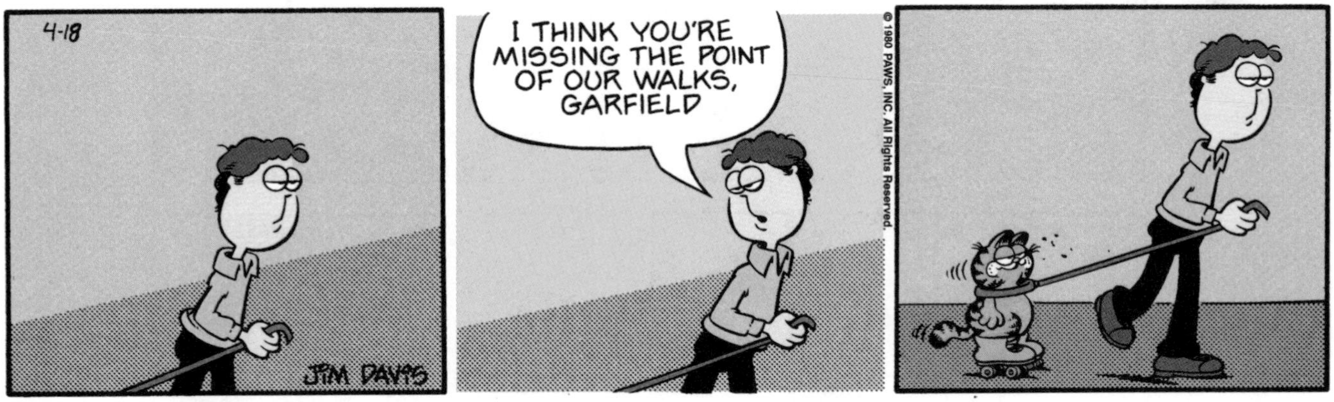
4-18
JIM DAVIS
I THINK YOU'RE MISSING THE POINT OF OUR WALKS, GARFIELD
© 1980 PAWS, INC. All Rights Reserved.

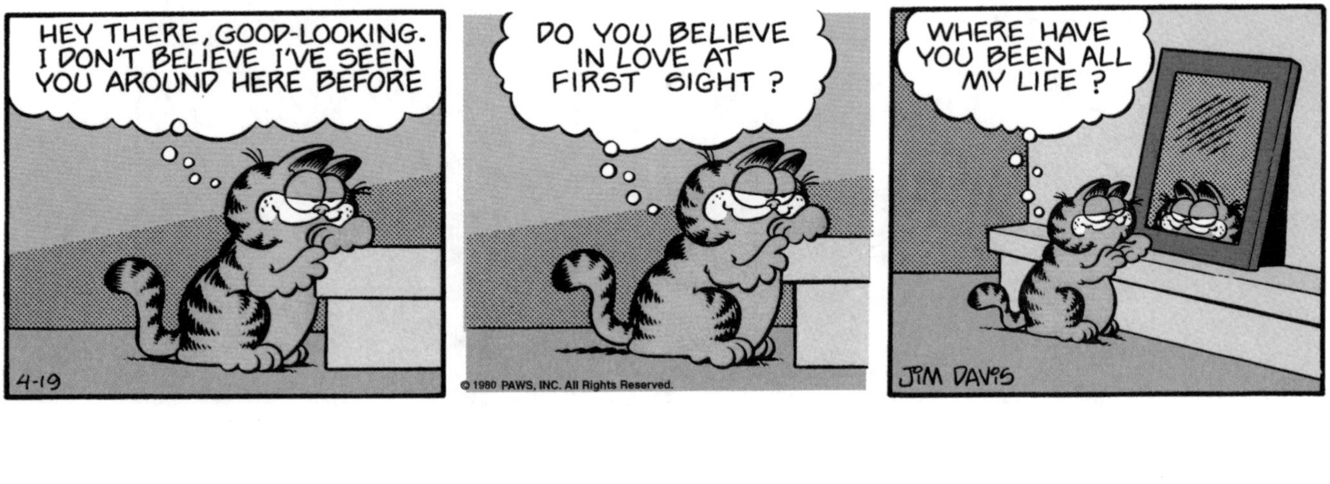
HEY THERE, GOOD-LOOKING. I DON'T BELIEVE I'VE SEEN YOU AROUND HERE BEFORE
4-19
DO YOU BELIEVE IN LOVE AT FIRST SIGHT ?
© 1980 PAWS, INC. All Rights Reserved.
WHERE HAVE YOU BEEN ALL MY LIFE ?
JIM DAVIS

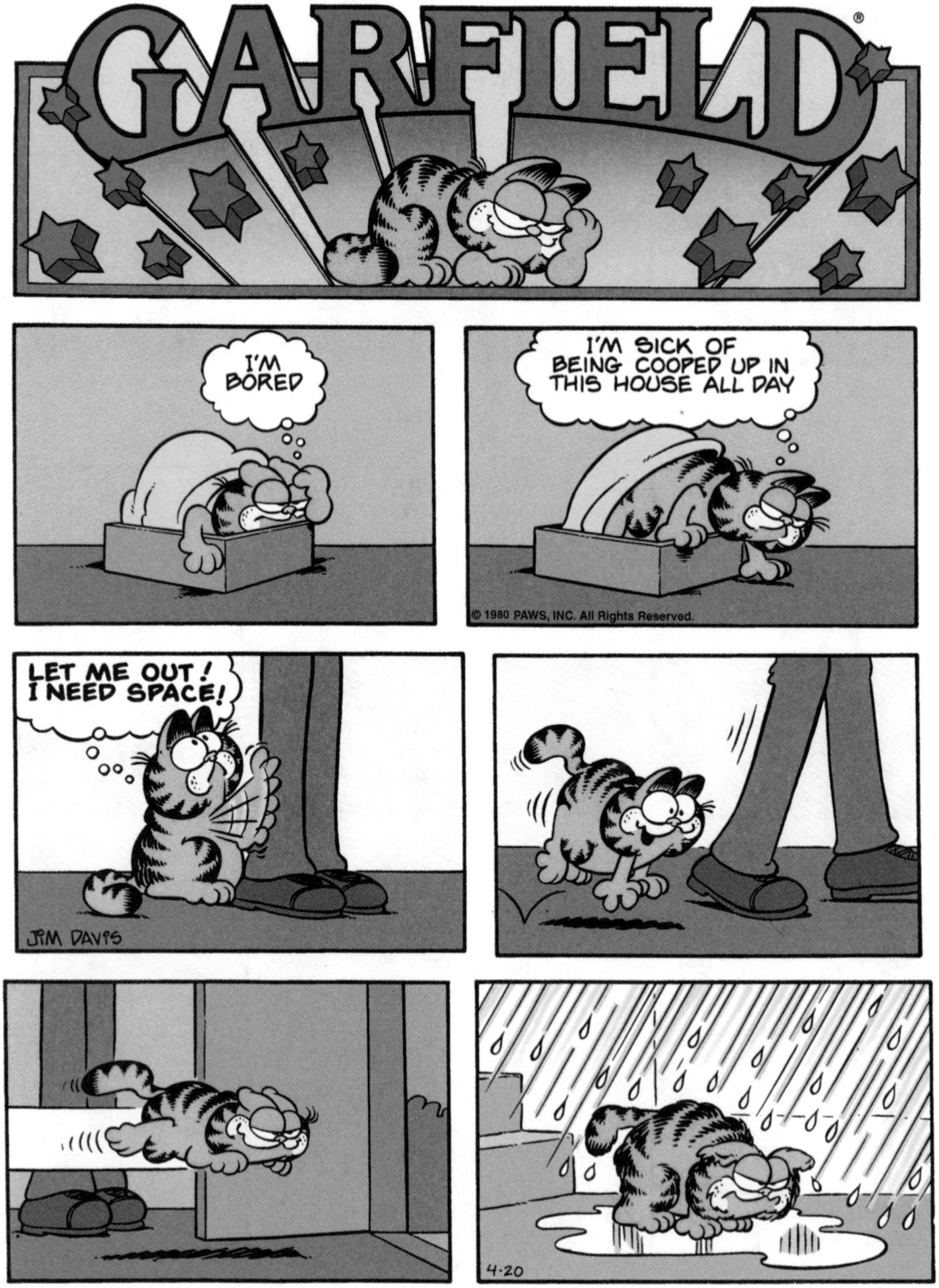
GARFIELD®
I'M BORED
I'M SICK OF BEING COOPED UP IN THIS HOUSE ALL DAY
© 1980 PAWS, INC. All Rights Reserved.
LET ME OUT! I NEED SPACE!
JIM DAVIS
4-20

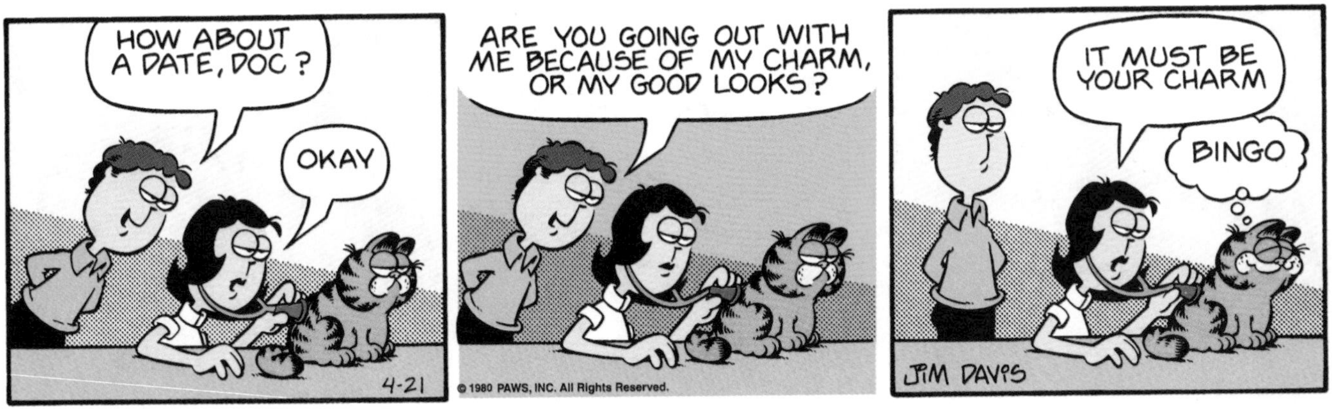
HOW ABOUT A DATE, DOC ?
OKAY
4-21
ARE YOU GOING OUT WITH ME BECAUSE OF MY CHARM, OR MY GOOD LOOKS ?
© 1980 PAWS, INC. All Rights Reserved.
IT MUST BE YOUR CHARM
BINGO
JIM DAVIS

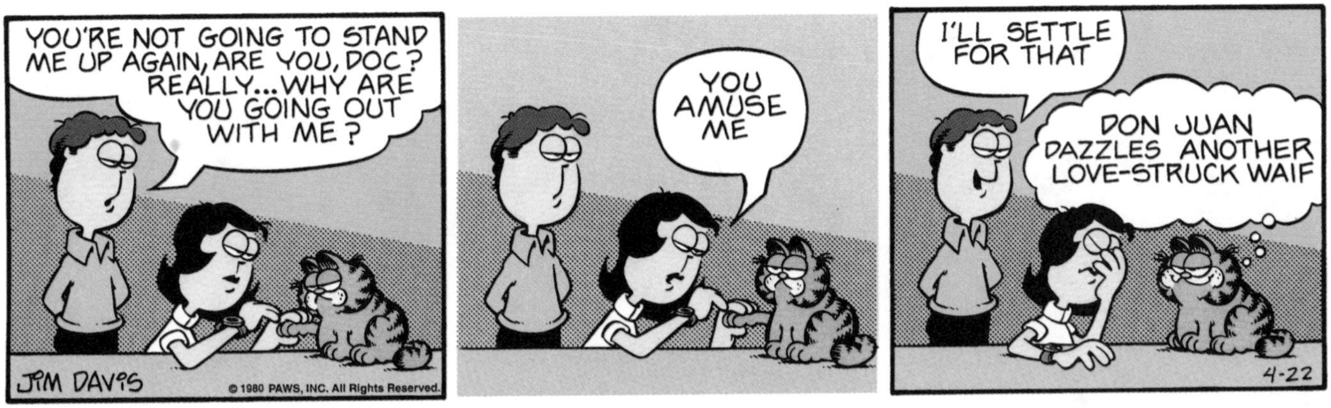
YOU'RE NOT GOING TO STAND ME UP AGAIN, ARE YOU, DOC ? REALLY...WHY ARE YOU GOING OUT WITH ME ?
JIM DAVIS
© 1980 PAWS, INC. All Rights Reserved.
YOU AMUSE ME
I'LL SETTLE FOR THAT
DON JUAN DAZZLES ANOTHER LOVE-STRUCK WAIF
4-22

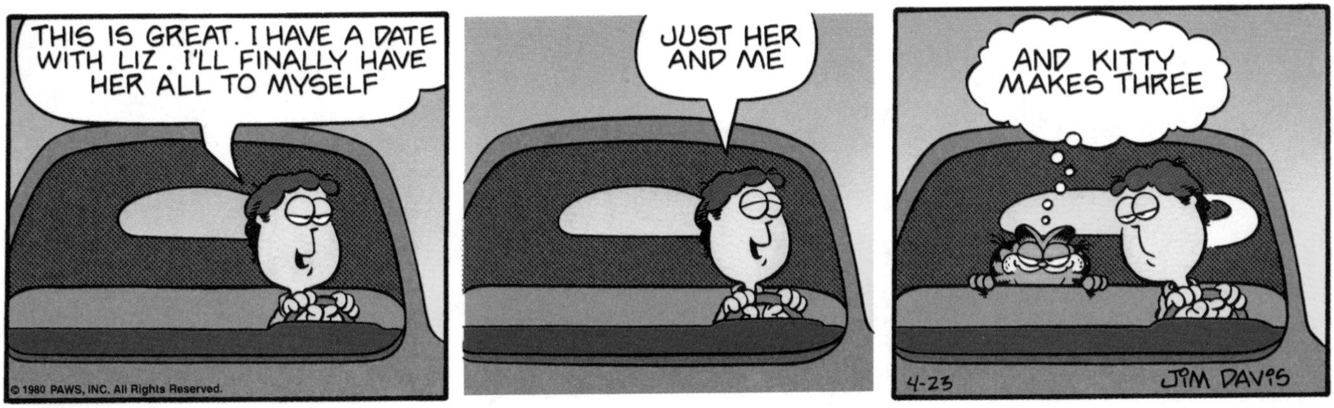
THIS IS GREAT. I HAVE A DATE WITH LIZ. I'LL FINALLY HAVE HER ALL TO MYSELF
© 1980 PAWS, INC. All Rights Reserved.
JUST HER AND ME
AND KITTY MAKES THREE
4-23
JIM DAVIS

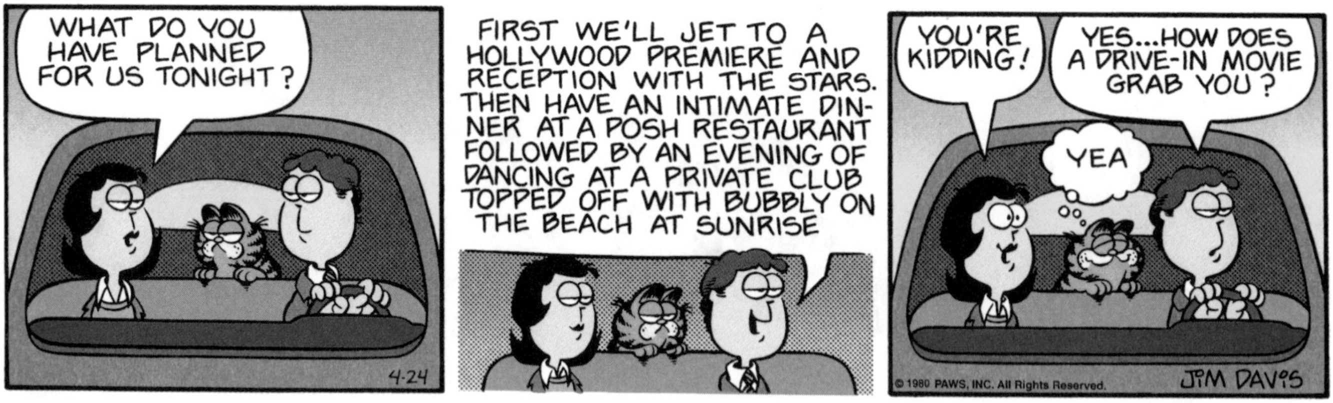
WHAT DO YOU HAVE PLANNED FOR US TONIGHT?
4-24
FIRST WE'LL JET TO A HOLLYWOOD PREMIERE AND RECEPTION WITH THE STARS. THEN HAVE AN INTIMATE DINNER AT A POSH RESTAURANT FOLLOWED BY AN EVENING OF DANCING AT A PRIVATE CLUB TOPPED OFF WITH BUBBLY ON THE BEACH AT SUNRISE
YOU'RE KIDDING!
YES...HOW DOES A DRIVE-IN MOVIE GRAB YOU?
YEA
© 1980 PAWS, INC. All Rights Reserved.
JIM DAVIS

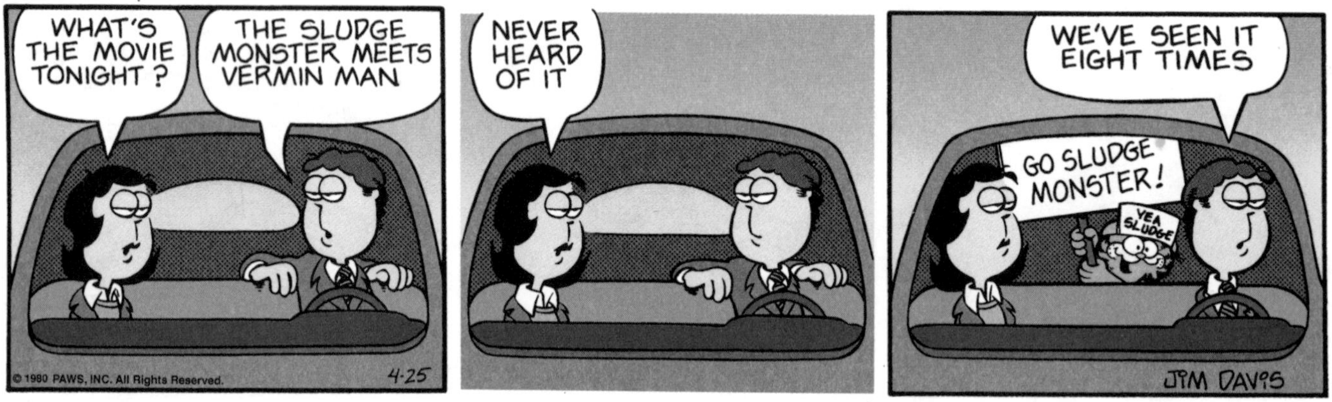
WHAT'S THE MOVIE TONIGHT?
THE SLUDGE MONSTER MEETS VERMIN MAN
© 1980 PAWS, INC. All Rights Reserved.
4-25
NEVER HEARD OF IT
WE'VE SEEN IT EIGHT TIMES
GO SLUDGE MONSTER!
YEA SLUDGE
JIM DAVIS

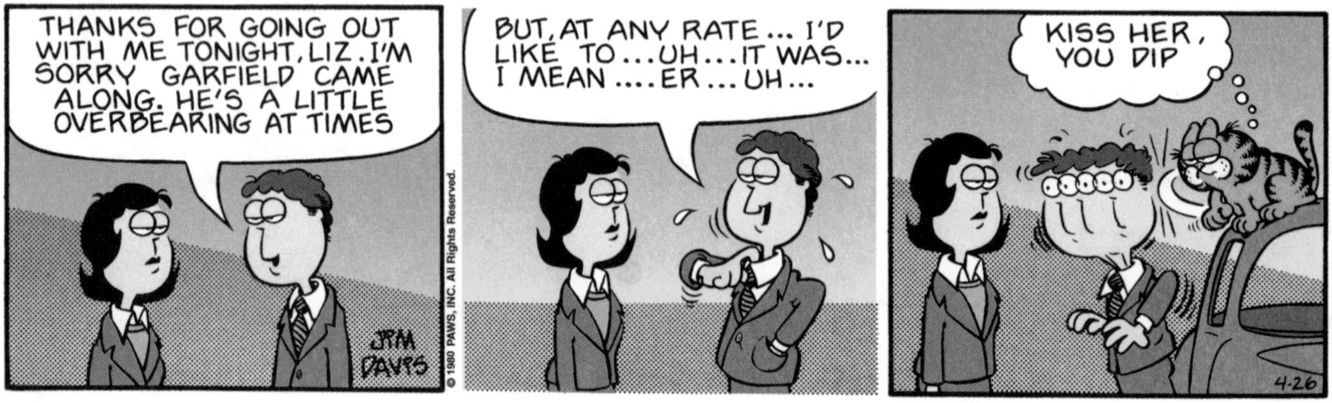
THANKS FOR GOING OUT WITH ME TONIGHT, LIZ. I'M SORRY GARFIELD CAME ALONG. HE'S A LITTLE OVERBEARING AT TIMES
JIM DAVIS
© 1980 PAWS, INC. All Rights Reserved.
BUT, AT ANY RATE... I'D LIKE TO...UH...IT WAS... I MEAN....ER...UH...
KISS HER, YOU DIP
4-26

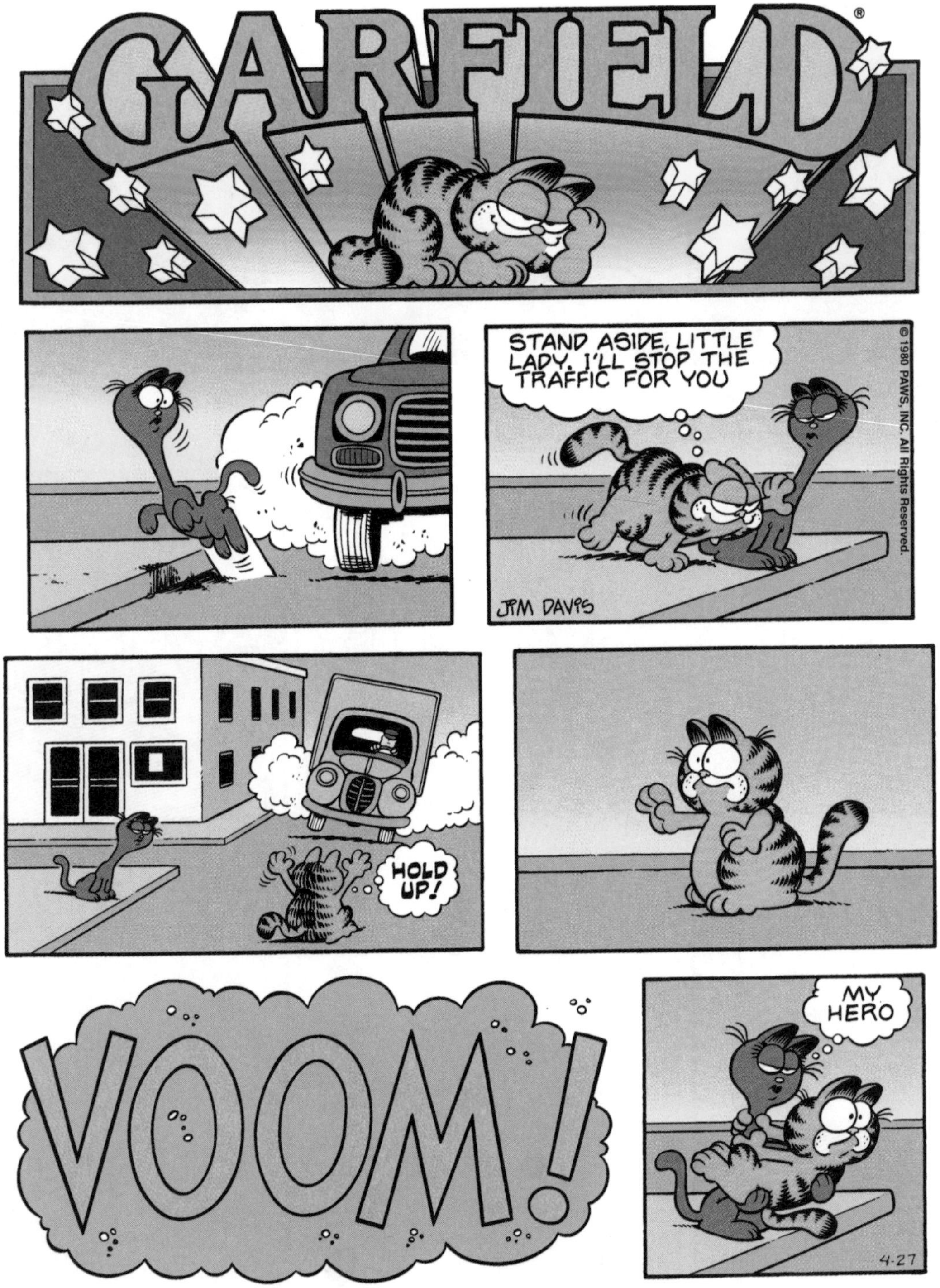
GARFIELD®
STAND ASIDE, LITTLE LADY. I'LL STOP THE TRAFFIC FOR YOU
JIM DAVIS
HOLD UP!
VOOM!
MY HERO
4-27

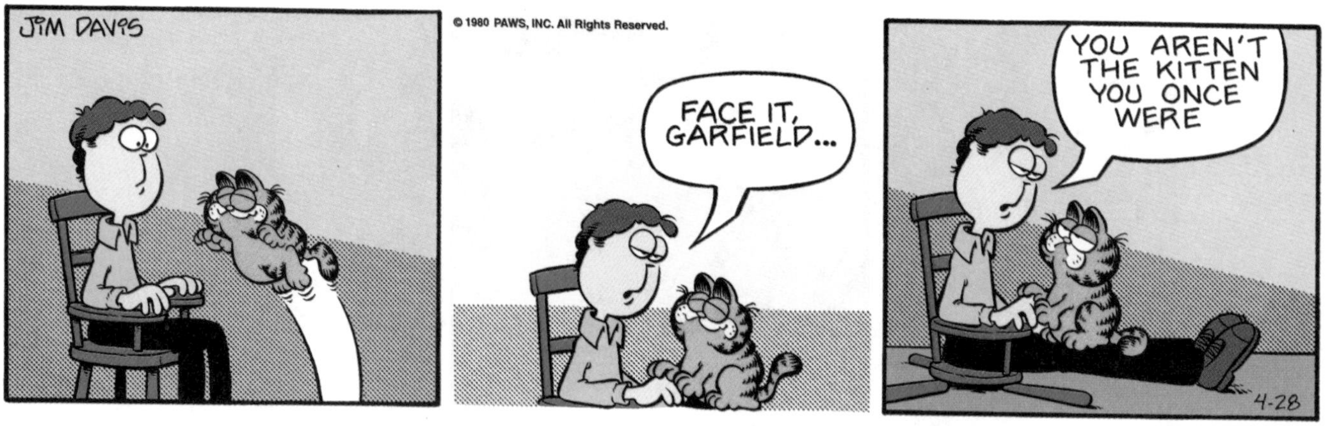
JIM DAVIS
© 1980 PAWS, INC. All Rights Reserved.
FACE IT, GARFIELD...
YOU AREN'T THE KITTEN YOU ONCE WERE
4-28

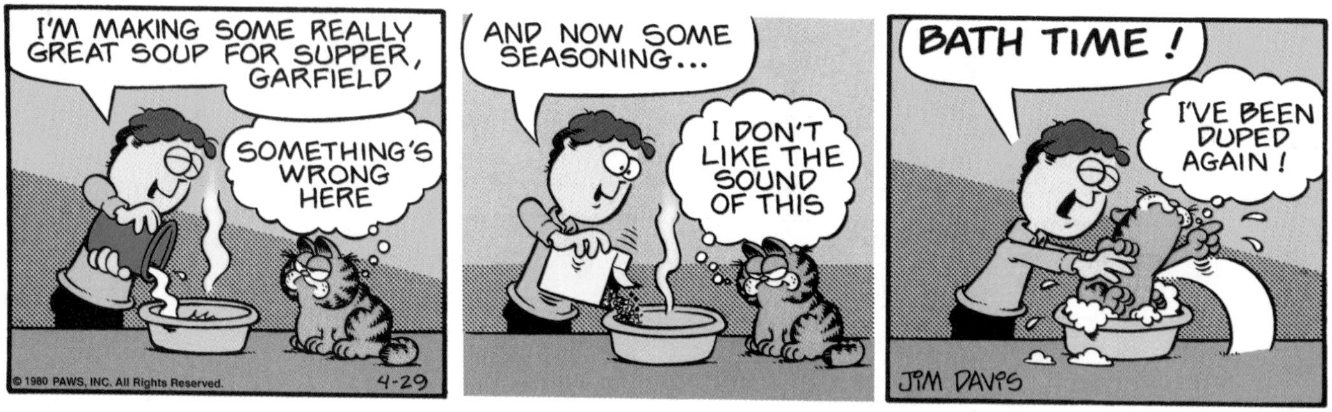
I'M MAKING SOME REALLY GREAT SOUP FOR SUPPER, GARFIELD
SOMETHING'S WRONG HERE
© 1980 PAWS, INC. All Rights Reserved.
4-29
AND NOW SOME SEASONING...
I DON'T LIKE THE SOUND OF THIS
BATH TIME !
I'VE BEEN DUPED AGAIN !
JIM DAVIS

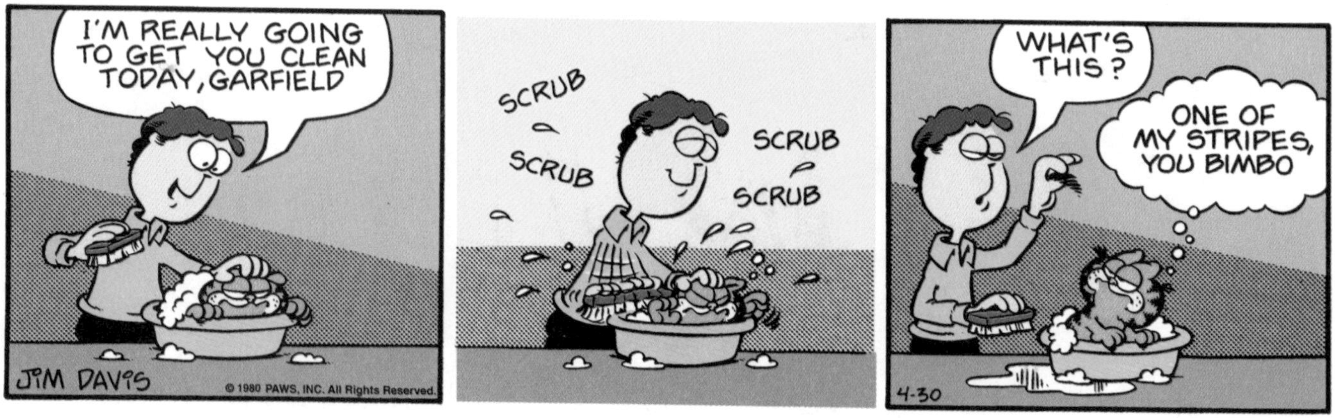
I'M REALLY GOING TO GET YOU CLEAN TODAY, GARFIELD
JIM DAVIS
© 1980 PAWS, INC. All Rights Reserved.
SCRUB
SCRUB
SCRUB
SCRUB
WHAT'S THIS ?
ONE OF MY STRIPES, YOU BIMBO
4-30

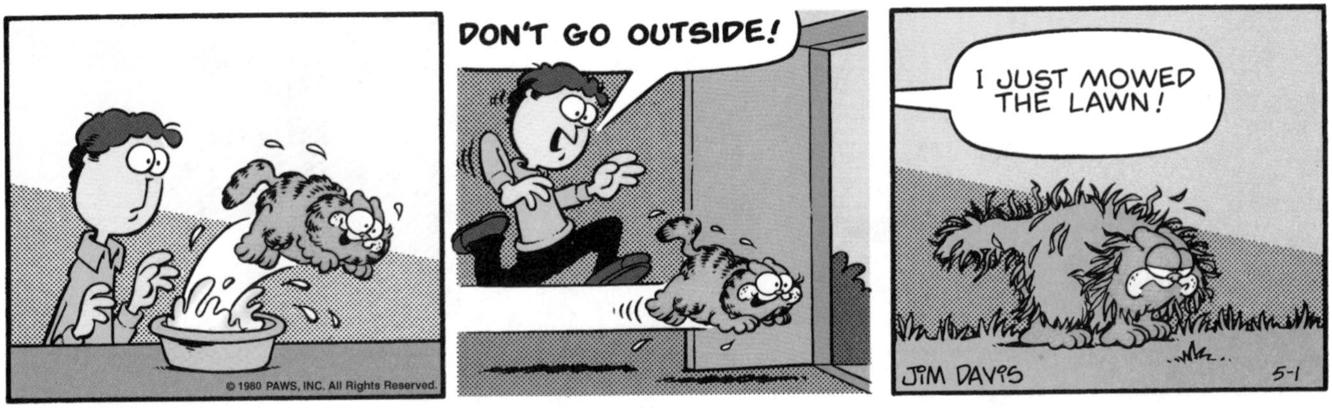
© 1980 PAWS, INC. All Rights Reserved.
DON'T GO OUTSIDE!
I JUST MOWED THE LAWN!
JIM DAVIS
5-1

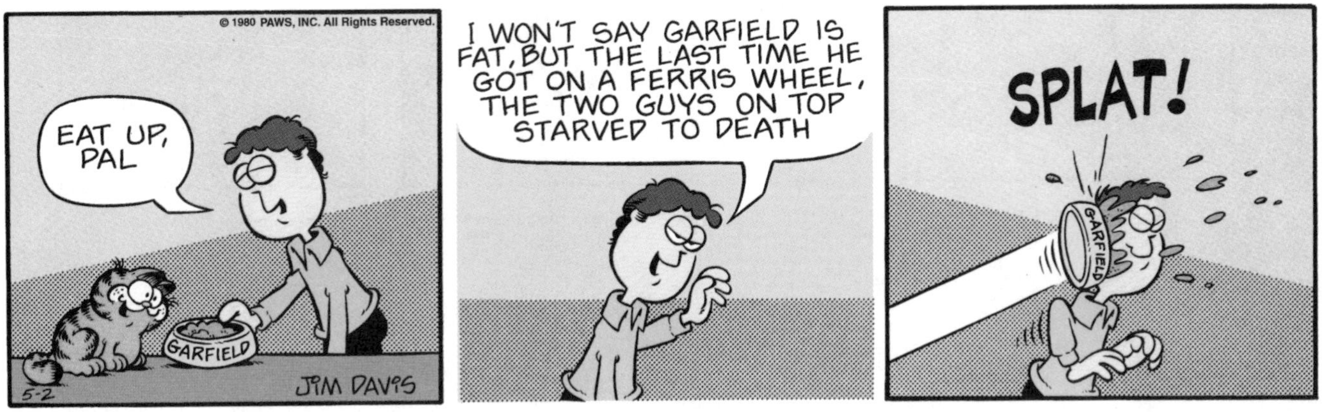
© 1980 PAWS, INC. All Rights Reserved.
EAT UP, PAL
GARFIELD
5-2
JIM DAVIS
I WON'T SAY GARFIELD IS FAT, BUT THE LAST TIME HE GOT ON A FERRIS WHEEL, THE TWO GUYS ON TOP STARVED TO DEATH
SPLAT!
GARFIELD

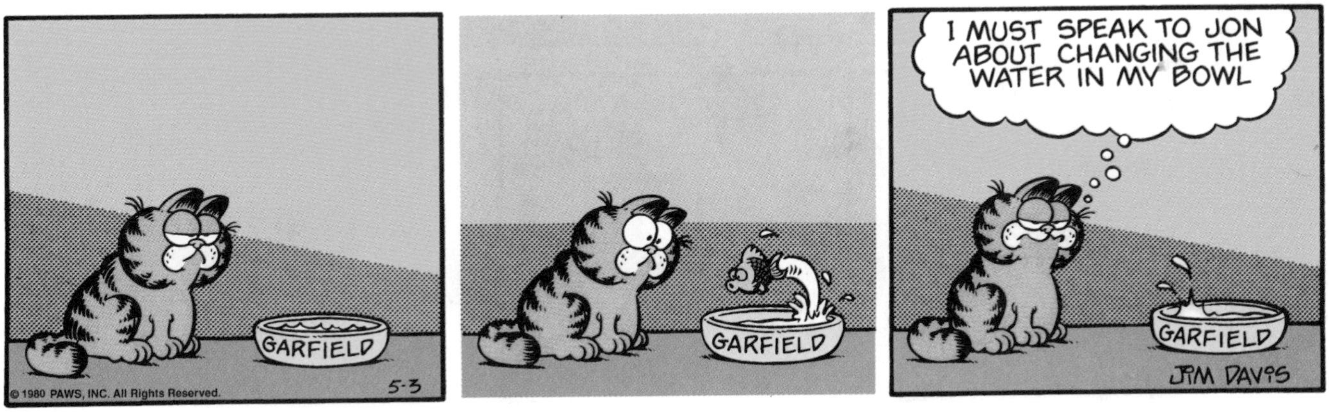
GARFIELD
© 1980 PAWS, INC. All Rights Reserved.
5-3
GARFIELD
I MUST SPEAK TO JON ABOUT CHANGING THE WATER IN MY BOWL
GARFIELD
JIM DAVIS

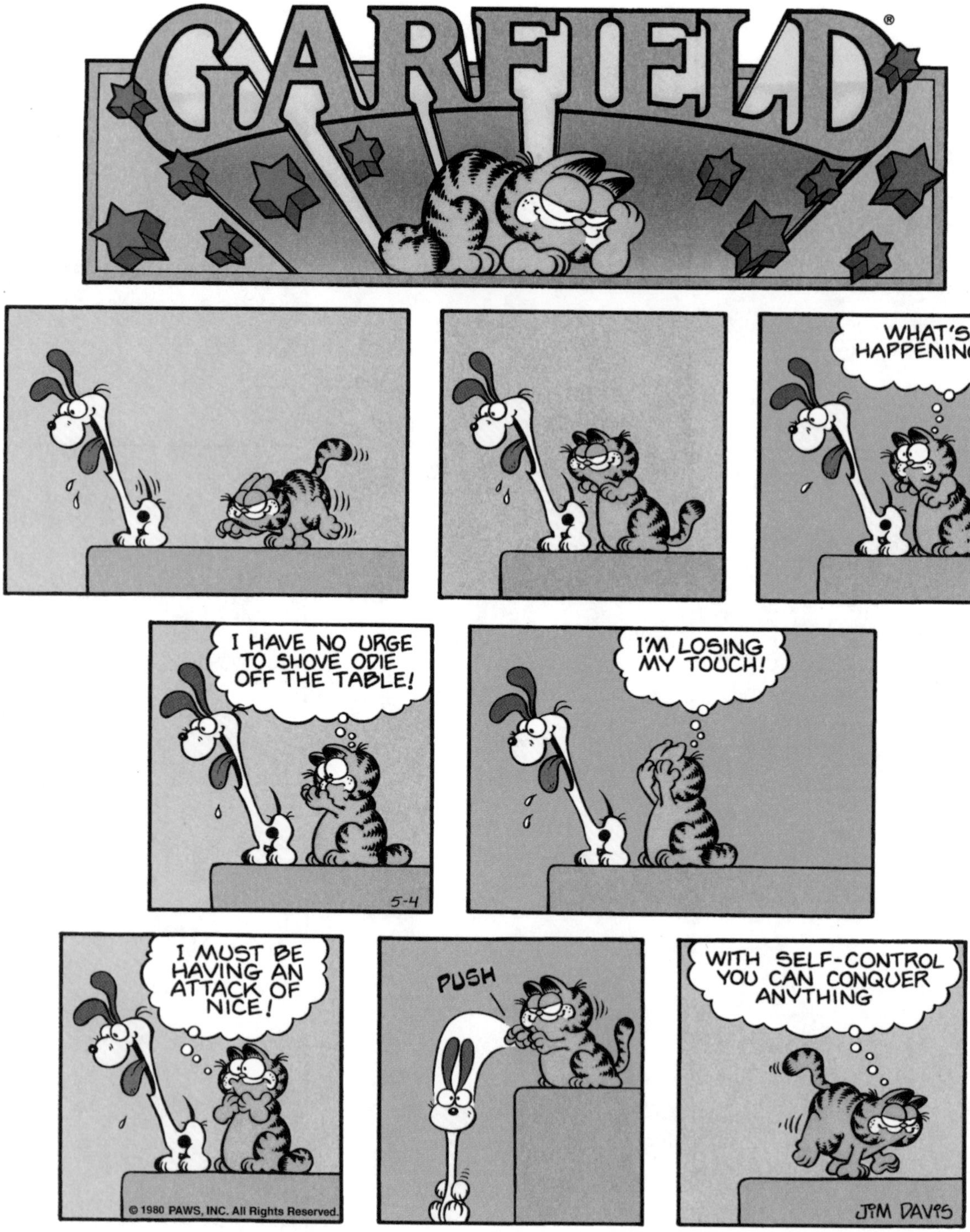
GARFIELD®
WHAT'S HAPPENING?
I HAVE NO URGE TO SHOVE ODIE OFF THE TABLE!
5-4
I'M LOSING MY TOUCH!
I MUST BE HAVING AN ATTACK OF NICE!
© 1980 PAWS, INC. All Rights Reserved.
PUSH
WITH SELF-CONTROL YOU CAN CONQUER ANYTHING
JIM DAVIS

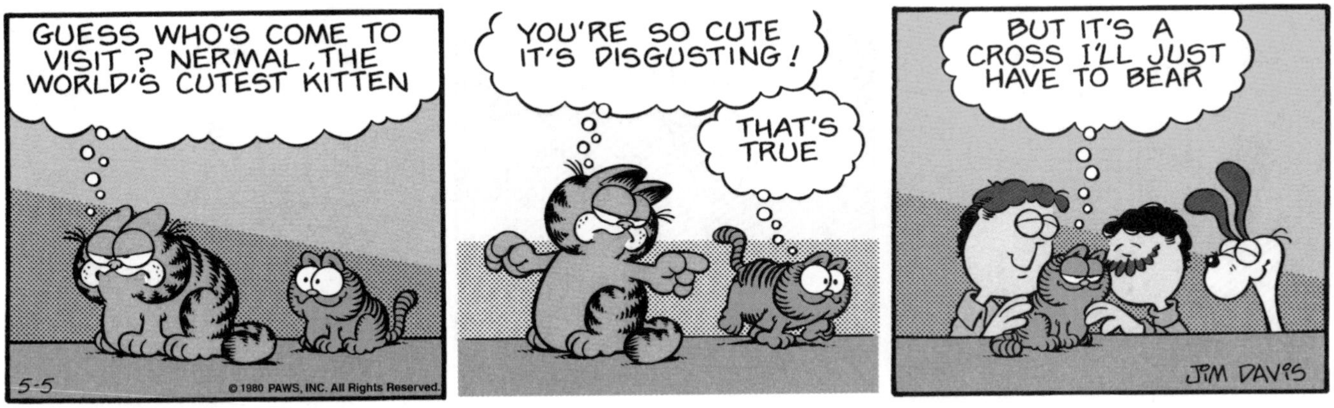
GUESS WHO'S COME TO VISIT ? NERMAL, THE WORLD'S CUTEST KITTEN
YOU'RE SO CUTE IT'S DISGUSTING !
THAT'S TRUE
BUT IT'S A CROSS I'LL JUST HAVE TO BEAR
5-5
© 1980 PAWS, INC. All Rights Reserved.
JIM DAVIS

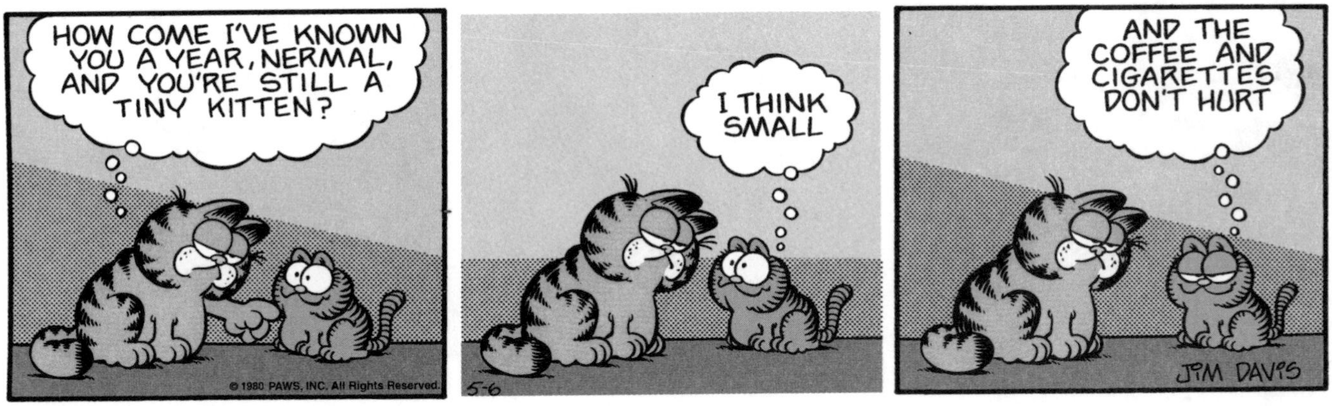
HOW COME I'VE KNOWN YOU A YEAR, NERMAL, AND YOU'RE STILL A TINY KITTEN?
I THINK SMALL
AND THE COFFEE AND CIGARETTES DON'T HURT
© 1980 PAWS, INC. All Rights Reserved.
5-6
JIM DAVIS

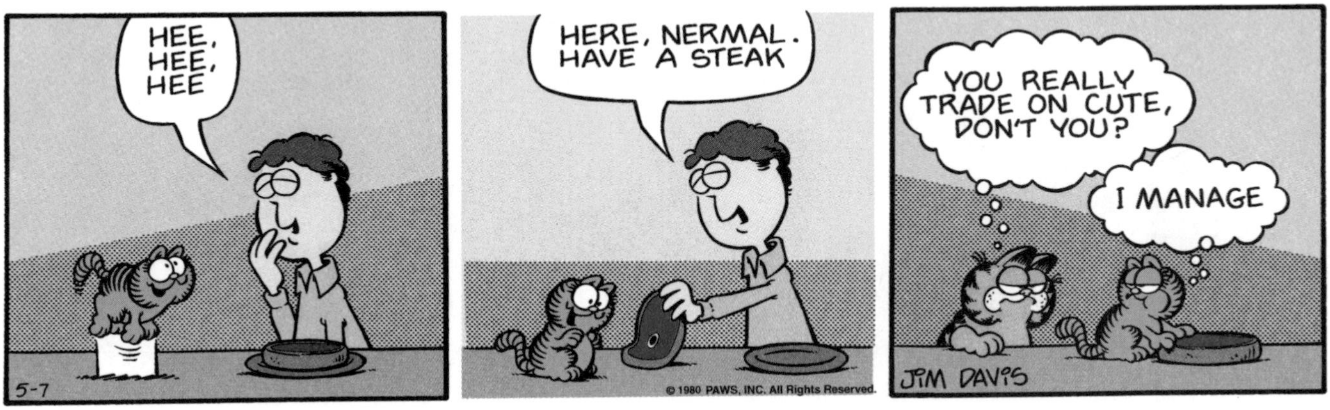
HEE, HEE, HEE
HERE, NERMAL. HAVE A STEAK
YOU REALLY TRADE ON CUTE, DON'T YOU?
I MANAGE
5-7
© 1980 PAWS, INC. All Rights Reserved.
JIM DAVIS

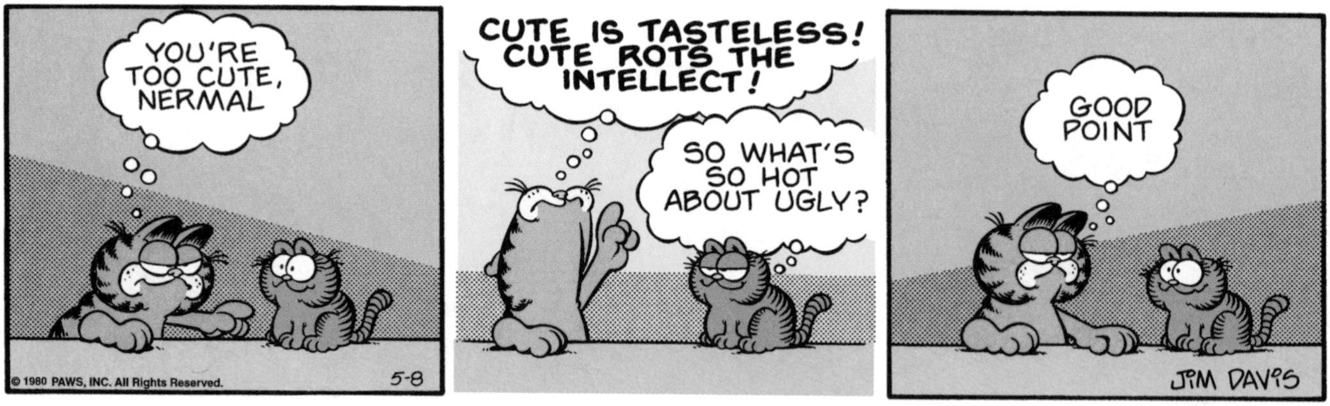
YOU'RE TOO CUTE, NERMAL
© 1980 PAWS, INC. All Rights Reserved.
5-8
CUTE IS TASTELESS! CUTE ROTS THE INTELLECT!
SO WHAT'S SO HOT ABOUT UGLY?
GOOD POINT
JIM DAVIS

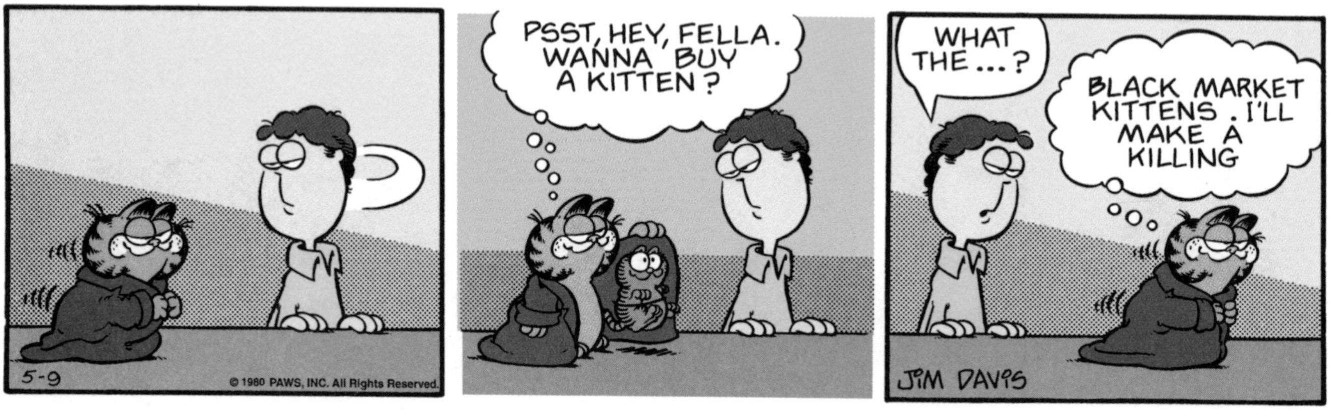
5-9
© 1980 PAWS, INC. All Rights Reserved.
PSST, HEY, FELLA. WANNA BUY A KITTEN?
WHAT THE ...?
BLACK MARKET KITTENS. I'LL MAKE A KILLING
JIM DAVIS

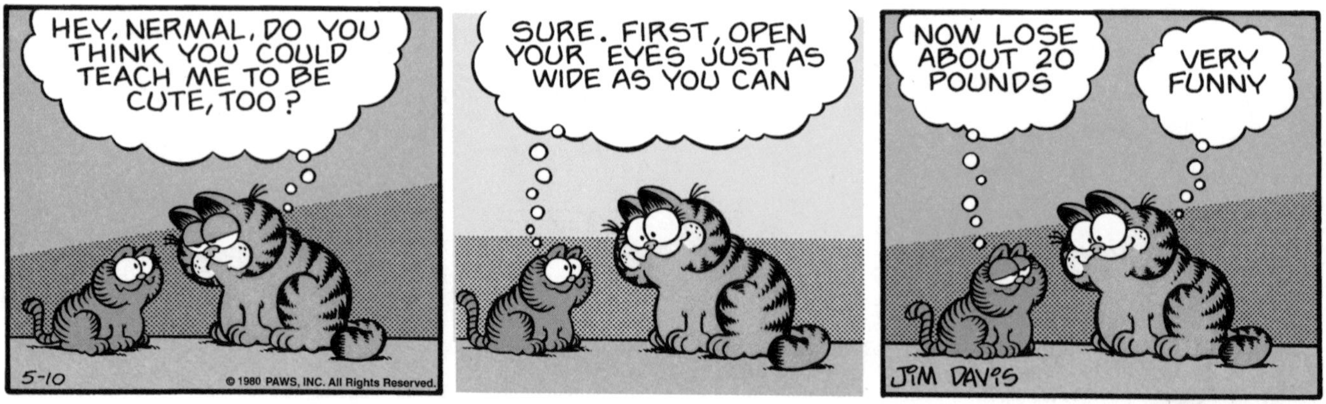
HEY, NERMAL, DO YOU THINK YOU COULD TEACH ME TO BE CUTE, TOO?
5-10
© 1980 PAWS, INC. All Rights Reserved.
SURE. FIRST, OPEN YOUR EYES JUST AS WIDE AS YOU CAN
NOW LOSE ABOUT 20 POUNDS
VERY FUNNY
JIM DAVIS

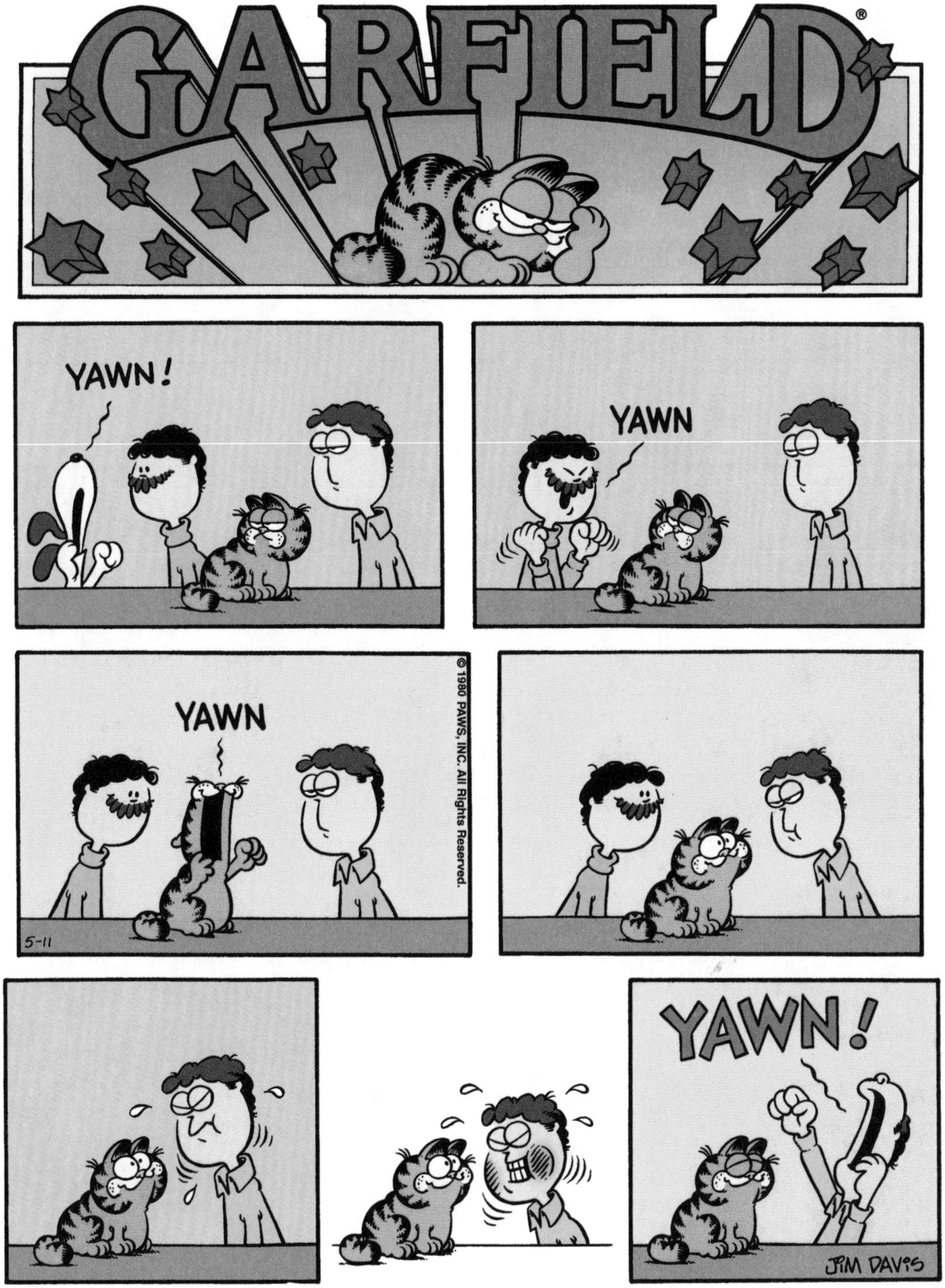
GARFIELD®
YAWN!
YAWN
YAWN
5-11
YAWN!
JIM DAVIS

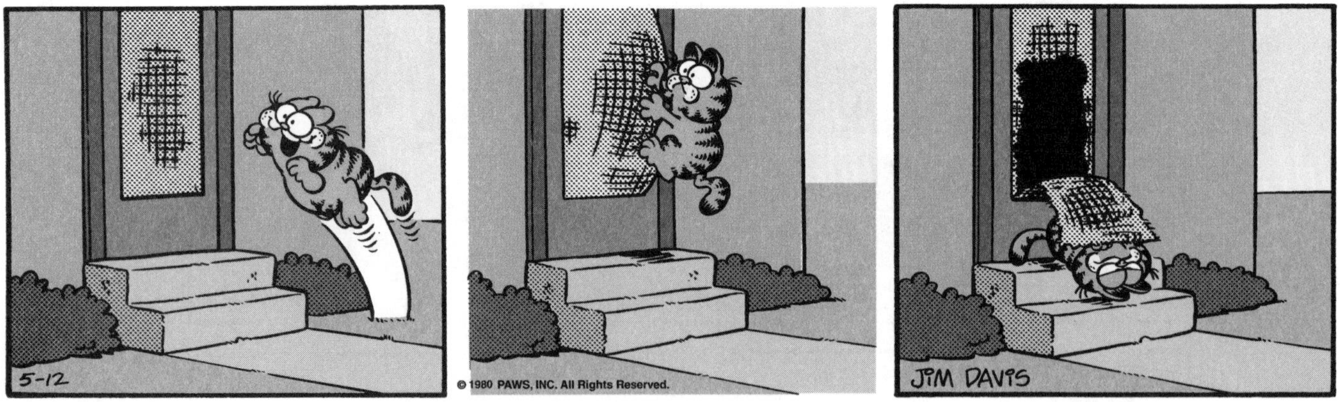
5-12
© 1980 PAWS, INC. All Rights Reserved.
JIM DAVIS

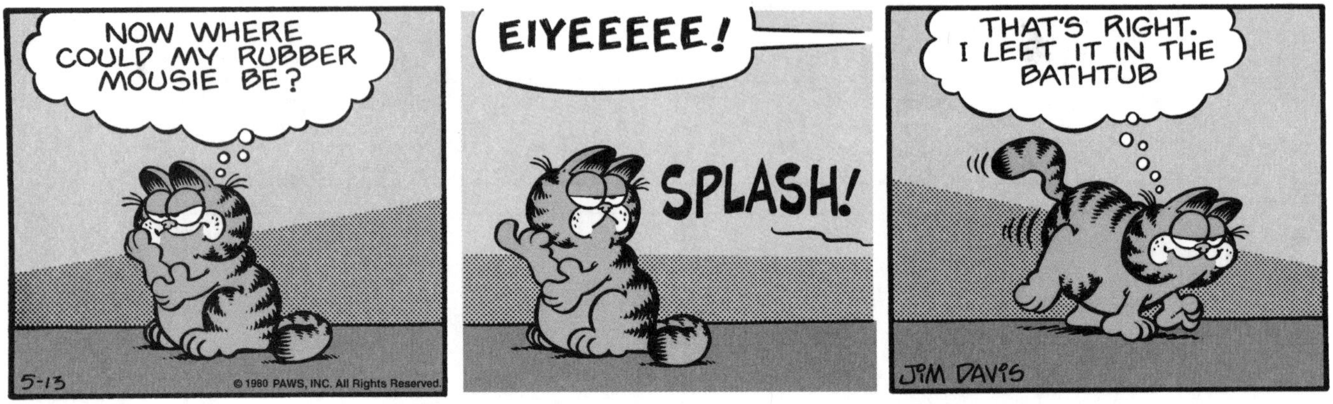
NOW WHERE COULD MY RUBBER MOUSIE BE?
5-13
© 1980 PAWS, INC. All Rights Reserved.
EIYEEEEE!
SPLASH!
THAT'S RIGHT. I LEFT IT IN THE BATHTUB
JIM DAVIS

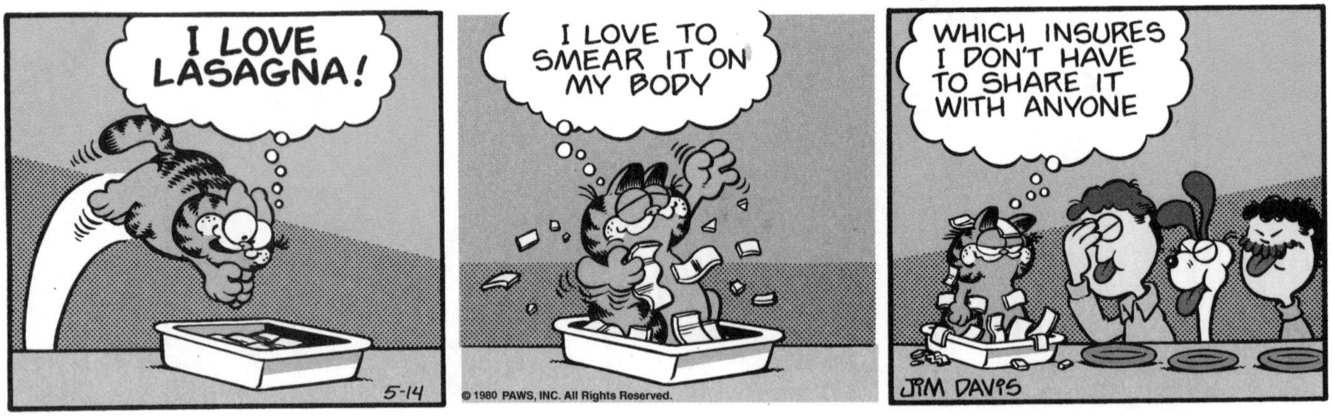
I LOVE LASAGNA!
5-14
I LOVE TO SMEAR IT ON MY BODY
© 1980 PAWS, INC. All Rights Reserved.
WHICH INSURES I DON'T HAVE TO SHARE IT WITH ANYONE
JIM DAVIS

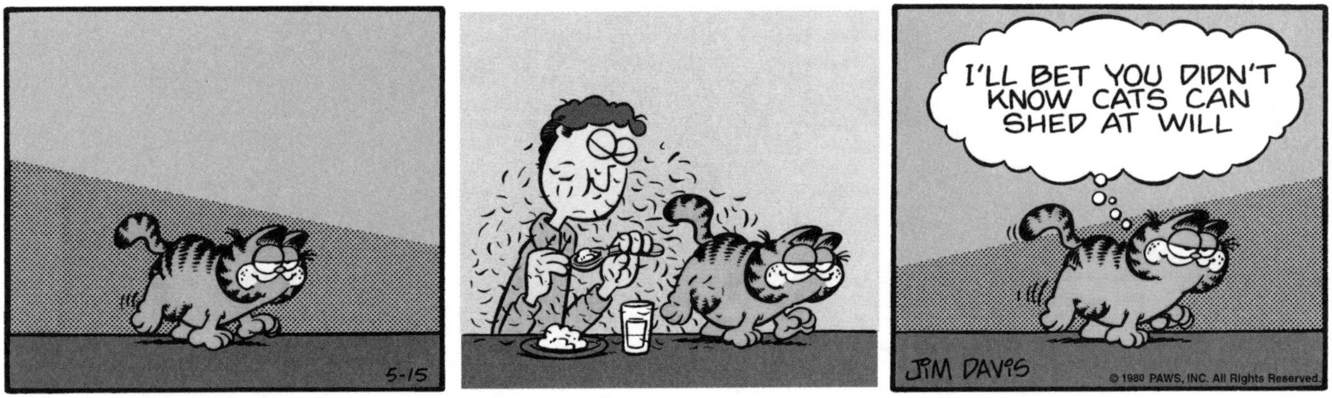
5-15
I'LL BET YOU DIDN'T KNOW CATS CAN SHED AT WILL
JIM DAVIS
© 1980 PAWS, INC. All Rights Reserved.

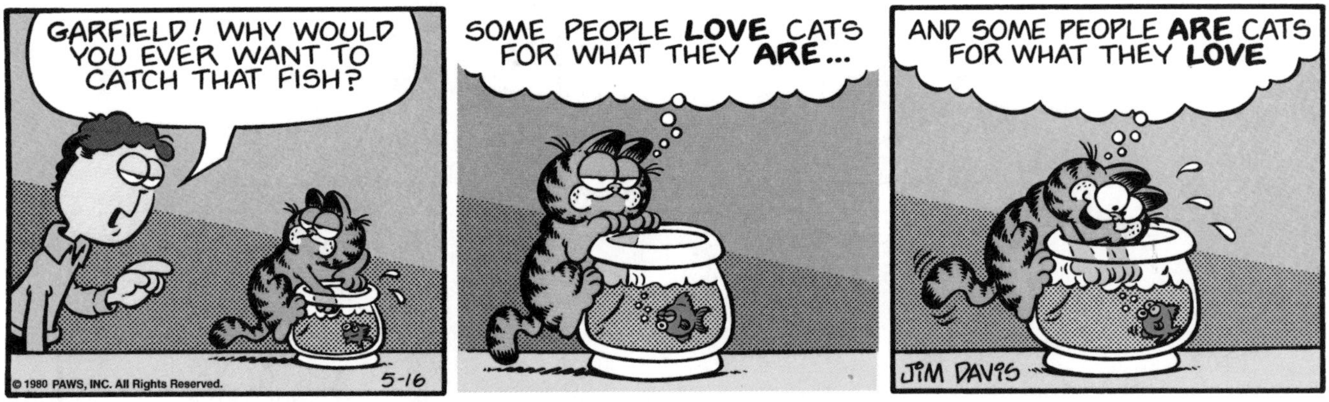
GARFIELD! WHY WOULD YOU EVER WANT TO CATCH THAT FISH?
© 1980 PAWS, INC. All Rights Reserved.
5-16
SOME PEOPLE **LOVE** CATS FOR WHAT THEY **ARE**...
AND SOME PEOPLE **ARE** CATS FOR WHAT THEY **LOVE**
JIM DAVIS

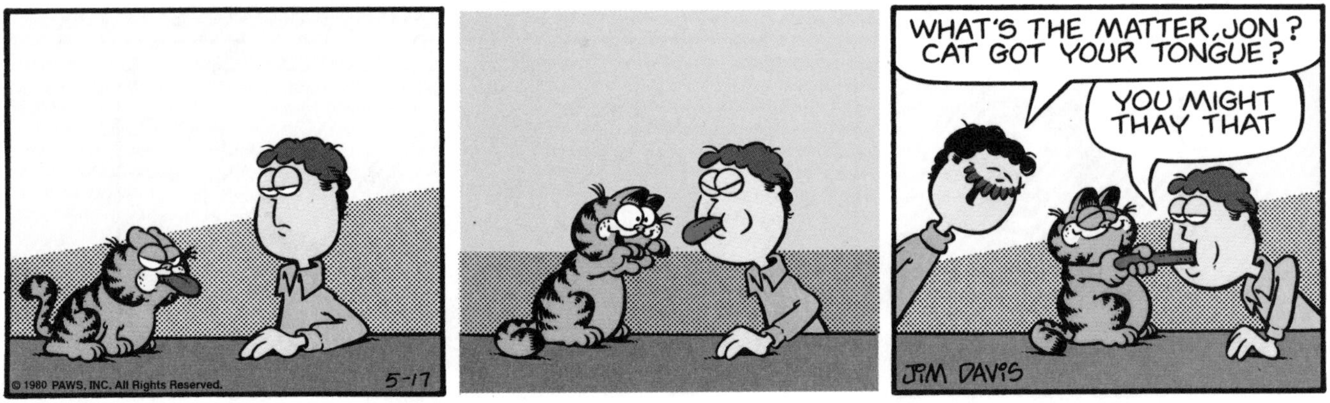
© 1980 PAWS, INC. All Rights Reserved.
5-17
WHAT'S THE MATTER, JON? CAT GOT YOUR TONGUE?
YOU MIGHT THAY THAT
JIM DAVIS

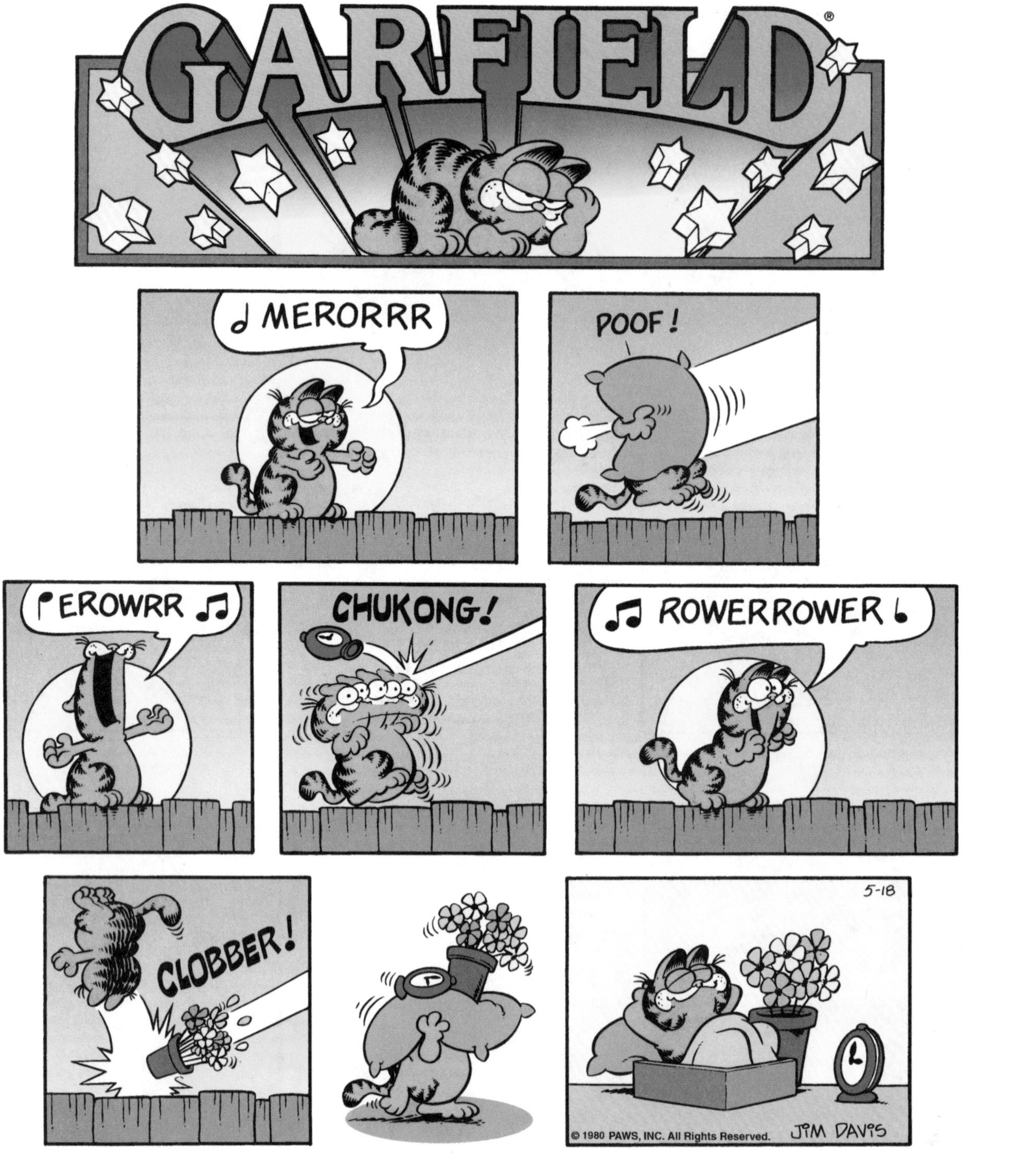
GARFIELD®
MERORRR
POOF!
EROWRR
CHUKONG!
ROWERROWER
CLOBBER!
5-18
© 1980 PAWS, INC. All Rights Reserved.
JIM DAVIS

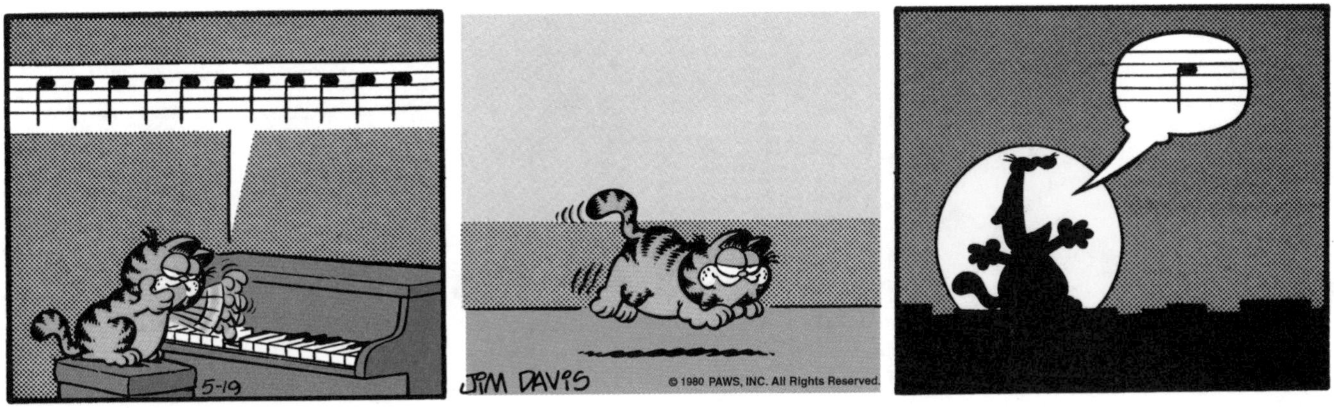
5-19
JIM DAVIS
© 1980 PAWS, INC. All Rights Reserved.

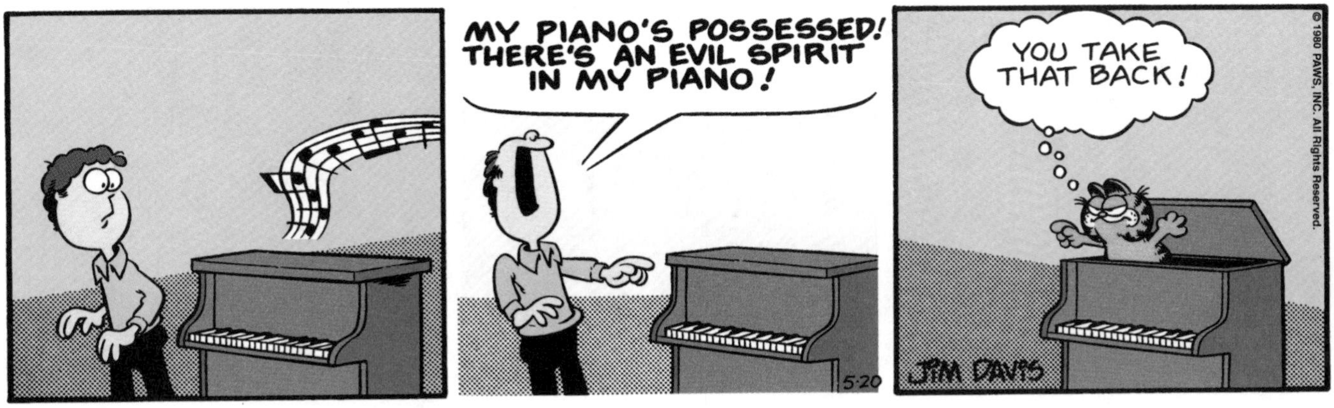
MY PIANO'S POSSESSED! THERE'S AN EVIL SPIRIT IN MY PIANO!
5-20
YOU TAKE THAT BACK!
© 1980 PAWS, INC. All Rights Reserved.
JIM DAVIS

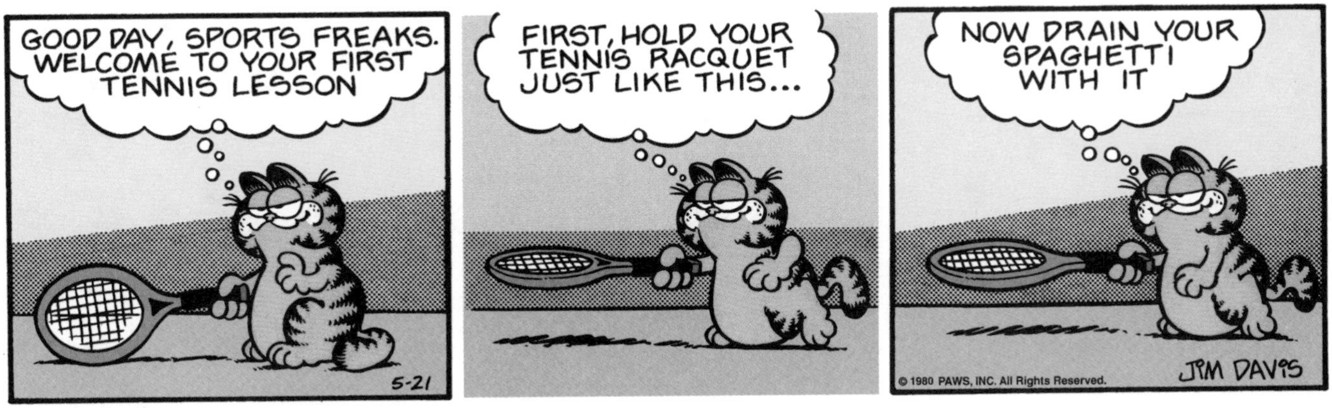
GOOD DAY, SPORTS FREAKS. WELCOME TO YOUR FIRST TENNIS LESSON
5-21
FIRST, HOLD YOUR TENNIS RACQUET JUST LIKE THIS...
NOW DRAIN YOUR SPAGHETTI WITH IT
© 1980 PAWS, INC. All Rights Reserved.
JIM DAVIS

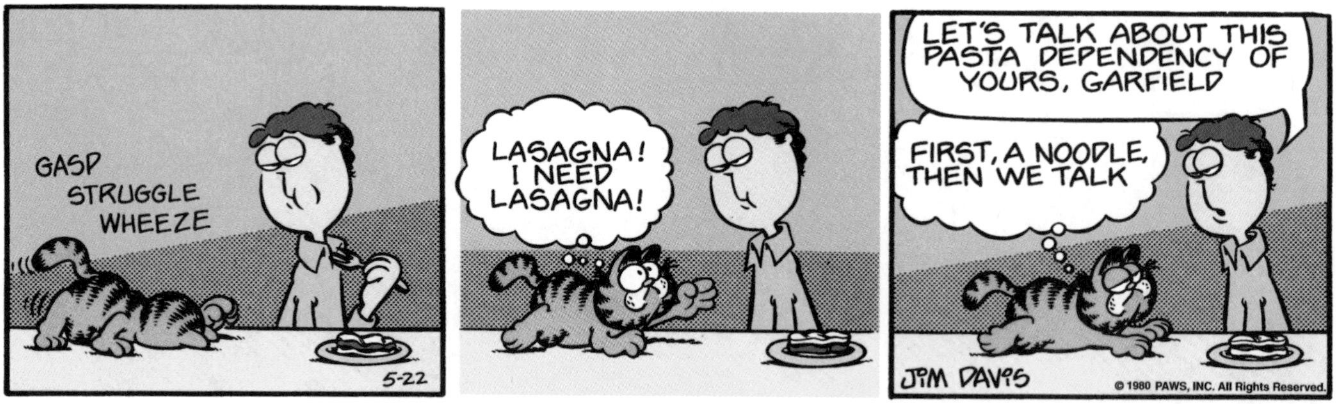
GASP
STRUGGLE
WHEEZE
5-22
LASAGNA! I NEED LASAGNA!
LET'S TALK ABOUT THIS PASTA DEPENDENCY OF YOURS, GARFIELD
FIRST, A NOODLE, THEN WE TALK
JIM DAVIS
© 1980 PAWS, INC. All Rights Reserved.

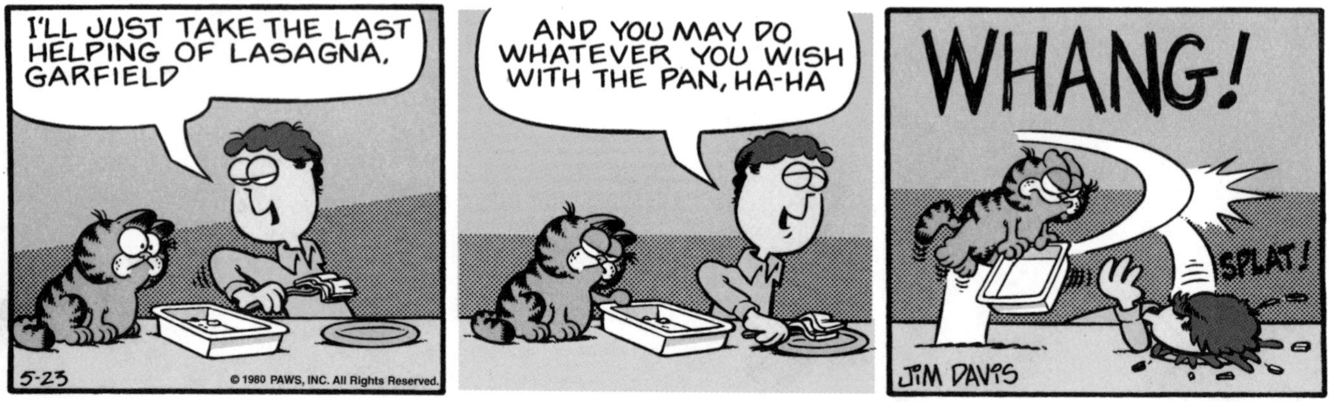
I'LL JUST TAKE THE LAST HELPING OF LASAGNA, GARFIELD
5-23
© 1980 PAWS, INC. All Rights Reserved.
AND YOU MAY DO WHATEVER YOU WISH WITH THE PAN, HA-HA
WHANG!
SPLAT!
JIM DAVIS

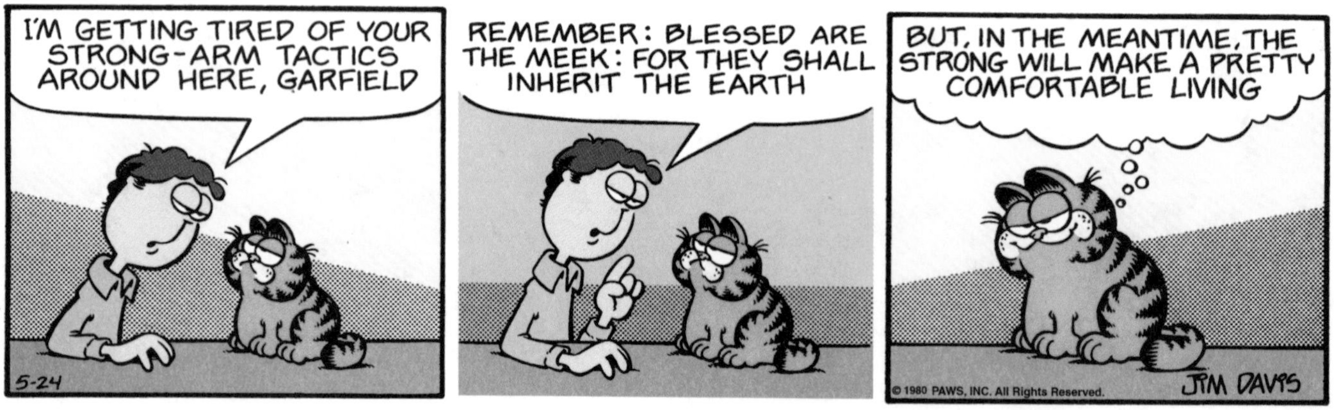
I'M GETTING TIRED OF YOUR STRONG-ARM TACTICS AROUND HERE, GARFIELD
5-24
REMEMBER: BLESSED ARE THE MEEK: FOR THEY SHALL INHERIT THE EARTH
BUT, IN THE MEANTIME, THE STRONG WILL MAKE A PRETTY COMFORTABLE LIVING
© 1980 PAWS, INC. All Rights Reserved.
JIM DAVIS

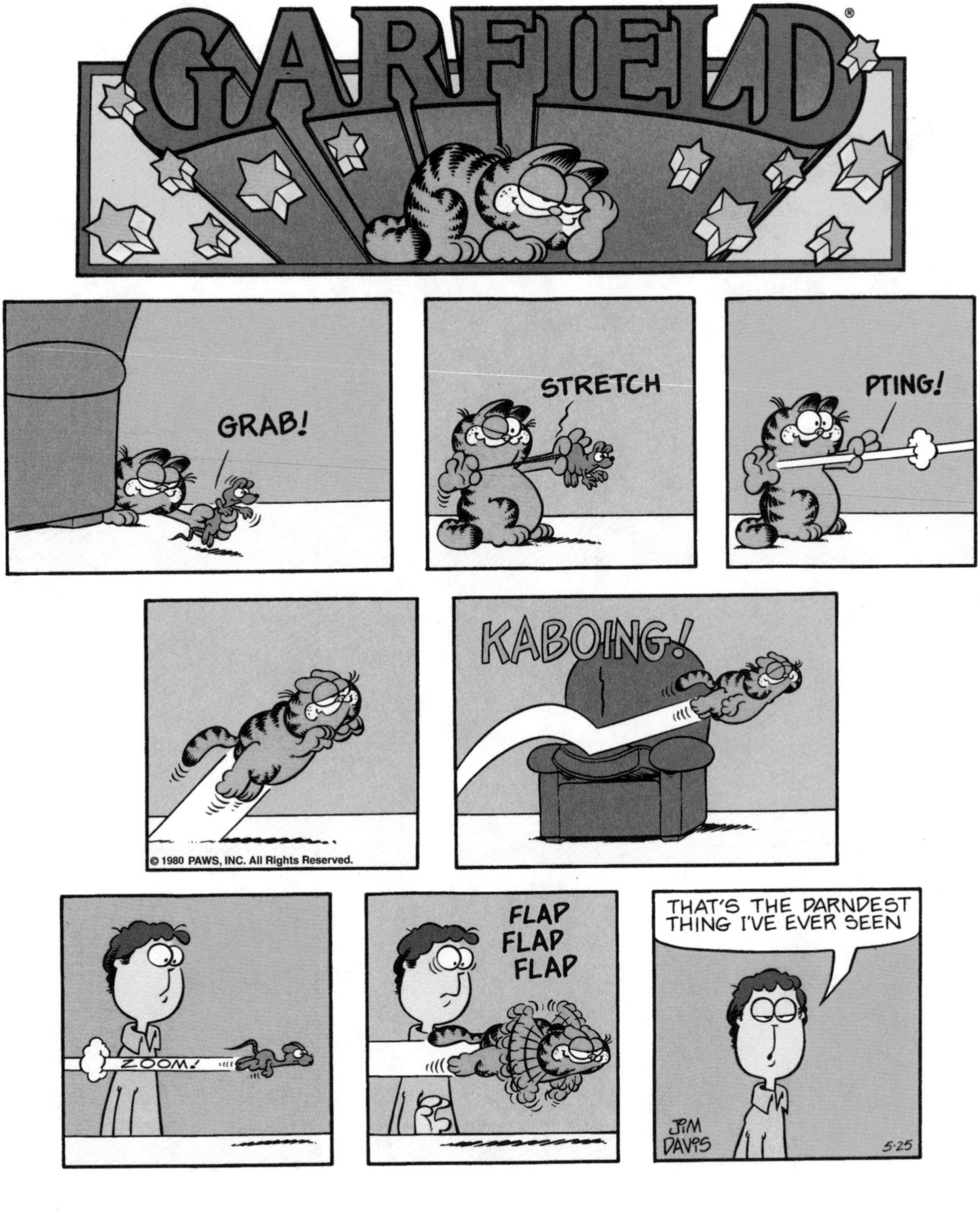
GARFIELD®
GRAB!
STRETCH
PTING!
KABOING!
© 1980 PAWS, INC. All Rights Reserved.
ZOOM!
FLAP
FLAP
FLAP
THAT'S THE DARNDEST THING I'VE EVER SEEN
JIM DAVIS
5-25

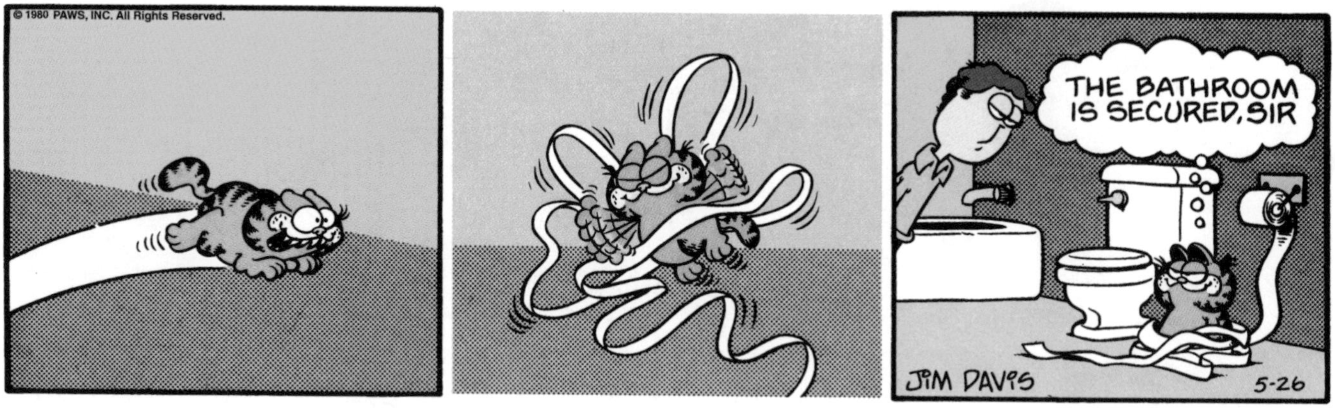
© 1980 PAWS, INC. All Rights Reserved.
THE BATHROOM IS SECURED, SIR
JIM DAVIS
5-26

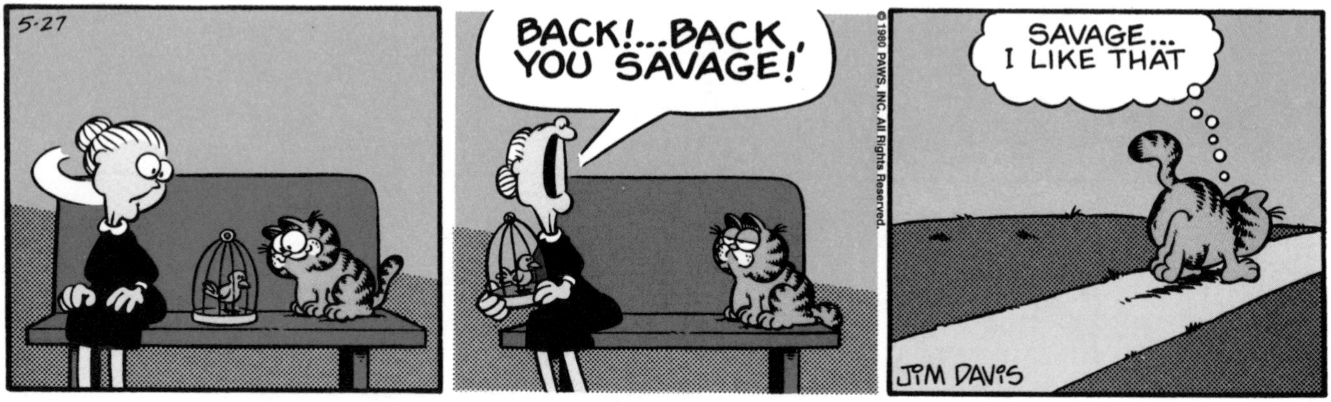
5-27
BACK!...BACK, YOU SAVAGE!
© 1980 PAWS, INC. All Rights Reserved.
SAVAGE... I LIKE THAT
JIM DAVIS

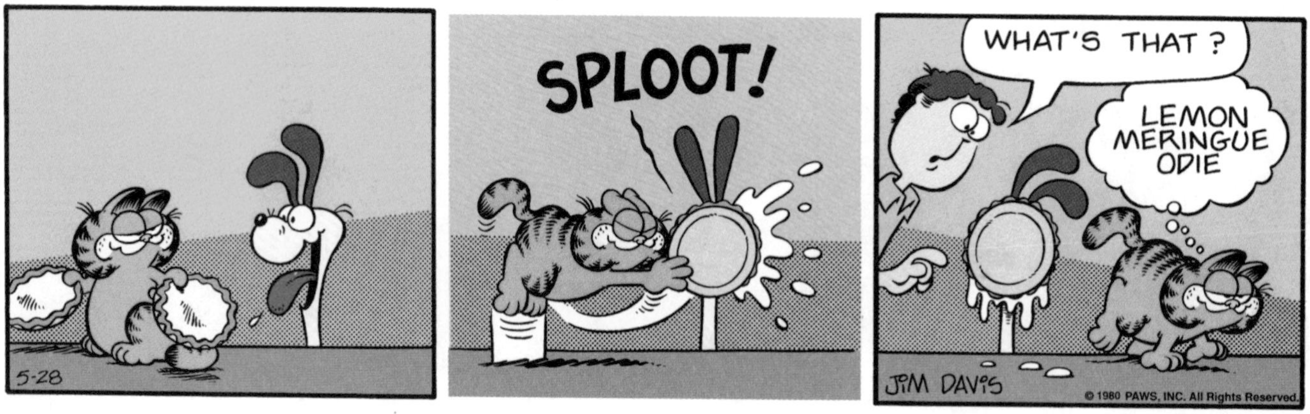
5-28
SPLOOT!
WHAT'S THAT ?
LEMON MERINGUE ODIE
JIM DAVIS
© 1980 PAWS, INC. All Rights Reserved.

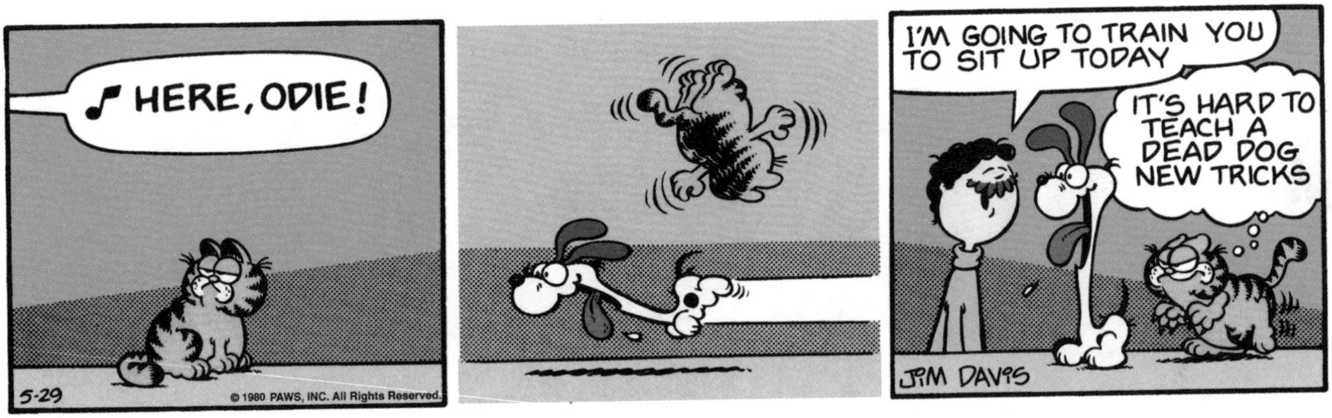
♪ HERE, ODIE!
I'M GOING TO TRAIN YOU TO SIT UP TODAY
IT'S HARD TO TEACH A DEAD DOG NEW TRICKS
JIM DAVIS
5-29
© 1980 PAWS, INC. All Rights Reserved.

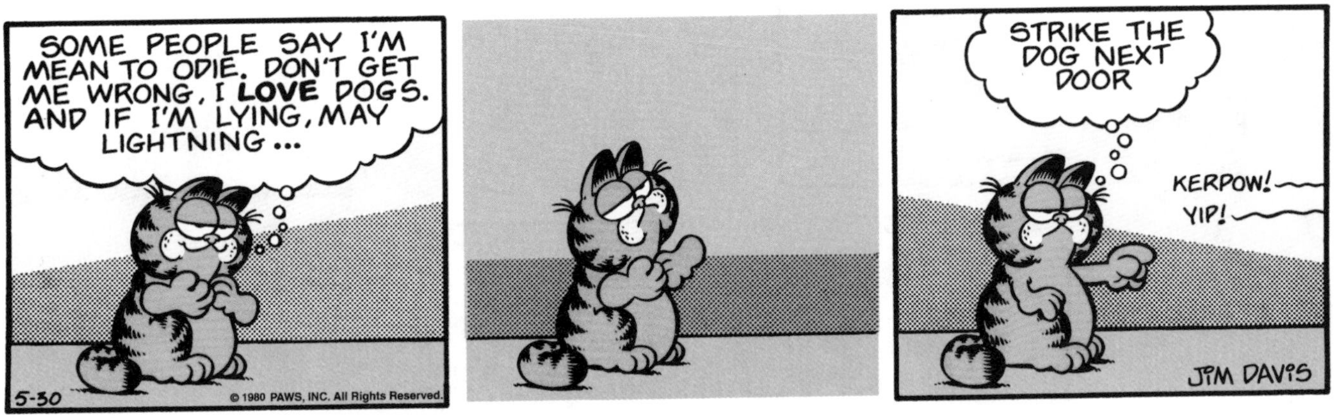
SOME PEOPLE SAY I'M MEAN TO ODIE. DON'T GET ME WRONG, I **LOVE** DOGS. AND IF I'M LYING, MAY LIGHTNING...
STRIKE THE DOG NEXT DOOR
KERPOW!
YIP!
JIM DAVIS
5-30
© 1980 PAWS, INC. All Rights Reserved.

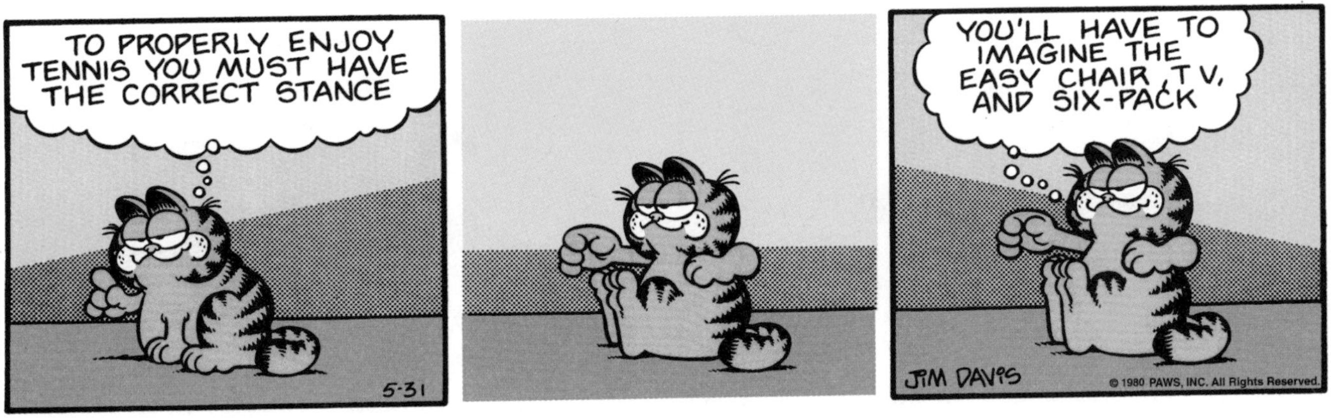
TO PROPERLY ENJOY TENNIS YOU MUST HAVE THE CORRECT STANCE
YOU'LL HAVE TO IMAGINE THE EASY CHAIR, T.V, AND SIX-PACK
5-31
JIM DAVIS
© 1980 PAWS, INC. All Rights Reserved.

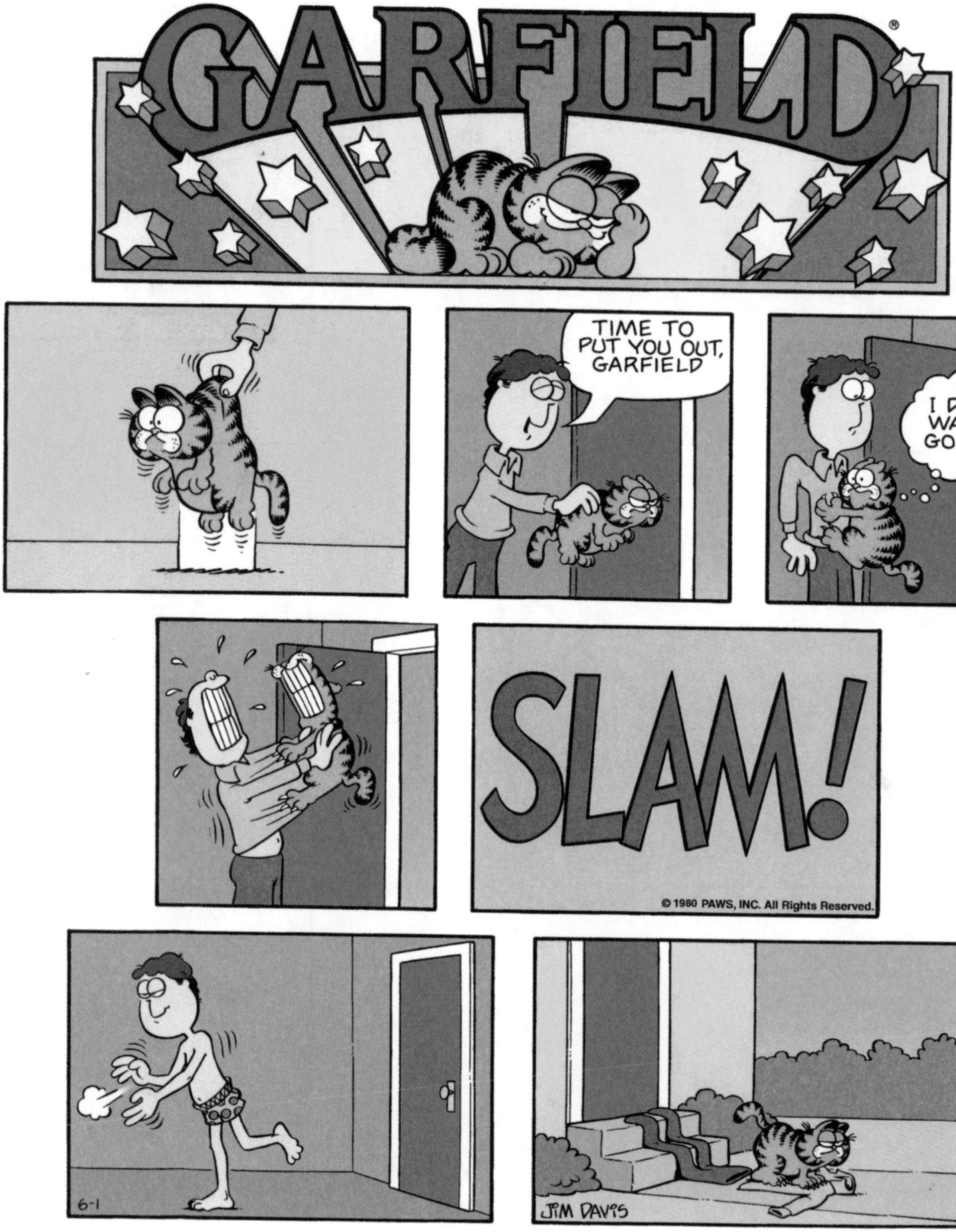
GARFIELD®
TIME TO PUT YOU OUT, GARFIELD
I DON'T WANNA GO OUT!
SLAM!
© 1980 PAWS, INC. All Rights Reserved.
6-1
JIM DAVIS

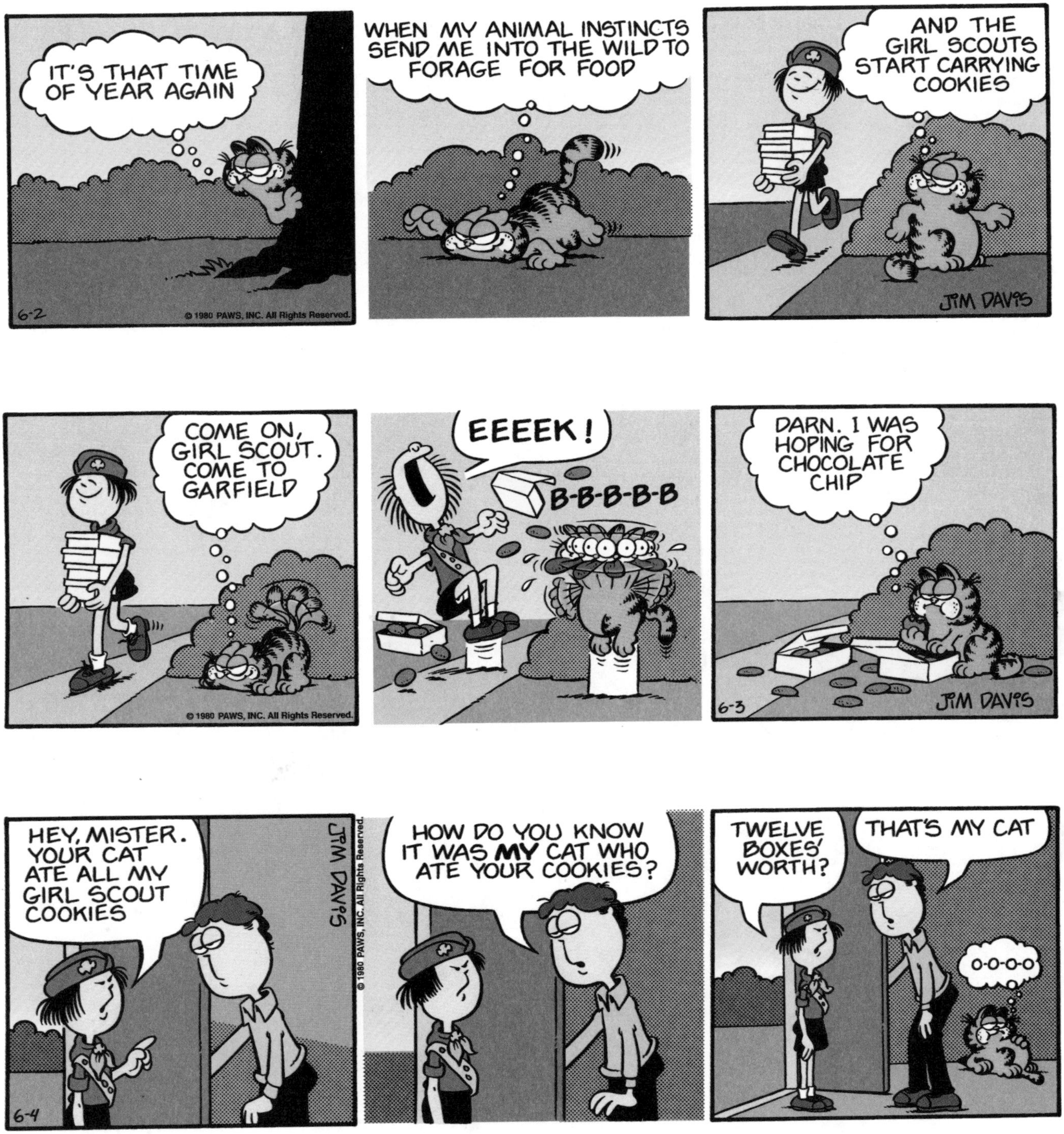

IT'S THAT TIME OF YEAR AGAIN
6-2
© 1980 PAWS, INC. All Rights Reserved.
WHEN MY ANIMAL INSTINCTS SEND ME INTO THE WILD TO FORAGE FOR FOOD
AND THE GIRL SCOUTS START CARRYING COOKIES
JIM DAVIS
COME ON, GIRL SCOUT. COME TO GARFIELD
© 1980 PAWS, INC. All Rights Reserved.
EEEEK!
B-B-B-B-B
DARN. I WAS HOPING FOR CHOCOLATE CHIP
6-3
JIM DAVIS
HEY, MISTER. YOUR CAT ATE ALL MY GIRL SCOUT COOKIES
6-4
JIM DAVIS
© 1980 PAWS, INC. All Rights Reserved.
HOW DO YOU KNOW IT WAS **MY** CAT WHO ATE YOUR COOKIES?
TWELVE BOXES' WORTH?
THAT'S MY CAT
O-O-O-O

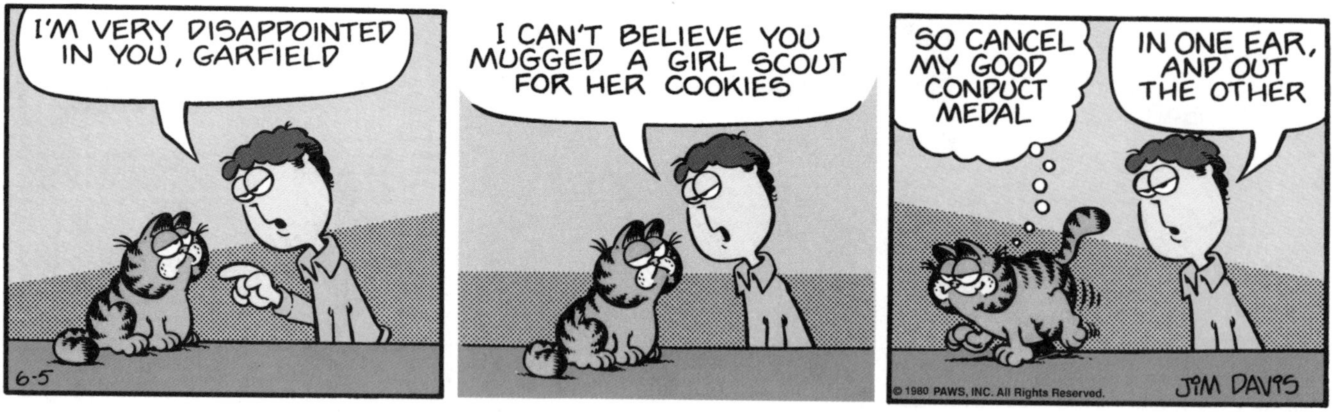
6-5
I'M VERY DISAPPOINTED IN YOU, GARFIELD
I CAN'T BELIEVE YOU MUGGED A GIRL SCOUT FOR HER COOKIES
SO CANCEL MY GOOD CONDUCT MEDAL
IN ONE EAR, AND OUT THE OTHER
© 1980 PAWS, INC. All Rights Reserved.
JIM DAVIS

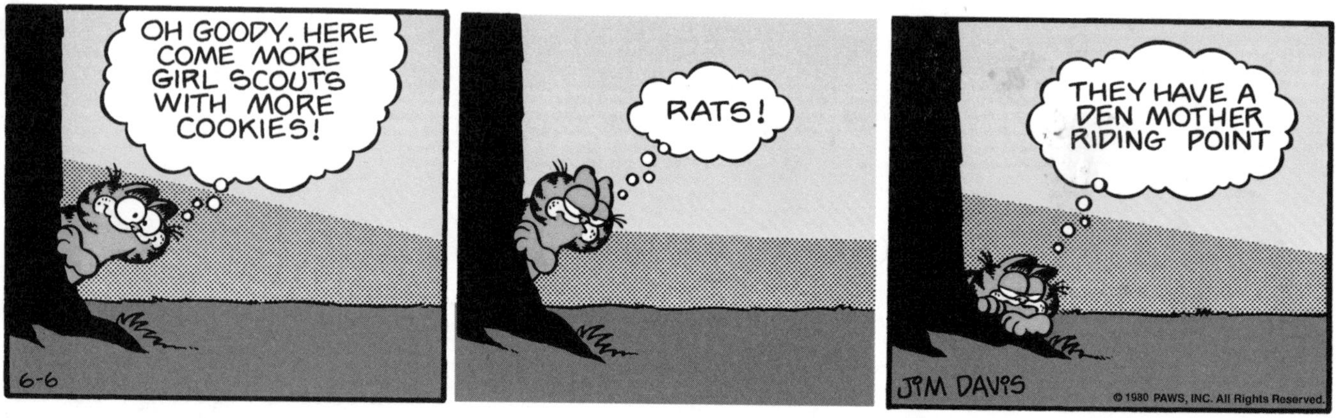
OH GOODY. HERE COME MORE GIRL SCOUTS WITH MORE COOKIES!
6-6
RATS!
THEY HAVE A DEN MOTHER RIDING POINT
JIM DAVIS
© 1980 PAWS, INC. All Rights Reserved.

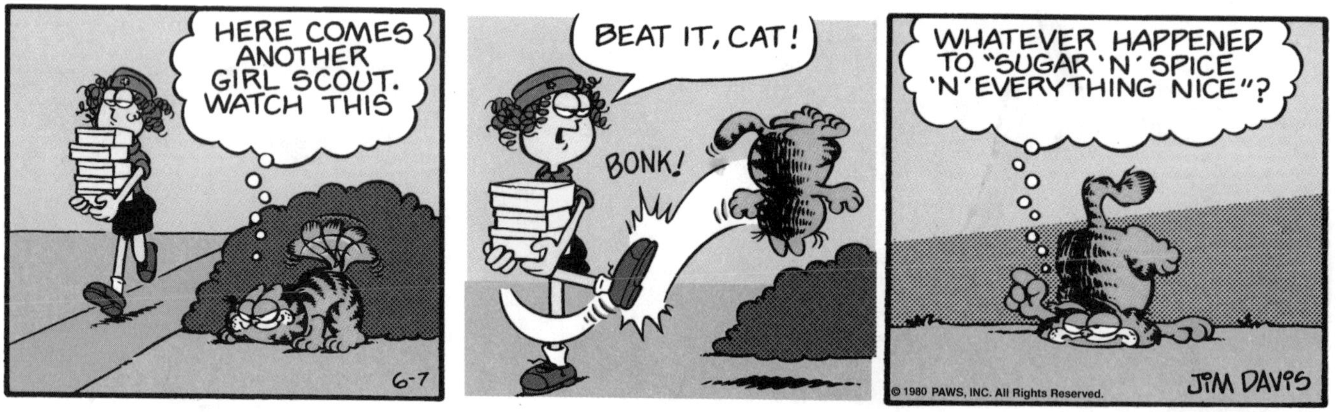
HERE COMES ANOTHER GIRL SCOUT. WATCH THIS
6-7
BEAT IT, CAT!
BONK!
WHATEVER HAPPENED TO "SUGAR 'N' SPICE 'N' EVERYTHING NICE"?
© 1980 PAWS, INC. All Rights Reserved.
JIM DAVIS

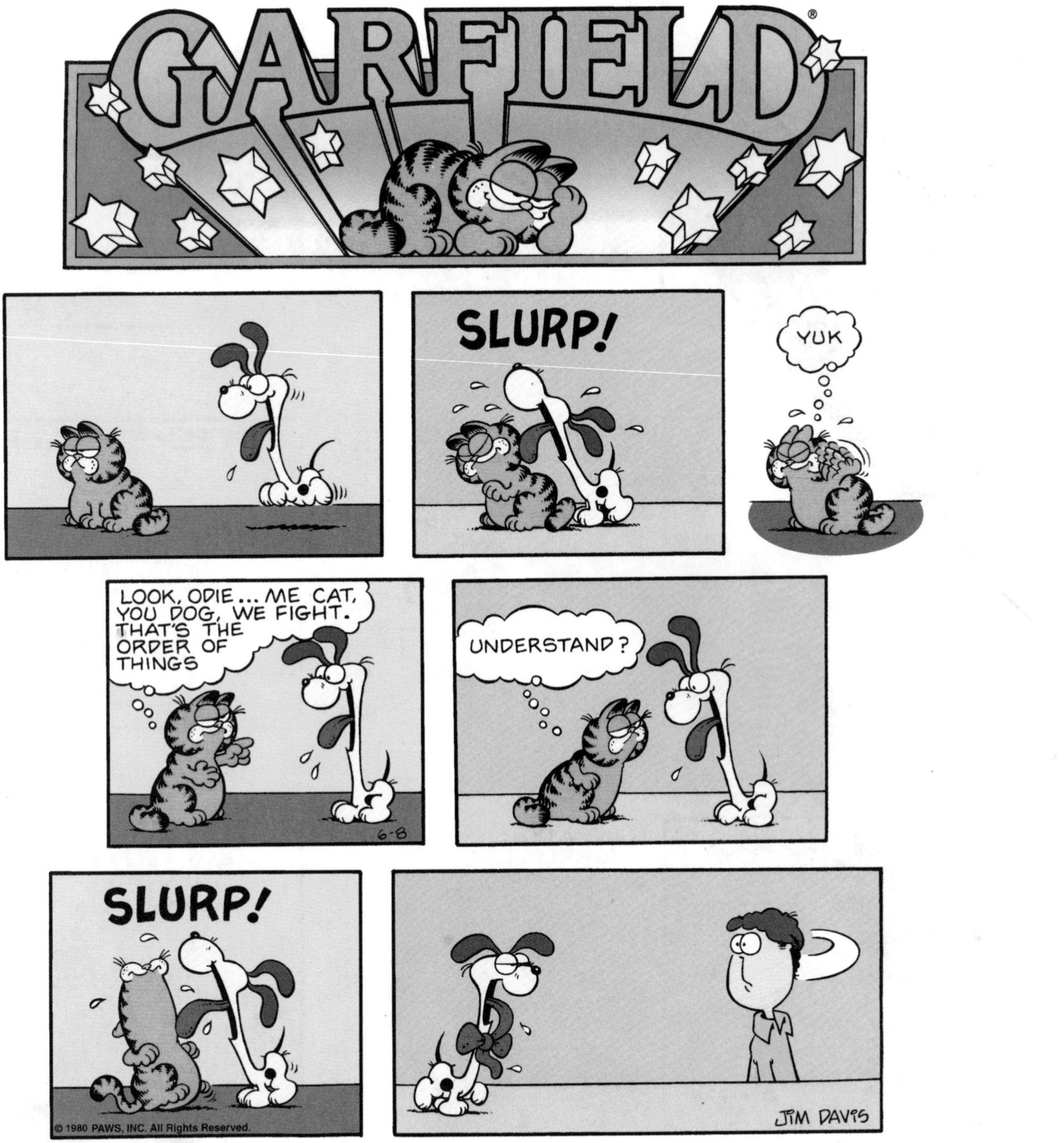
GARFIELD®
SLURP!
YUK
LOOK, ODIE... ME CAT, YOU DOG, WE FIGHT. THAT'S THE ORDER OF THINGS
6-8
UNDERSTAND?
SLURP!
© 1980 PAWS, INC. All Rights Reserved.
JIM DAVIS

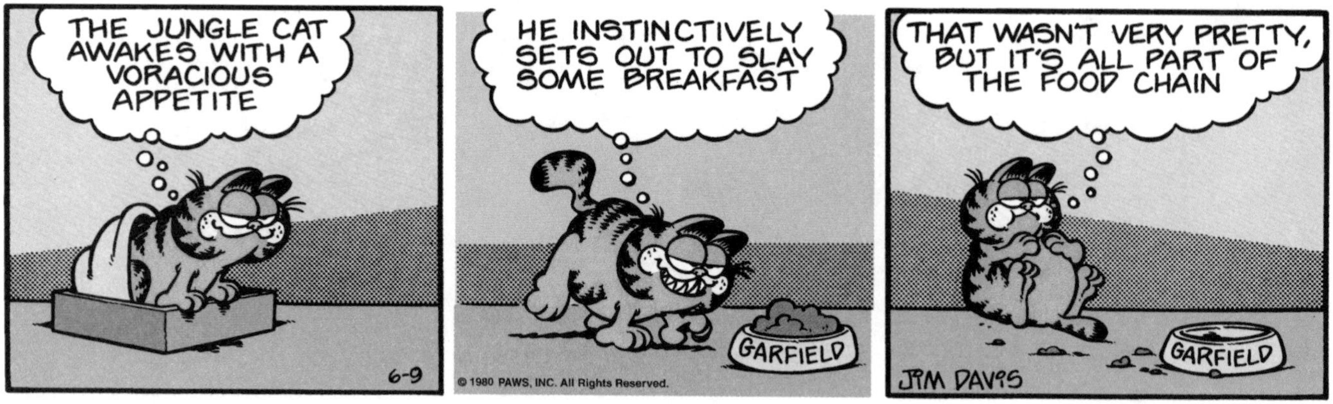
THE JUNGLE CAT AWAKES WITH A VORACIOUS APPETITE
6-9
HE INSTINCTIVELY SETS OUT TO SLAY SOME BREAKFAST
GARFIELD
© 1980 PAWS, INC. All Rights Reserved.
THAT WASN'T VERY PRETTY, BUT IT'S ALL PART OF THE FOOD CHAIN
GARFIELD
JIM DAVIS

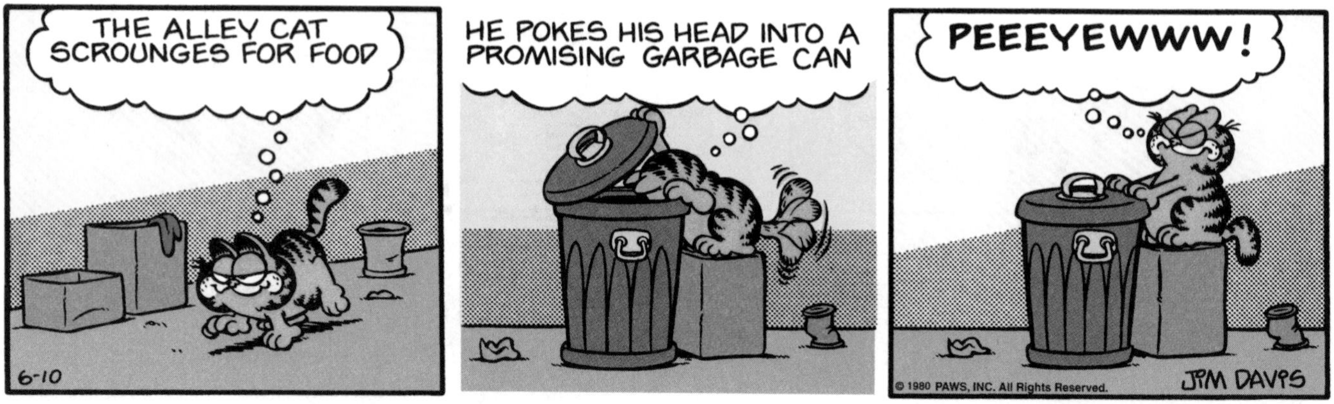
THE ALLEY CAT SCROUNGES FOR FOOD
6-10
HE POKES HIS HEAD INTO A PROMISING GARBAGE CAN
PEEEYEWWW!
© 1980 PAWS, INC. All Rights Reserved.
JIM DAVIS

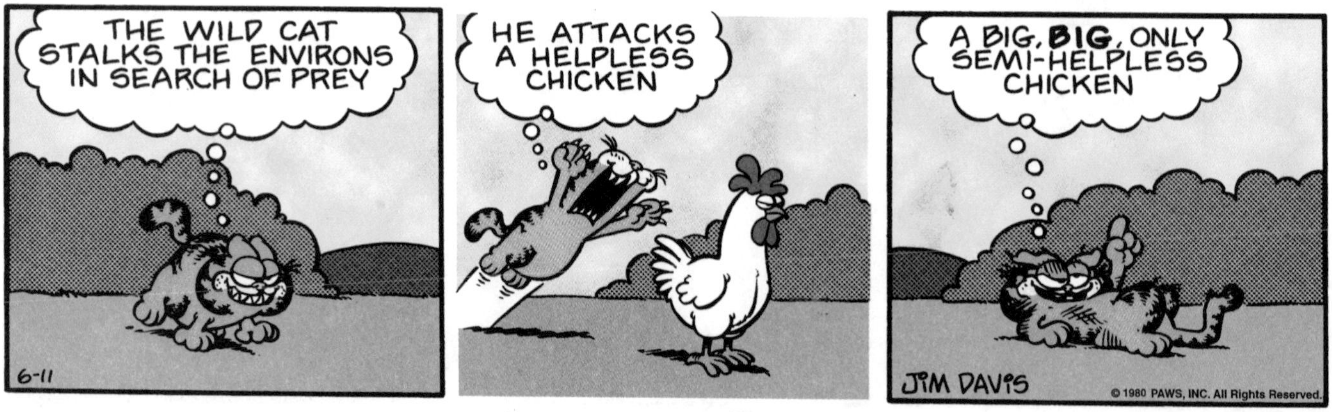
THE WILD CAT STALKS THE ENVIRONS IN SEARCH OF PREY
6-11
HE ATTACKS A HELPLESS CHICKEN
A BIG, **BIG**, ONLY SEMI-HELPLESS CHICKEN
JIM DAVIS
© 1980 PAWS, INC. All Rights Reserved.

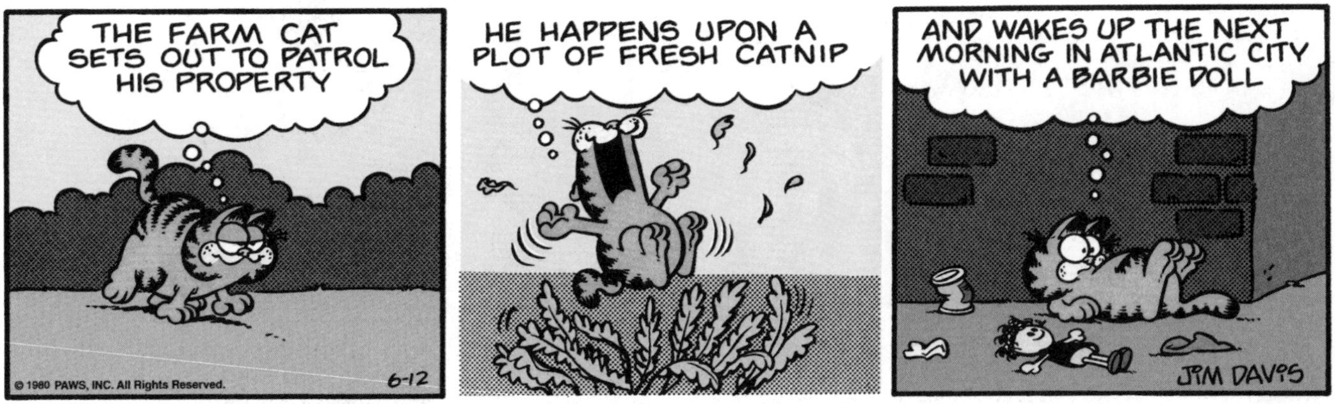
THE FARM CAT SETS OUT TO PATROL HIS PROPERTY
HE HAPPENS UPON A PLOT OF FRESH CATNIP
AND WAKES UP THE NEXT MORNING IN ATLANTIC CITY WITH A BARBIE DOLL
© 1980 PAWS, INC. All Rights Reserved.
6-12
JIM DAVIS

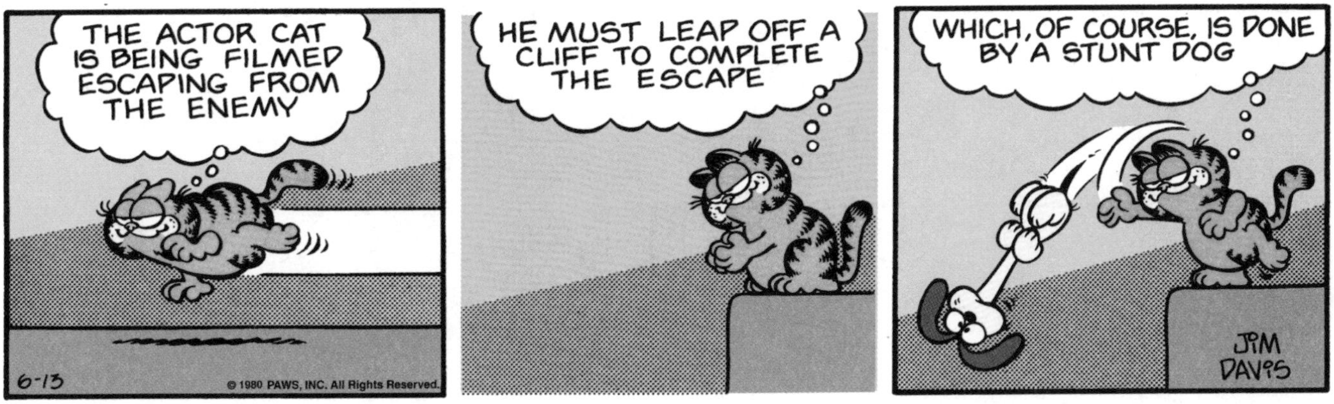
THE ACTOR CAT IS BEING FILMED ESCAPING FROM THE ENEMY
HE MUST LEAP OFF A CLIFF TO COMPLETE THE ESCAPE
WHICH, OF COURSE, IS DONE BY A STUNT DOG
6-13
© 1980 PAWS, INC. All Rights Reserved.
JIM DAVIS

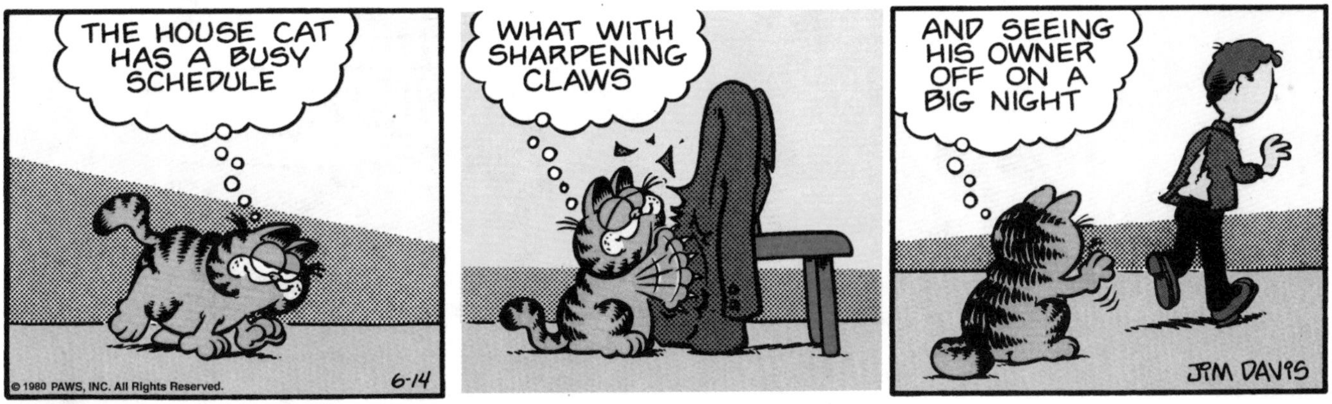
THE HOUSE CAT HAS A BUSY SCHEDULE
WHAT WITH SHARPENING CLAWS
AND SEEING HIS OWNER OFF ON A BIG NIGHT
© 1980 PAWS, INC. All Rights Reserved.
6-14
JIM DAVIS

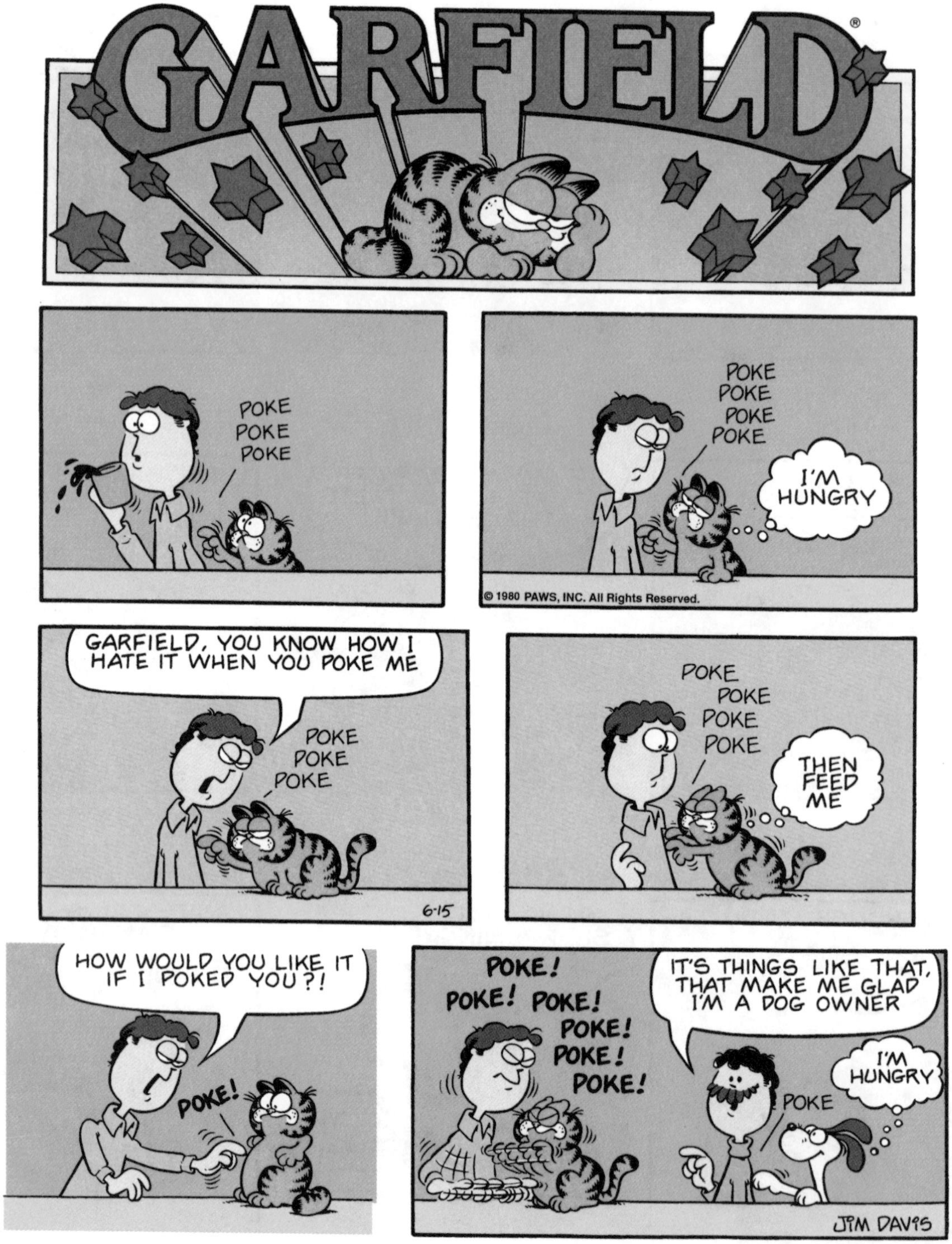
GARFIELD®
POKE POKE POKE
POKE POKE POKE POKE
I'M HUNGRY
© 1980 PAWS, INC. All Rights Reserved.
GARFIELD, YOU KNOW HOW I HATE IT WHEN YOU POKE ME
POKE POKE POKE
6-15
POKE POKE POKE POKE
THEN FEED ME
HOW WOULD YOU LIKE IT IF I POKED YOU?!
POKE!
POKE! POKE! POKE! POKE! POKE! POKE!
IT'S THINGS LIKE THAT, THAT MAKE ME GLAD I'M A DOG OWNER
POKE
I'M HUNGRY
JIM DAVIS

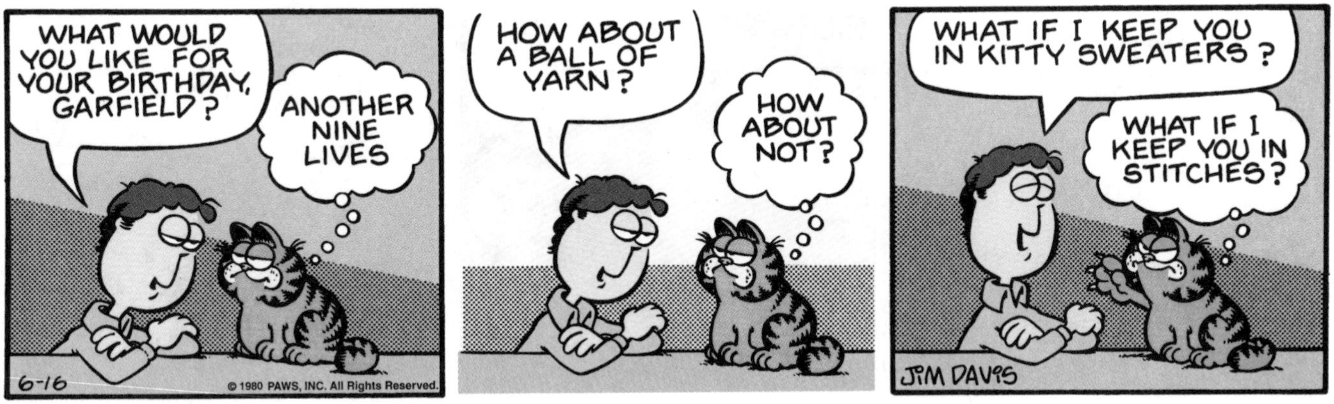
WHAT WOULD YOU LIKE FOR YOUR BIRTHDAY, GARFIELD?
ANOTHER NINE LIVES
HOW ABOUT A BALL OF YARN?
HOW ABOUT NOT?
WHAT IF I KEEP YOU IN KITTY SWEATERS?
WHAT IF I KEEP YOU IN STITCHES?
6-16
© 1980 PAWS, INC. All Rights Reserved.
JIM DAVIS

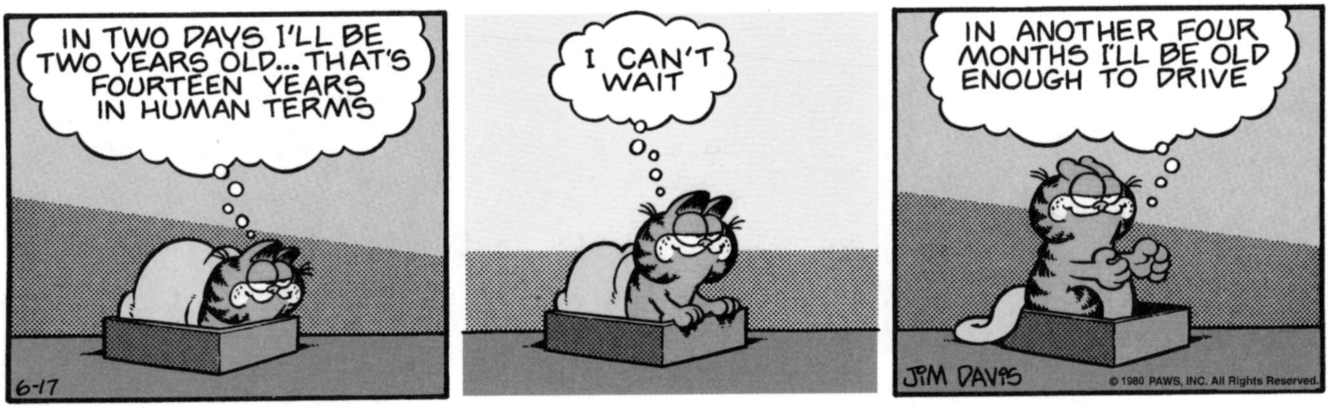
IN TWO DAYS I'LL BE TWO YEARS OLD... THAT'S FOURTEEN YEARS IN HUMAN TERMS
I CAN'T WAIT
IN ANOTHER FOUR MONTHS I'LL BE OLD ENOUGH TO DRIVE
6-17
JIM DAVIS
© 1980 PAWS, INC. All Rights Reserved.

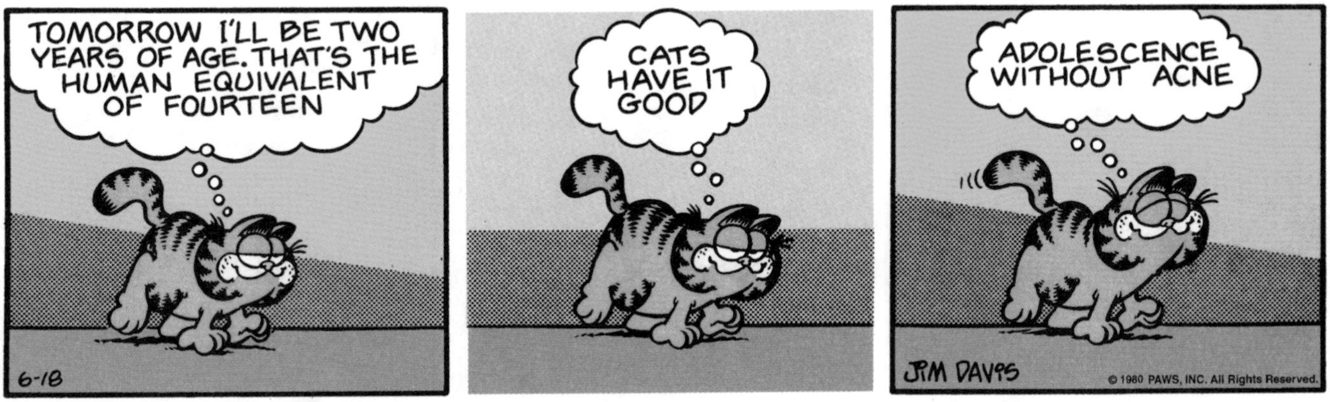
TOMORROW I'LL BE TWO YEARS OF AGE. THAT'S THE HUMAN EQUIVALENT OF FOURTEEN
CATS HAVE IT GOOD
ADOLESCENCE WITHOUT ACNE
6-18
JIM DAVIS
© 1980 PAWS, INC. All Rights Reserved.

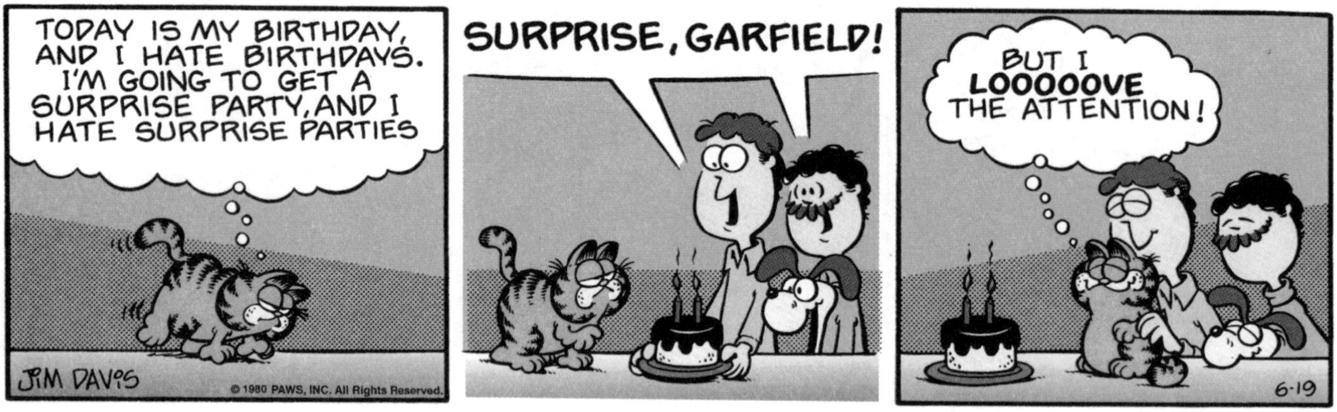
TODAY IS MY BIRTHDAY, AND I HATE BIRTHDAYS. I'M GOING TO GET A SURPRISE PARTY, AND I HATE SURPRISE PARTIES
JIM DAVIS
© 1980 PAWS, INC. All Rights Reserved.
SURPRISE, GARFIELD!
BUT I LOOOOOVE THE ATTENTION!
6-19

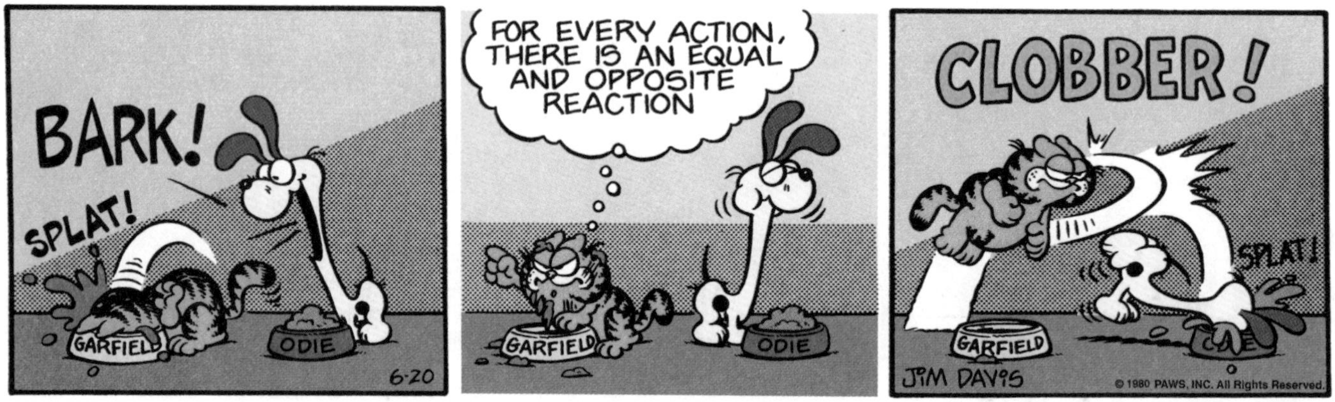
BARK!
SPLAT!
GARFIELD
ODIE
6-20
FOR EVERY ACTION, THERE IS AN EQUAL AND OPPOSITE REACTION
GARFIELD
ODIE
CLOBBER!
SPLAT!
GARFIELD
JIM DAVIS
© 1980 PAWS, INC. All Rights Reserved.

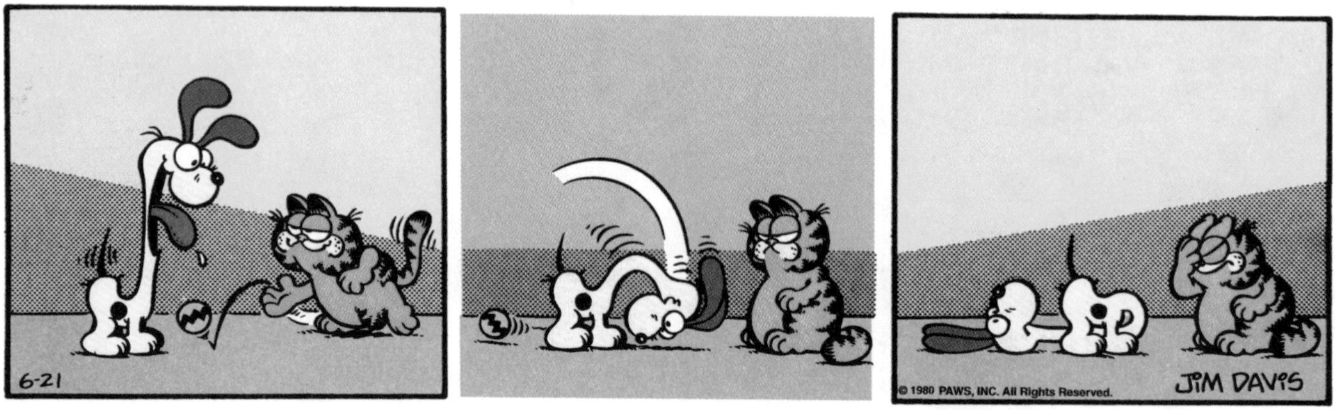
6-21
© 1980 PAWS, INC. All Rights Reserved.
JIM DAVIS

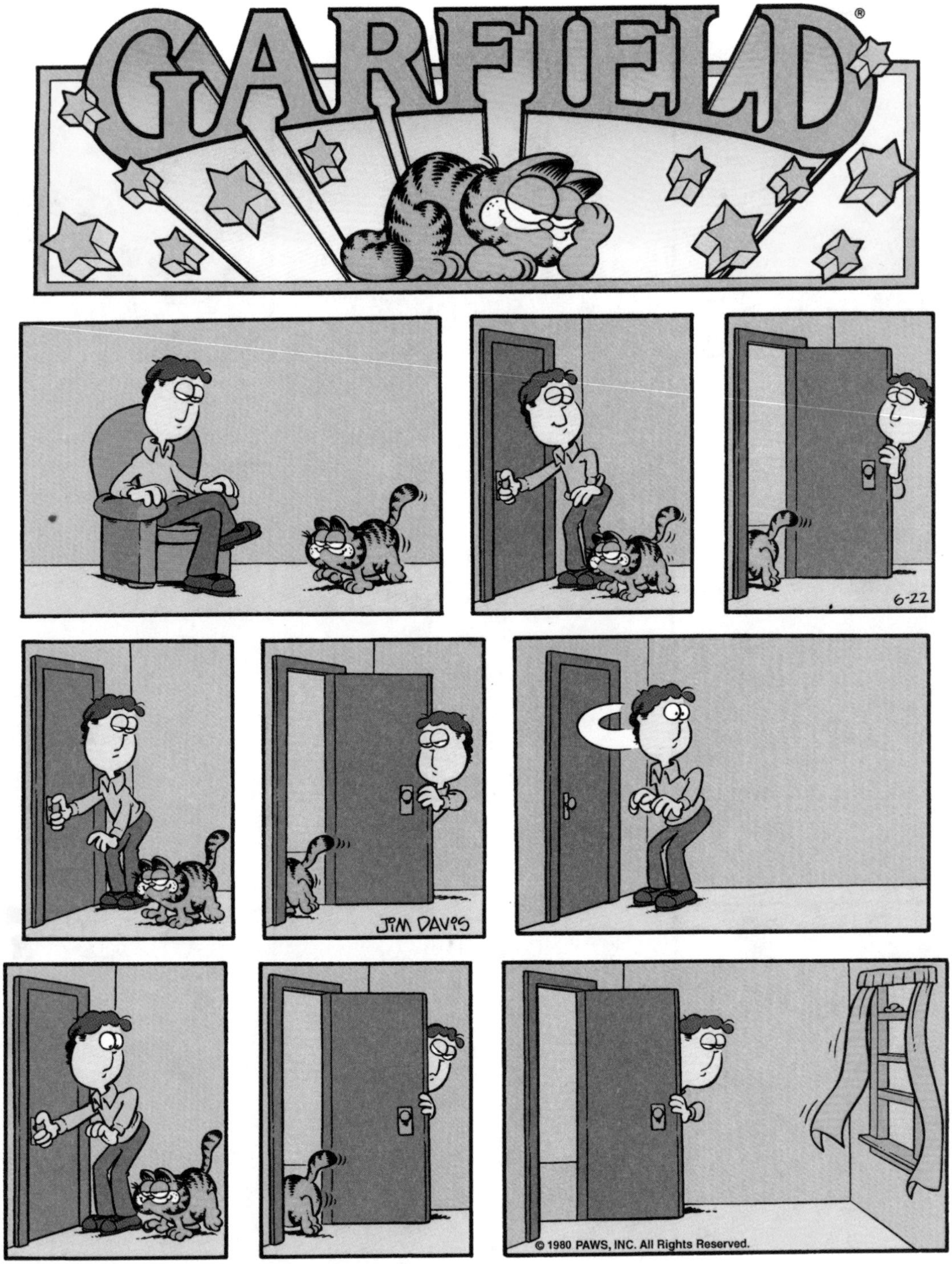
GARFIELD®
6-22
JIM DAVIS
© 1980 PAWS, INC. All Rights Reserved.

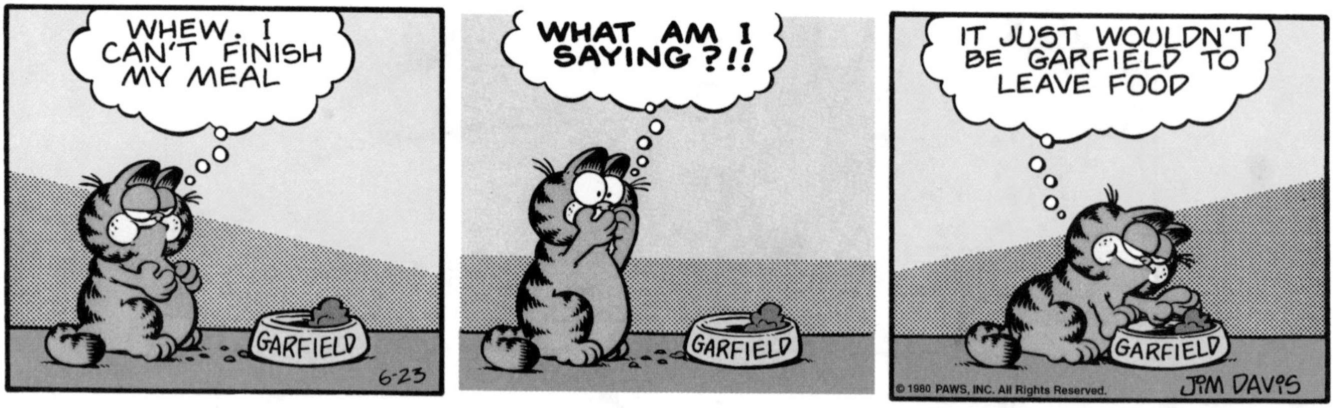
WHEW. I CAN'T FINISH MY MEAL
GARFIELD
6-23
WHAT AM I SAYING?!!
GARFIELD
IT JUST WOULDN'T BE GARFIELD TO LEAVE FOOD
GARFIELD
© 1980 PAWS, INC. All Rights Reserved.
JIM DAVIS

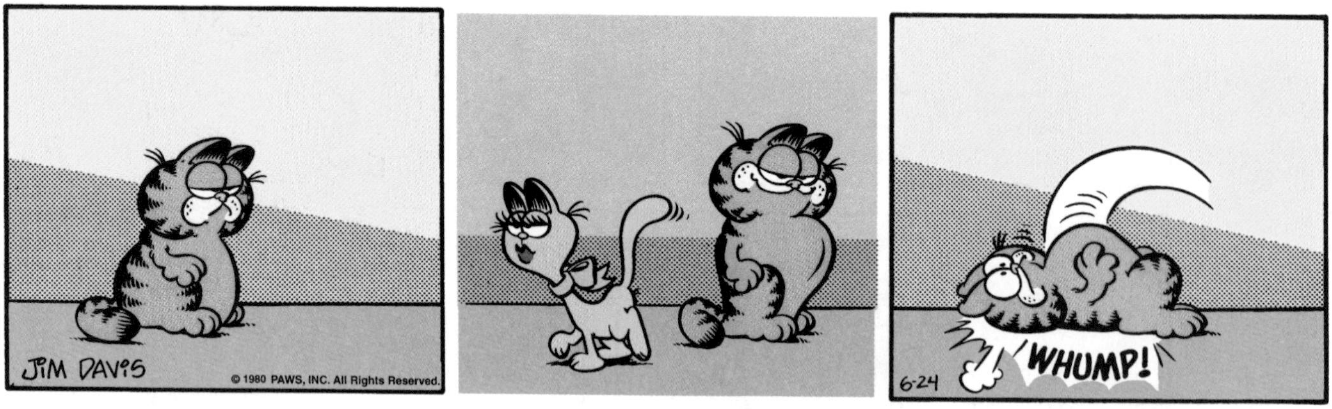
JIM DAVIS
© 1980 PAWS, INC. All Rights Reserved.
WHUMP!
6-24

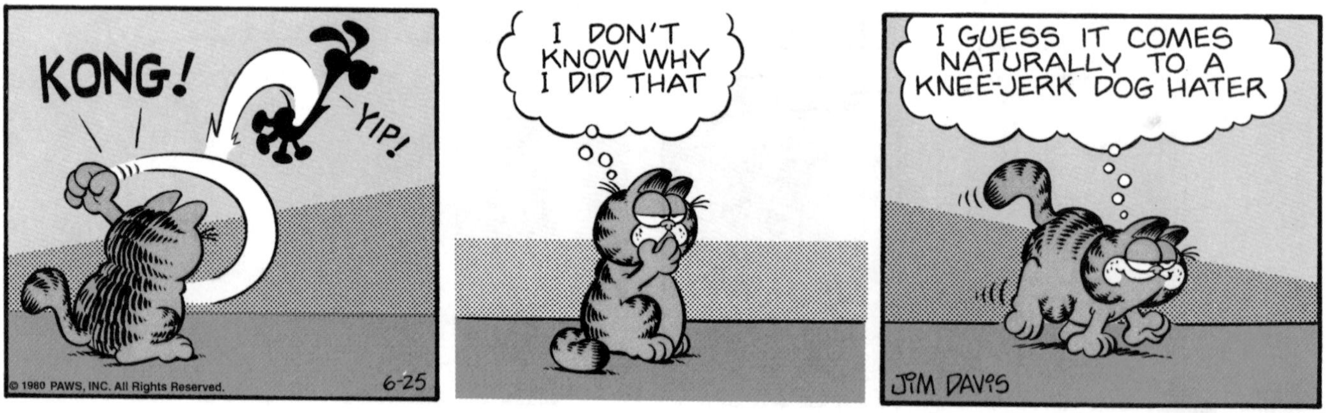
KONG!
YIP!
© 1980 PAWS, INC. All Rights Reserved.
6-25
I DON'T KNOW WHY I DID THAT
I GUESS IT COMES NATURALLY TO A KNEE-JERK DOG HATER
JIM DAVIS

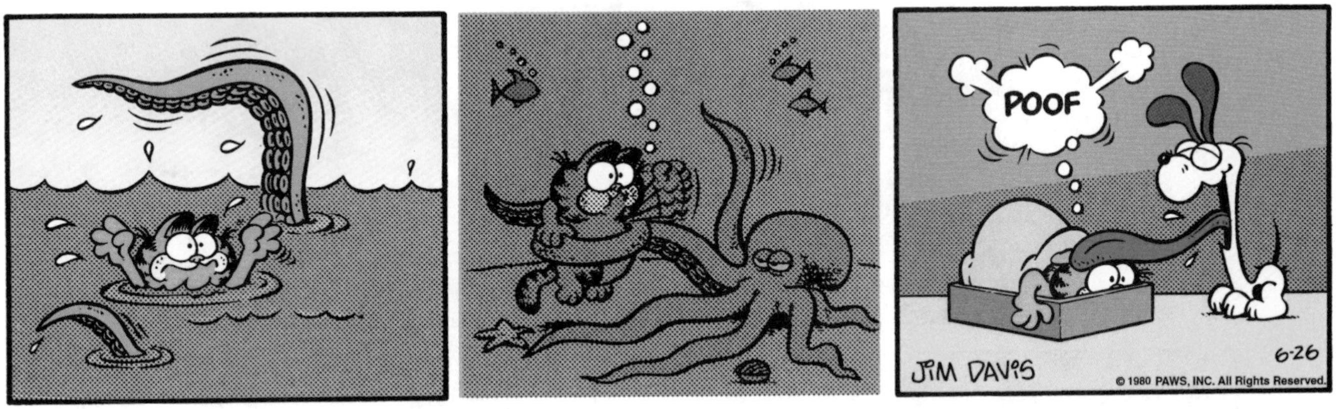
POOF
JIM DAVIS
6-26
© 1980 PAWS, INC. All Rights Reserved.

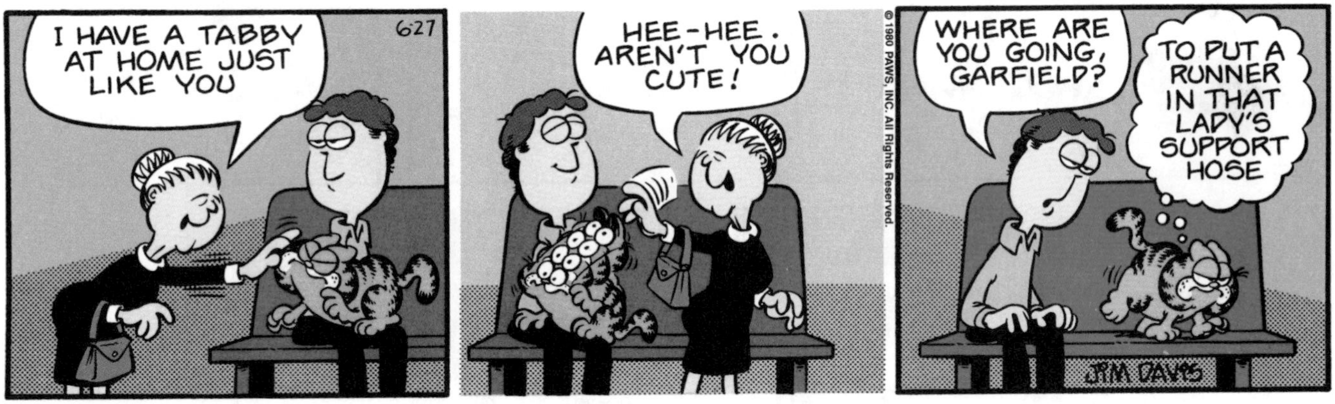
I HAVE A TABBY AT HOME JUST LIKE YOU
6-27
HEE-HEE. AREN'T YOU CUTE!
© 1980 PAWS, INC. All Rights Reserved.
WHERE ARE YOU GOING, GARFIELD?
TO PUT A RUNNER IN THAT LADY'S SUPPORT HOSE
JIM DAVIS

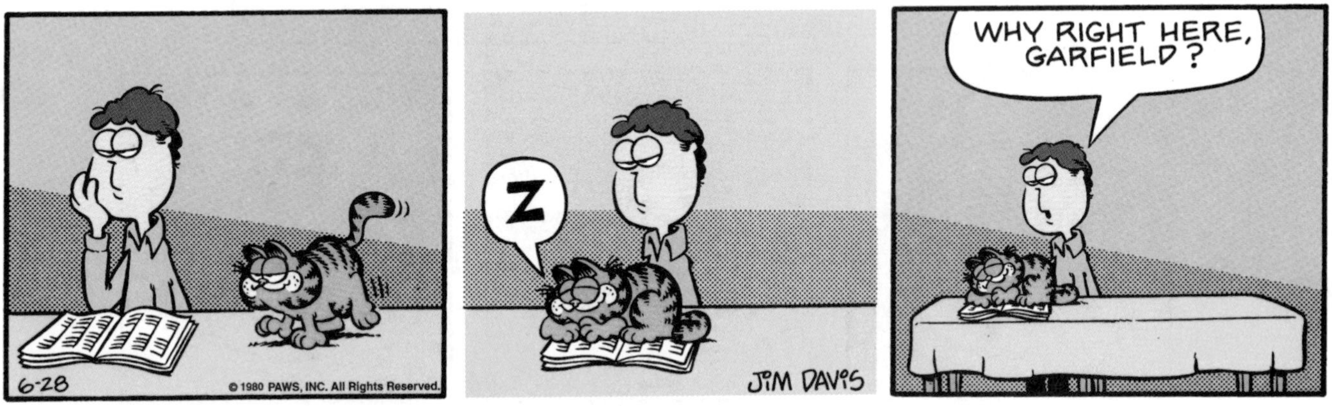
6-28
© 1980 PAWS, INC. All Rights Reserved.
Z
JIM DAVIS
WHY RIGHT HERE, GARFIELD?

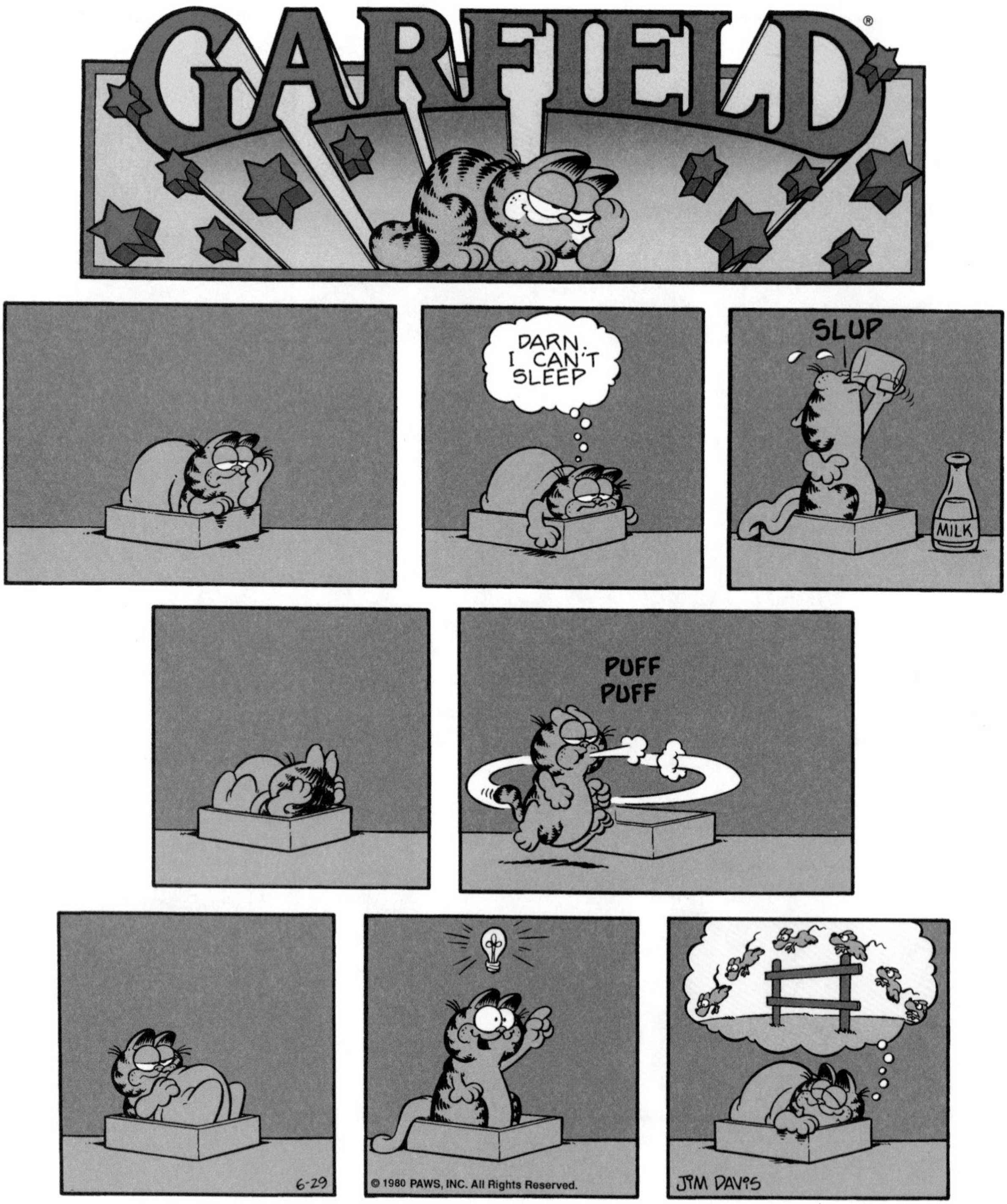
GARFIELD®
DARN. I CAN'T SLEEP
SLUP
MILK
PUFF PUFF
6-29
© 1980 PAWS, INC. All Rights Reserved.
JIM DAVIS

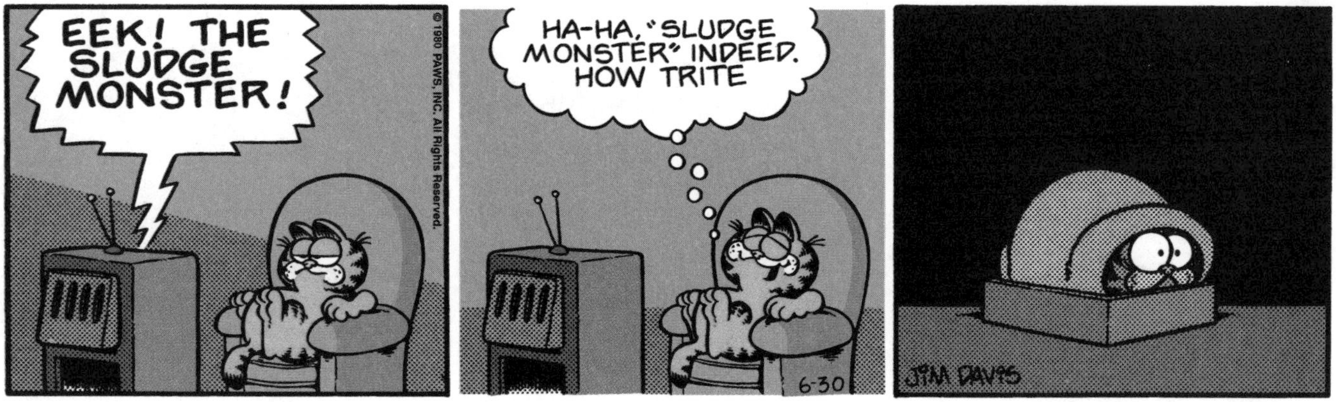
EEK! THE SLUDGE MONSTER!
© 1980 PAWS, INC. All Rights Reserved.
HA-HA, "SLUDGE MONSTER" INDEED. HOW TRITE
6-30
JIM DAVIS

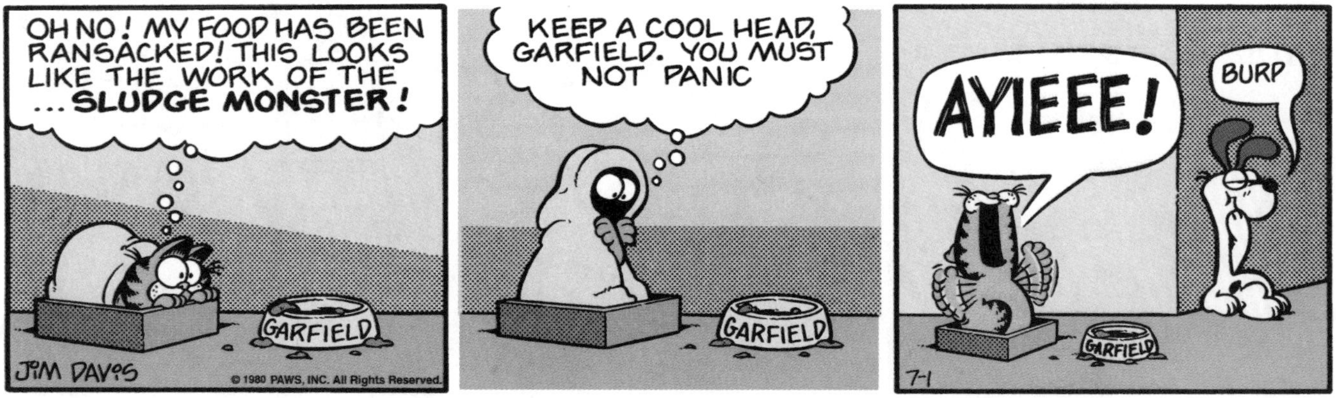
OH NO! MY FOOD HAS BEEN RANSACKED! THIS LOOKS LIKE THE WORK OF THE ...SLUDGE MONSTER!
GARFIELD
JIM DAVIS
© 1980 PAWS, INC. All Rights Reserved.
KEEP A COOL HEAD, GARFIELD. YOU MUST NOT PANIC
GARFIELD
AYIEEE!
BURP
GARFIELD
7-1

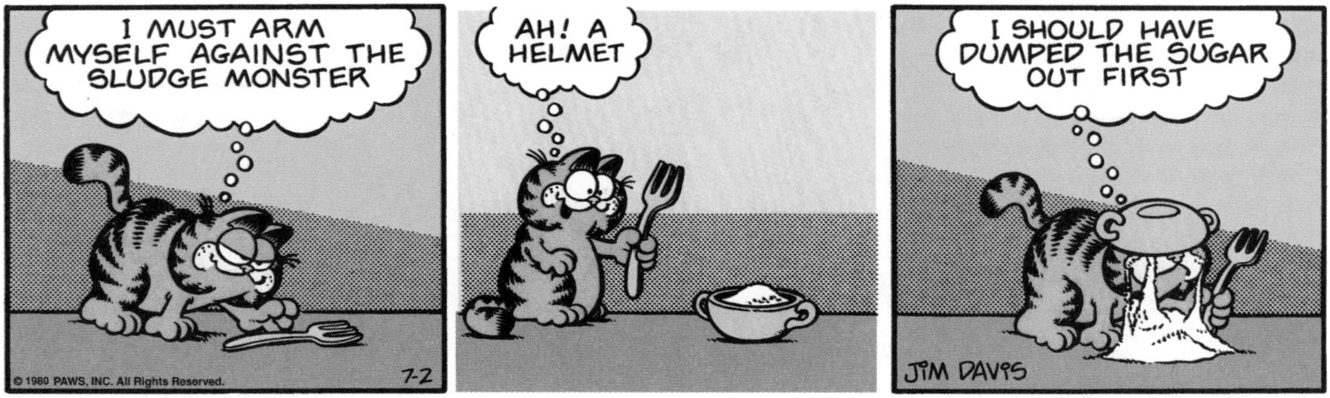
I MUST ARM MYSELF AGAINST THE SLUDGE MONSTER
© 1980 PAWS, INC. All Rights Reserved.
7-2
AH! A HELMET
I SHOULD HAVE DUMPED THE SUGAR OUT FIRST
JIM DAVIS

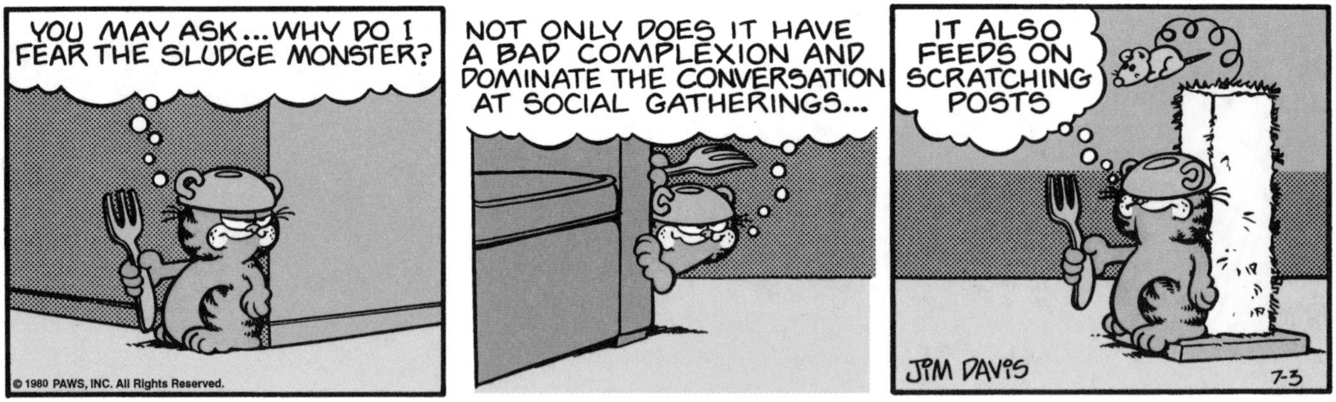
YOU MAY ASK...WHY DO I FEAR THE SLUDGE MONSTER?
© 1980 PAWS, INC. All Rights Reserved.
NOT ONLY DOES IT HAVE A BAD COMPLEXION AND DOMINATE THE CONVERSATION AT SOCIAL GATHERINGS...
IT ALSO FEEDS ON SCRATCHING POSTS
JIM DAVIS
7-3

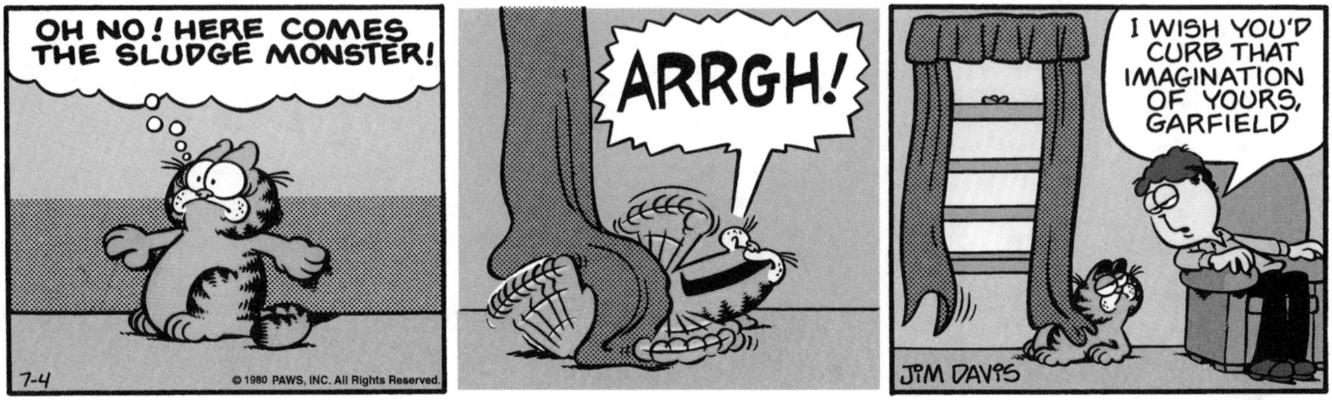
OH NO! HERE COMES THE SLUDGE MONSTER!
7-4
© 1980 PAWS, INC. All Rights Reserved.
ARRGH!
I WISH YOU'D CURB THAT IMAGINATION OF YOURS, GARFIELD
JIM DAVIS

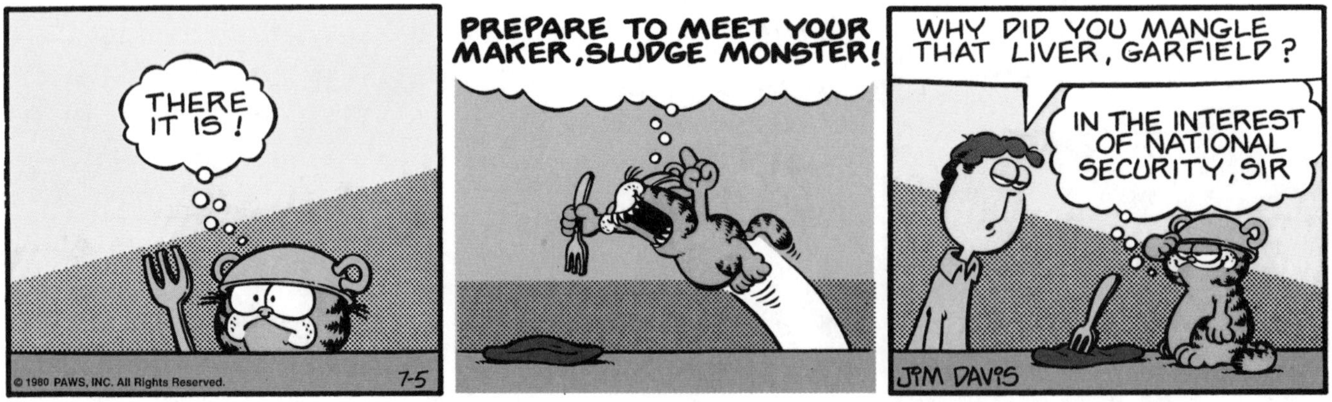
THERE IT IS!
© 1980 PAWS, INC. All Rights Reserved.
7-5
PREPARE TO MEET YOUR MAKER, SLUDGE MONSTER!
WHY DID YOU MANGLE THAT LIVER, GARFIELD?
IN THE INTEREST OF NATIONAL SECURITY, SIR
JIM DAVIS

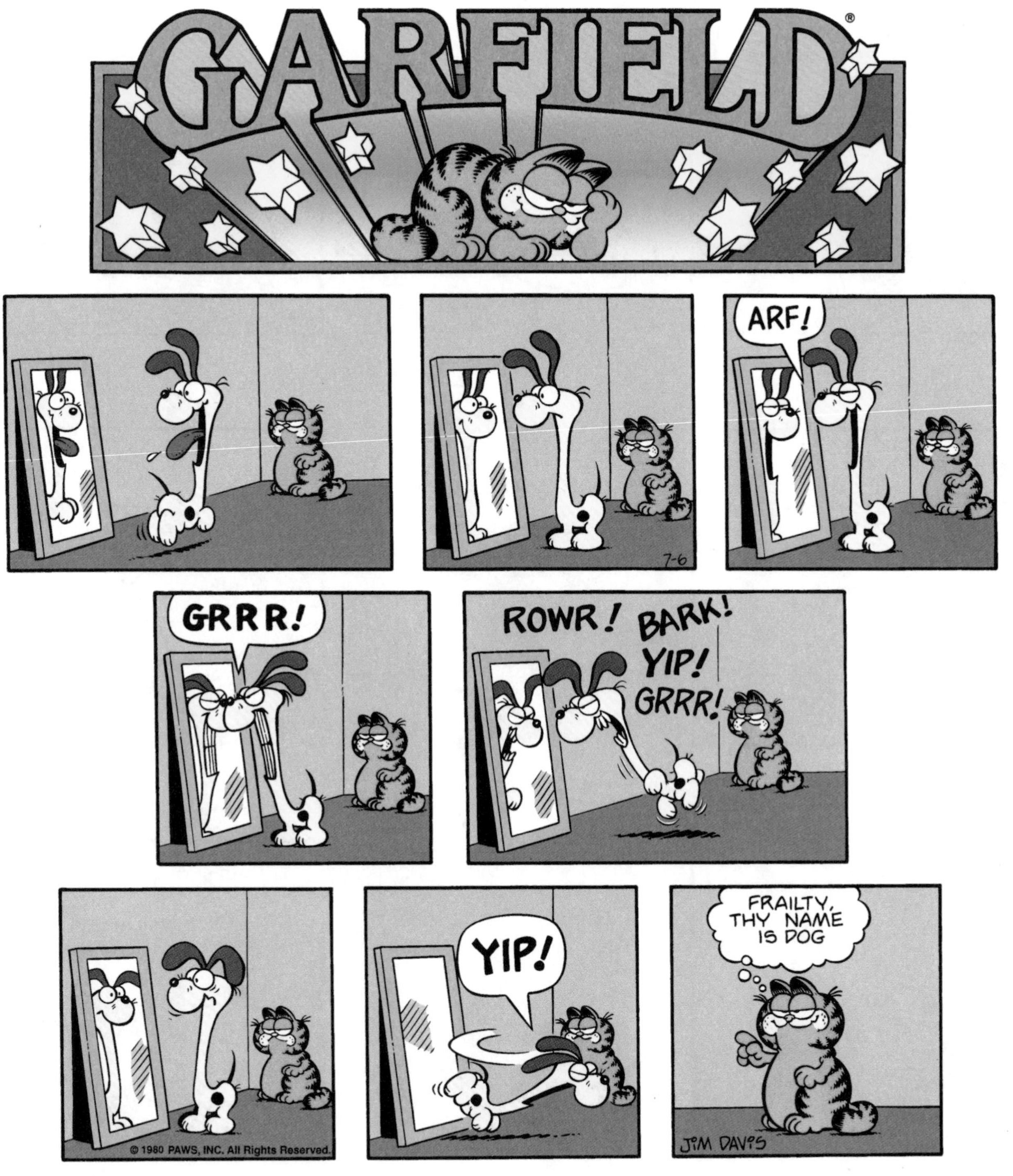
GARFIELD
ARF!
GRRR!
ROWR!
BARK!
YIP!
GRRR!
© 1980 PAWS, INC. All Rights Reserved.
YIP!
FRAILTY, THY NAME IS DOG
JIM DAVIS

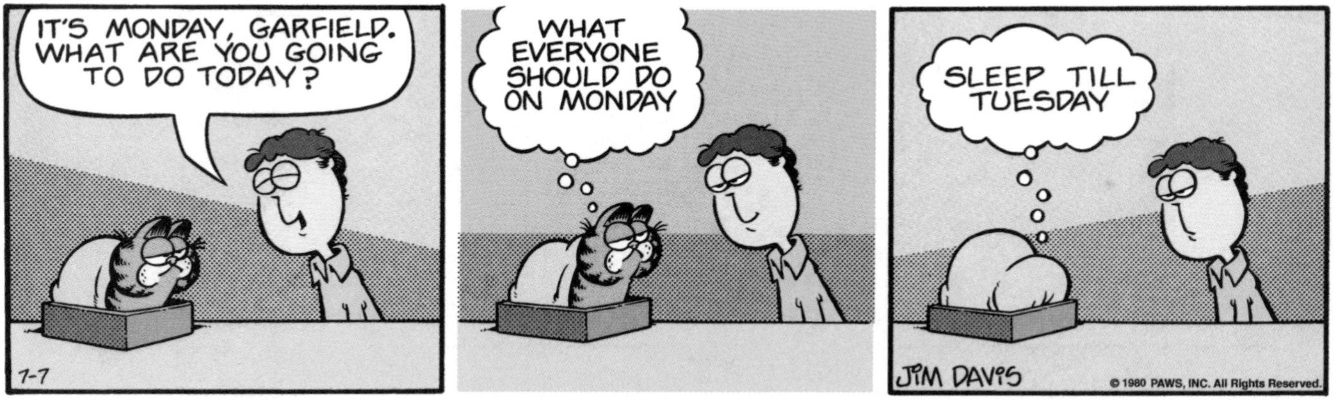
7-7
IT'S MONDAY, GARFIELD. WHAT ARE YOU GOING TO DO TODAY?
WHAT EVERYONE SHOULD DO ON MONDAY
SLEEP TILL TUESDAY
JIM DAVIS
© 1980 PAWS, INC. All Rights Reserved.

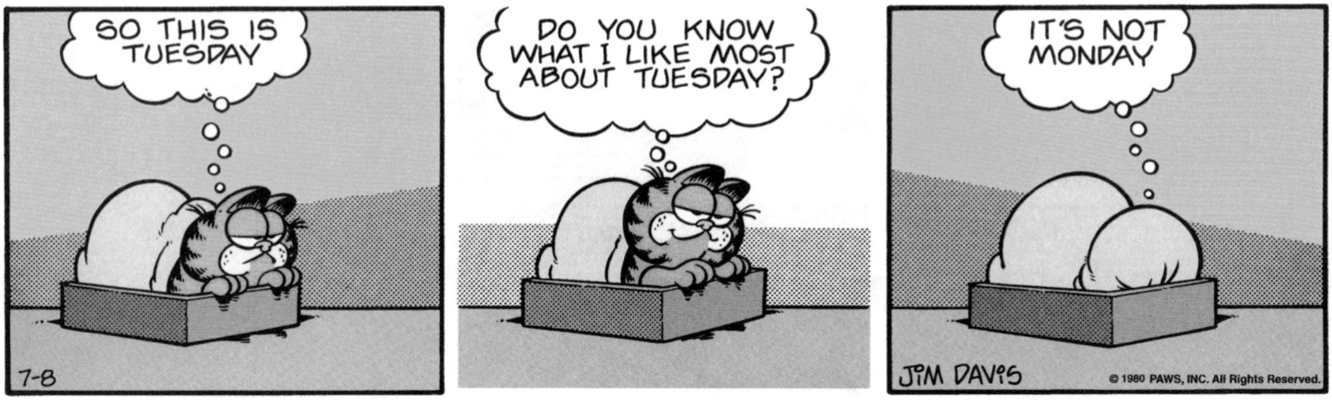
7-8
SO THIS IS TUESDAY
DO YOU KNOW WHAT I LIKE MOST ABOUT TUESDAY?
IT'S NOT MONDAY
JIM DAVIS
© 1980 PAWS, INC. All Rights Reserved.

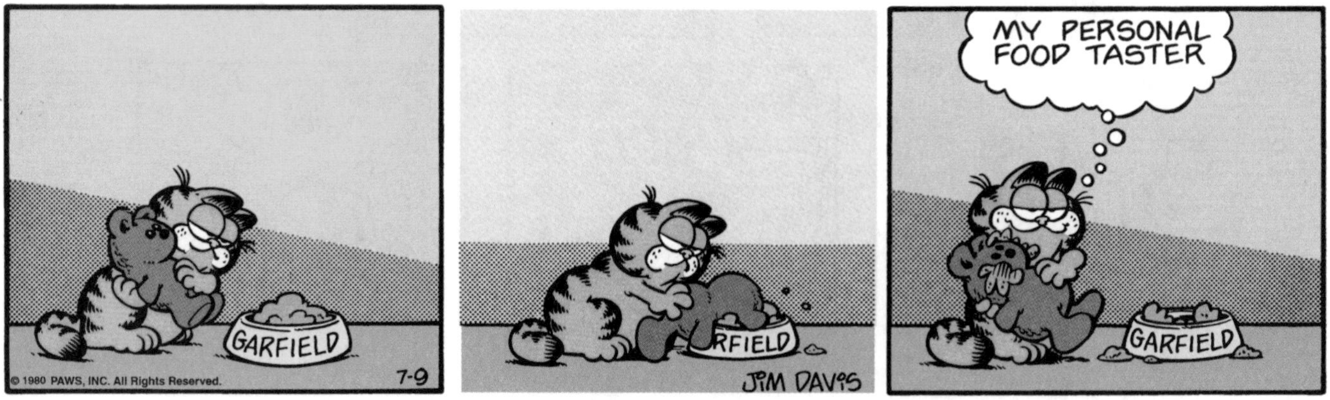
GARFIELD
© 1980 PAWS, INC. All Rights Reserved.
7-9
RFIELD
JIM DAVIS
MY PERSONAL FOOD TASTER
GARFIELD

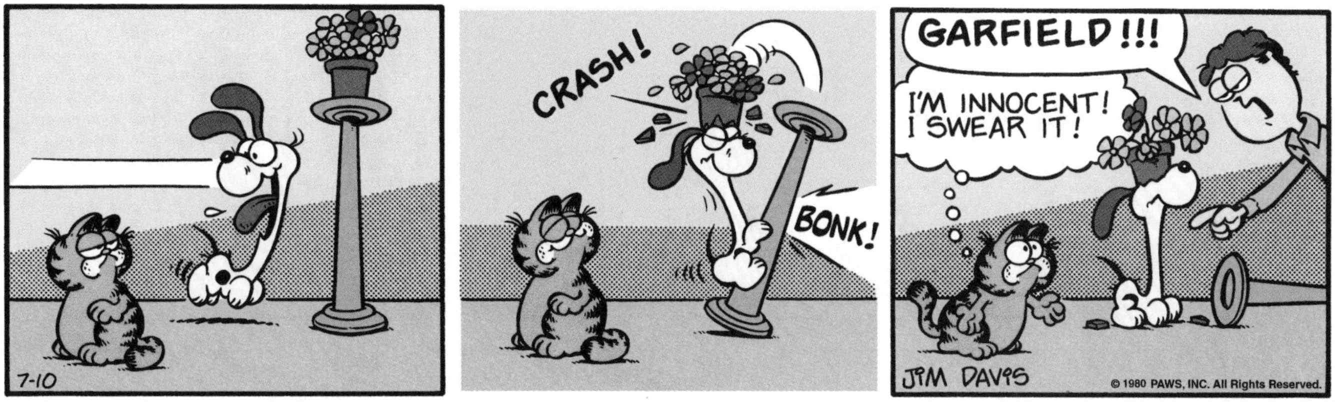
CRASH!
BONK!
GARFIELD!!!
I'M INNOCENT! I SWEAR IT!
7-10
JIM DAVIS
© 1980 PAWS, INC. All Rights Reserved.

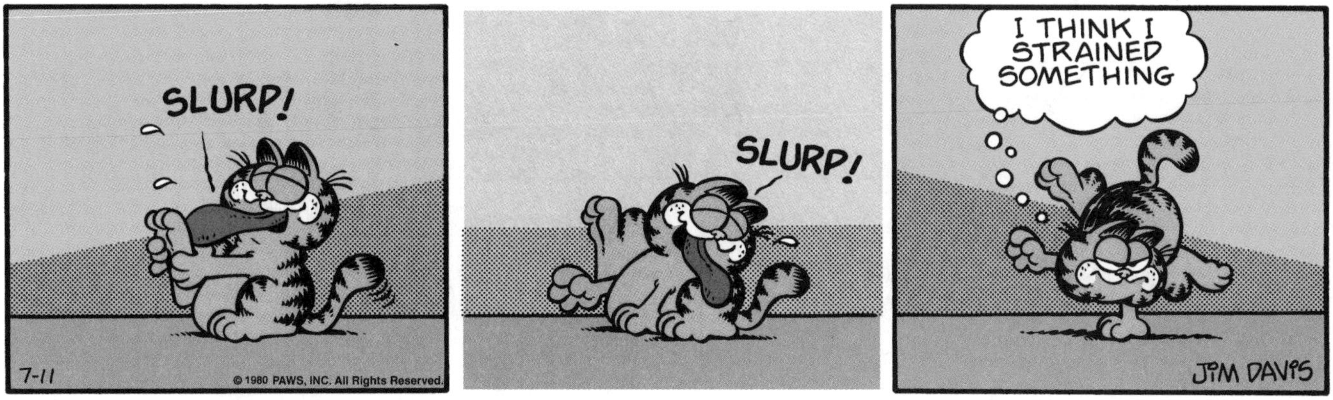
SLURP!
SLURP!
I THINK I STRAINED SOMETHING
7-11
© 1980 PAWS, INC. All Rights Reserved.
JIM DAVIS

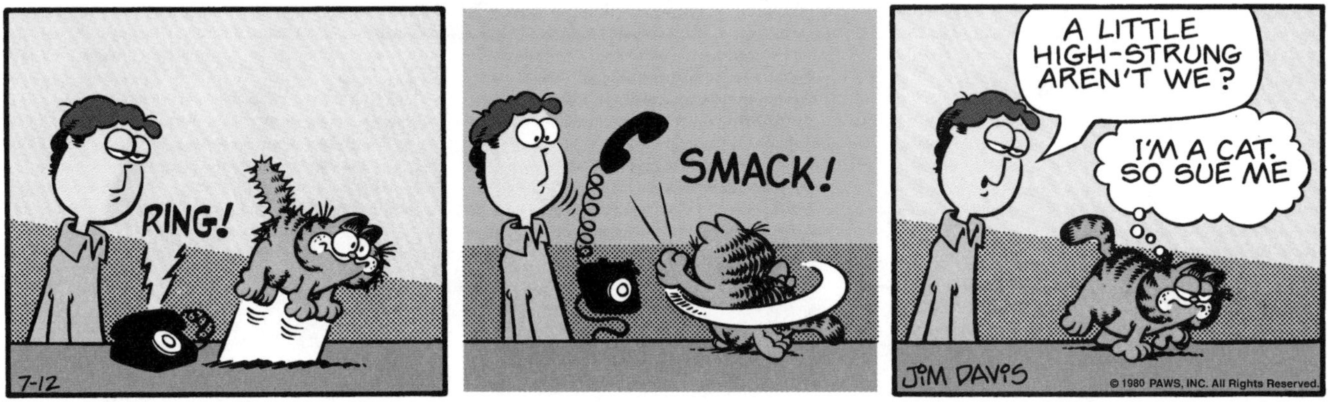
RING!
SMACK!
A LITTLE HIGH-STRUNG AREN'T WE?
I'M A CAT. SO SUE ME
7-12
JIM DAVIS
© 1980 PAWS, INC. All Rights Reserved.

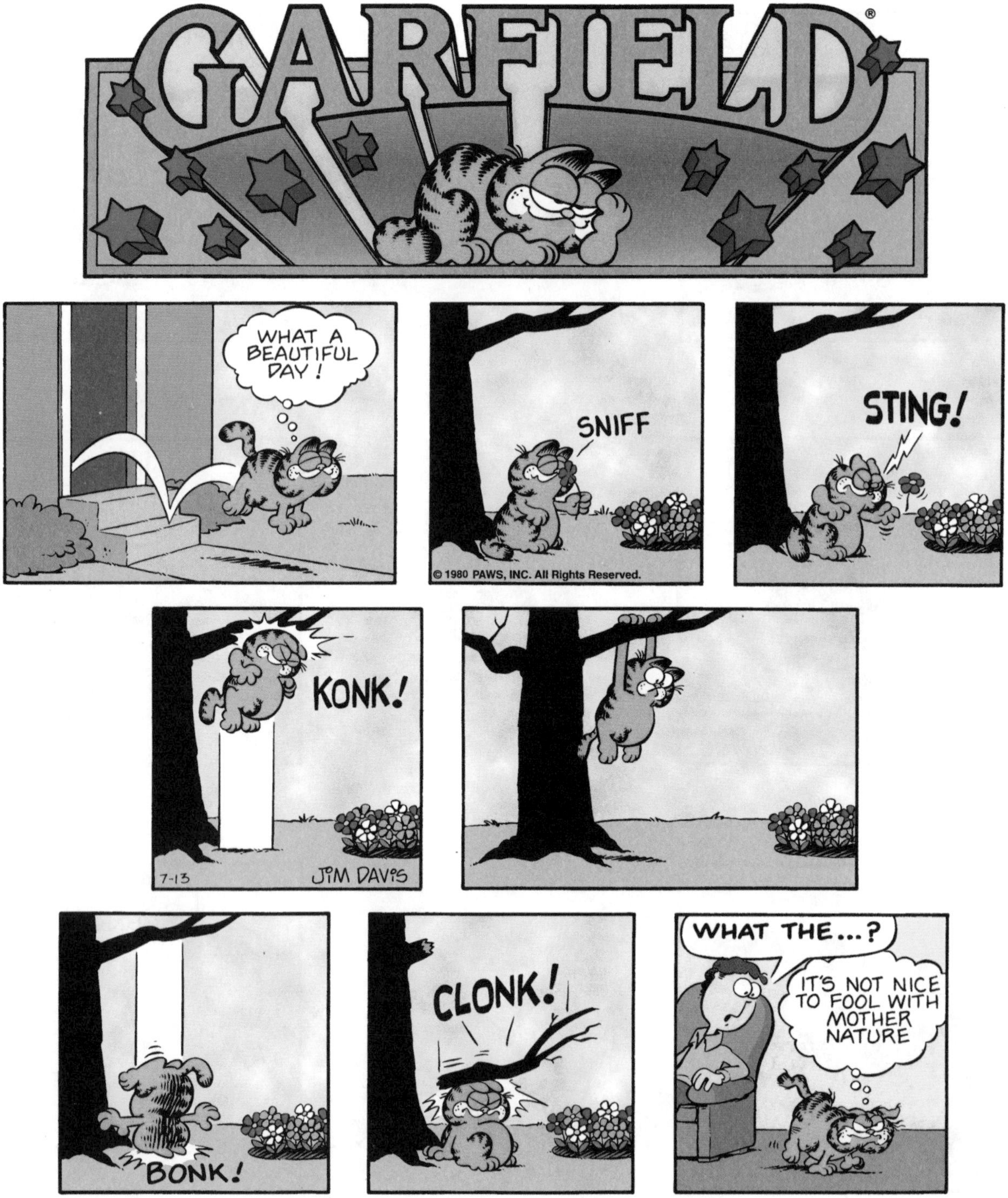
GARFIELD®
WHAT A BEAUTIFUL DAY!
SNIFF
© 1980 PAWS, INC. All Rights Reserved.
STING!
KONK!
7-13
JIM DAVIS
BONK!
CLONK!
WHAT THE...?
IT'S NOT NICE TO FOOL WITH MOTHER NATURE

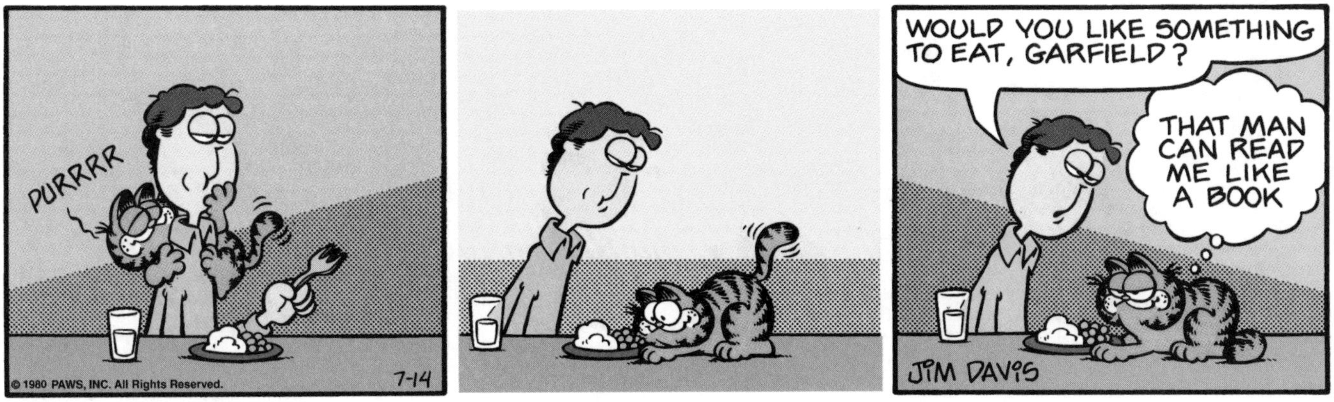
PURRRR
© 1980 PAWS, INC. All Rights Reserved.
7-14
WOULD YOU LIKE SOMETHING TO EAT, GARFIELD?
THAT MAN CAN READ ME LIKE A BOOK
JIM DAVIS

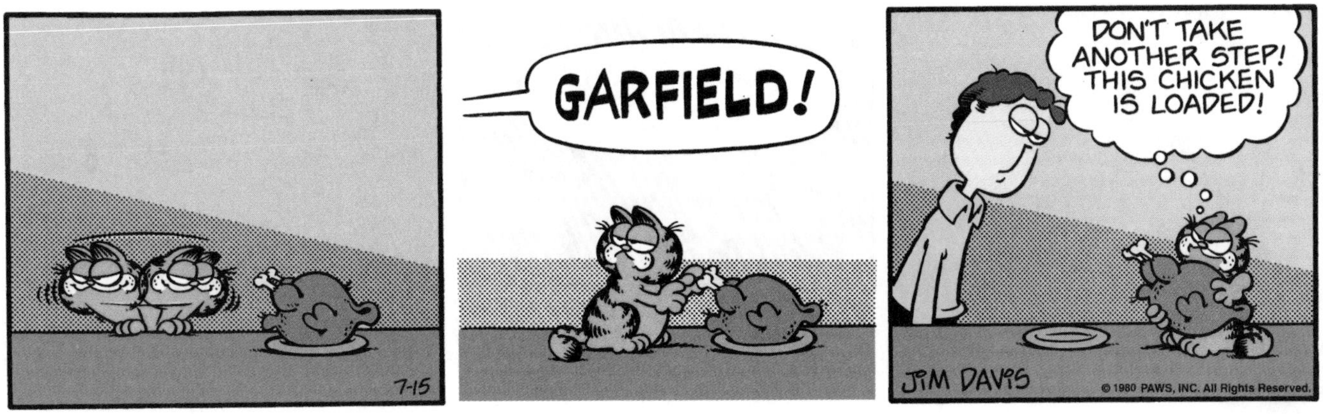
7-15
GARFIELD!
DON'T TAKE ANOTHER STEP! THIS CHICKEN IS LOADED!
JIM DAVIS
© 1980 PAWS, INC. All Rights Reserved.

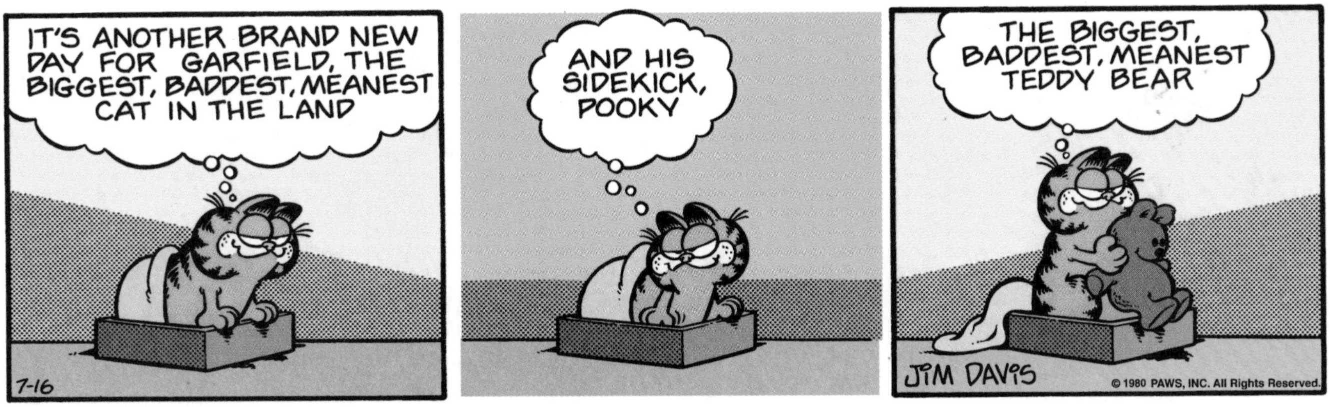
IT'S ANOTHER BRAND NEW DAY FOR GARFIELD, THE BIGGEST, BADDEST, MEANEST CAT IN THE LAND
7-16
AND HIS SIDEKICK, POOKY
THE BIGGEST, BADDEST, MEANEST TEDDY BEAR
JIM DAVIS
© 1980 PAWS, INC. All Rights Reserved.

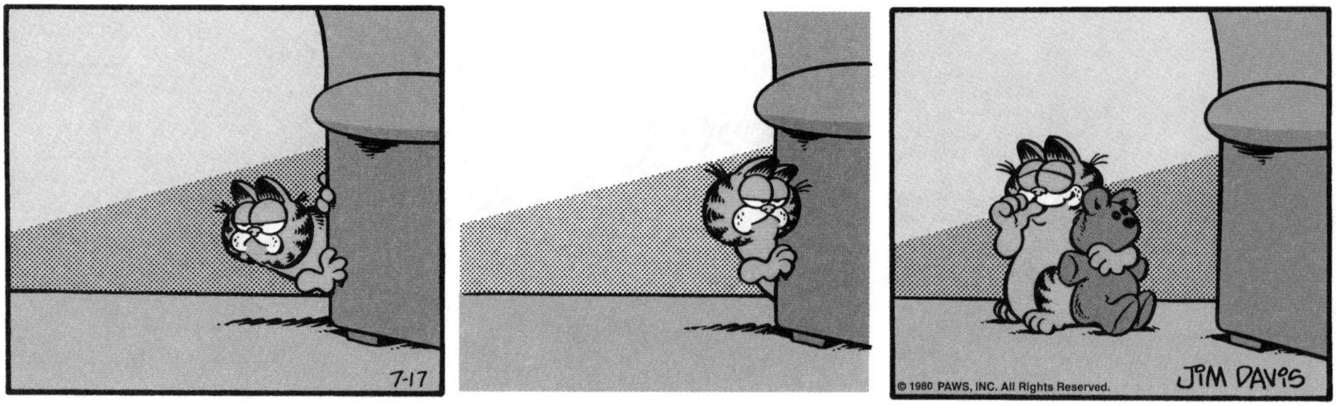
7-17
© 1980 PAWS, INC. All Rights Reserved.
JIM DAVIS

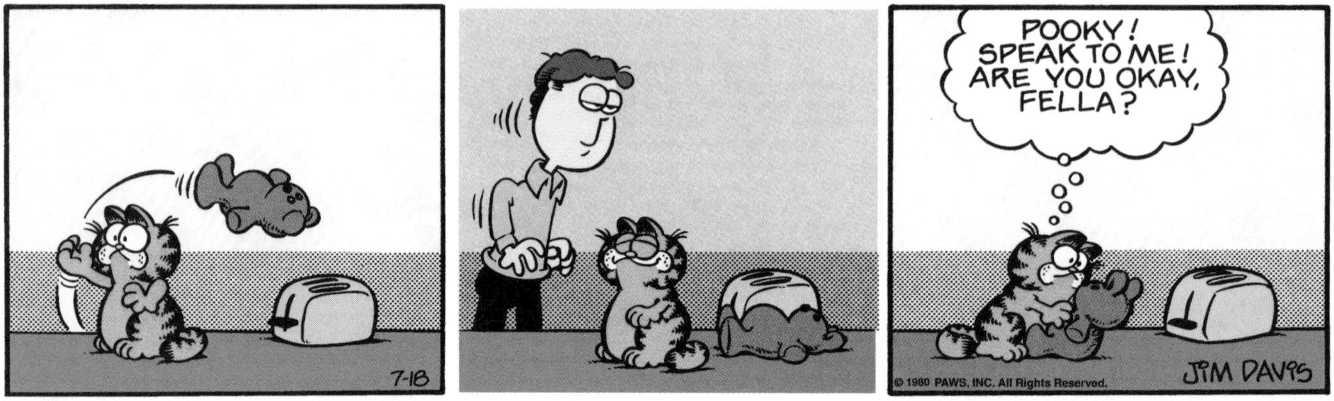
7-18
POOKY! SPEAK TO ME! ARE YOU OKAY, FELLA?
© 1980 PAWS, INC. All Rights Reserved.
JIM DAVIS

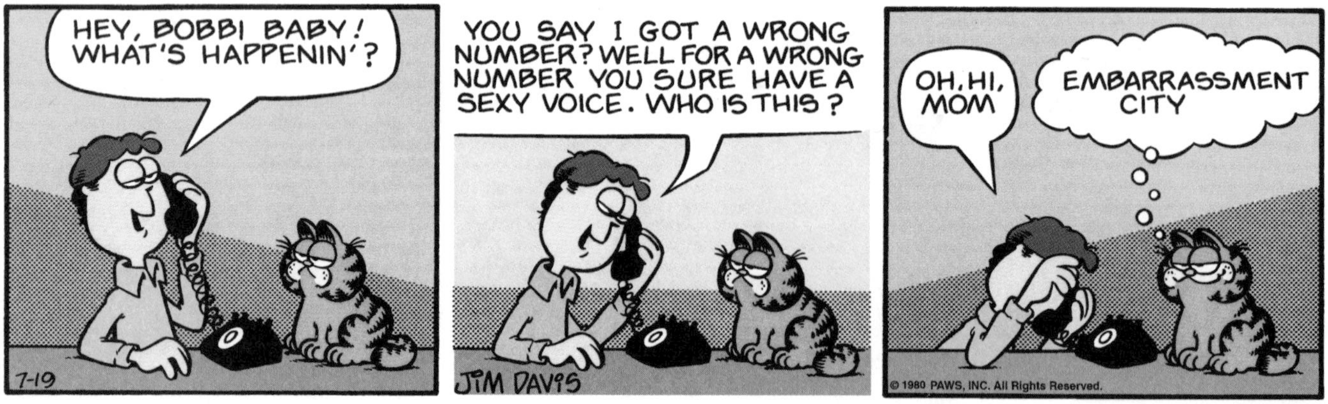
HEY, BOBBI BABY! WHAT'S HAPPENIN'?
7-19
YOU SAY I GOT A WRONG NUMBER? WELL FOR A WRONG NUMBER YOU SURE HAVE A SEXY VOICE. WHO IS THIS?
JIM DAVIS
OH, HI, MOM
EMBARRASSMENT CITY
© 1980 PAWS, INC. All Rights Reserved.

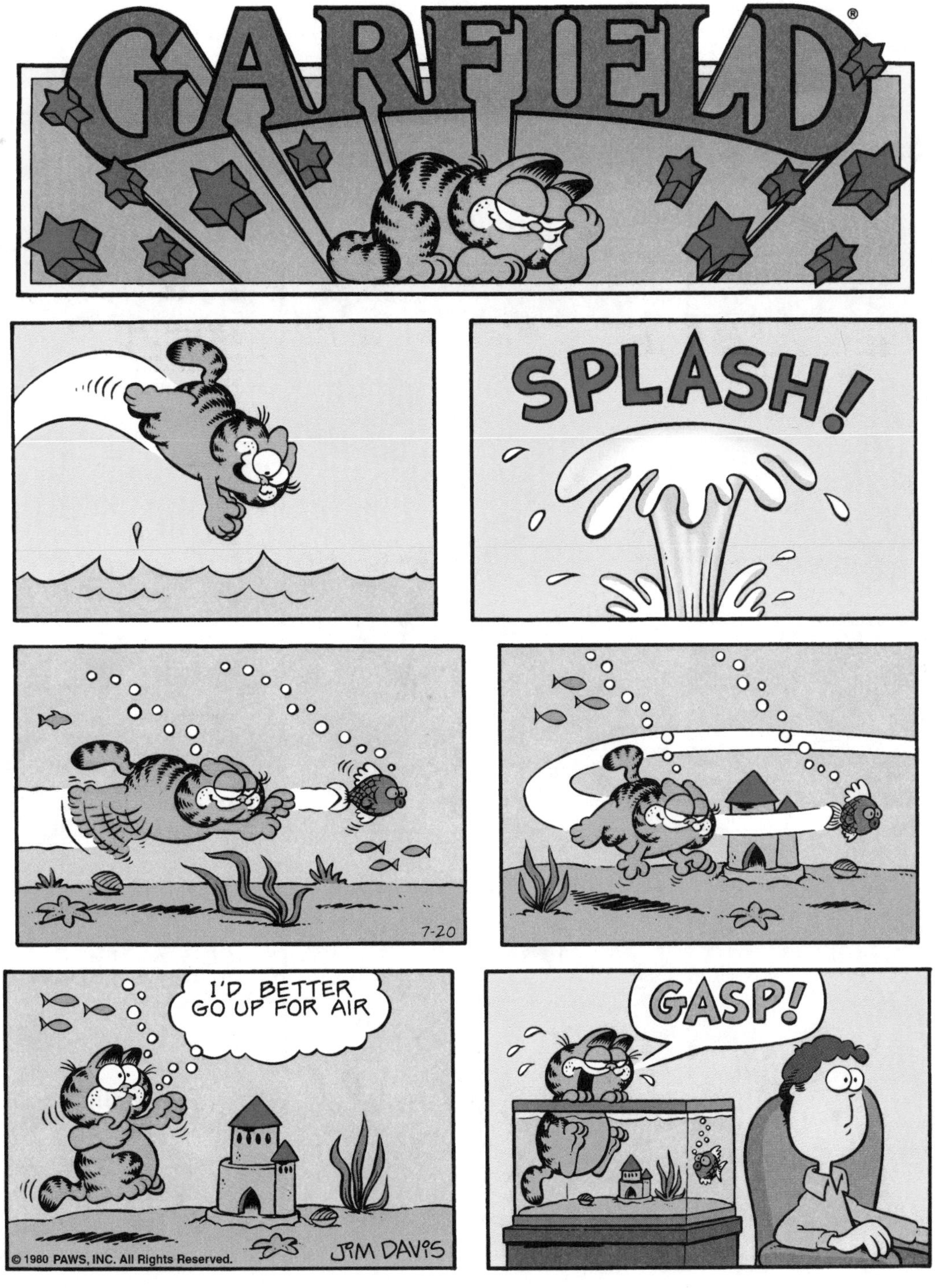

GARFIELD®
SPLASH!
7-20
I'D BETTER GO UP FOR AIR
GASP!
JIM DAVIS

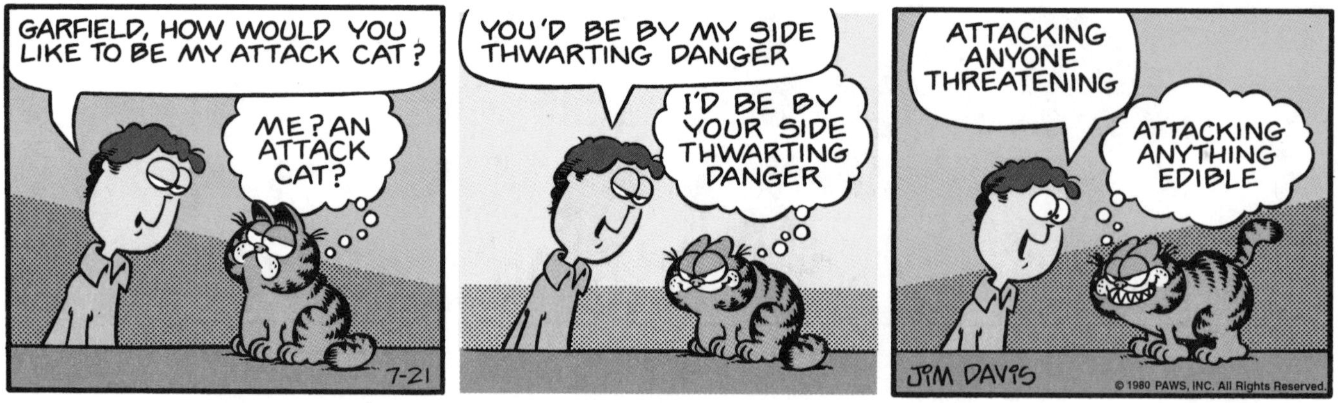
GARFIELD, HOW WOULD YOU LIKE TO BE MY ATTACK CAT?
ME? AN ATTACK CAT?
7-21
YOU'D BE BY MY SIDE THWARTING DANGER
I'D BE BY YOUR SIDE THWARTING DANGER
ATTACKING ANYONE THREATENING
ATTACKING ANYTHING EDIBLE
JIM DAVIS
© 1980 PAWS, INC. All Rights Reserved.

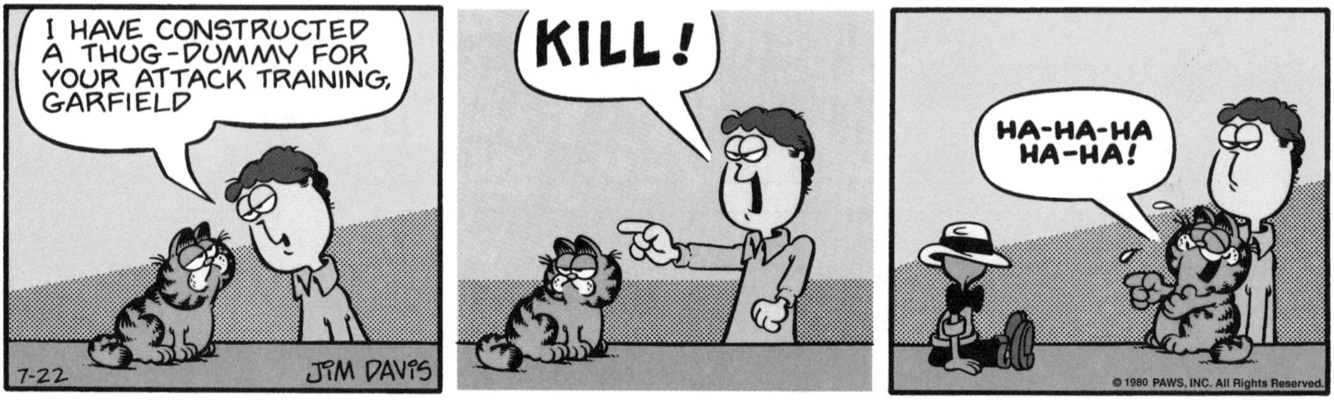
I HAVE CONSTRUCTED A THUG-DUMMY FOR YOUR ATTACK TRAINING, GARFIELD
7-22
JIM DAVIS
KILL!
HA-HA-HA HA-HA!
© 1980 PAWS, INC. All Rights Reserved.

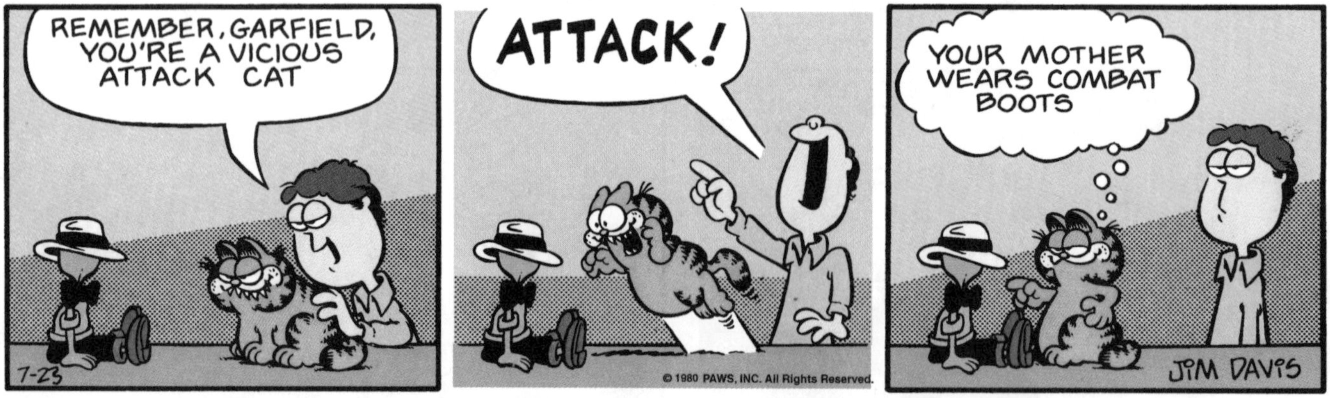
REMEMBER, GARFIELD, YOU'RE A VICIOUS ATTACK CAT
7-23
ATTACK!
© 1980 PAWS, INC. All Rights Reserved.
YOUR MOTHER WEARS COMBAT BOOTS
JIM DAVIS

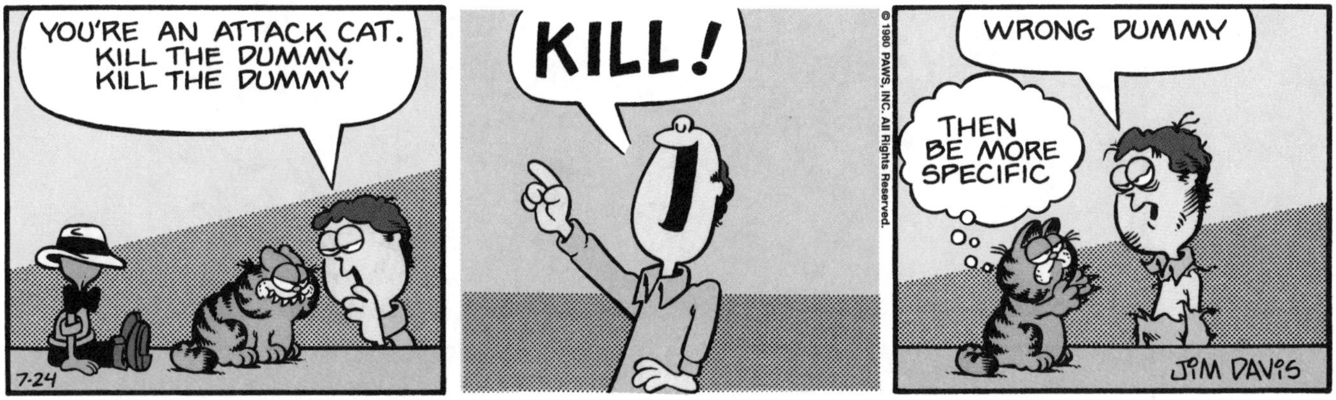
YOU'RE AN ATTACK CAT. KILL THE DUMMY. KILL THE DUMMY
7-24
KILL!
© 1980 PAWS, INC. All Rights Reserved.
WRONG DUMMY
THEN BE MORE SPECIFIC
JIM DAVIS

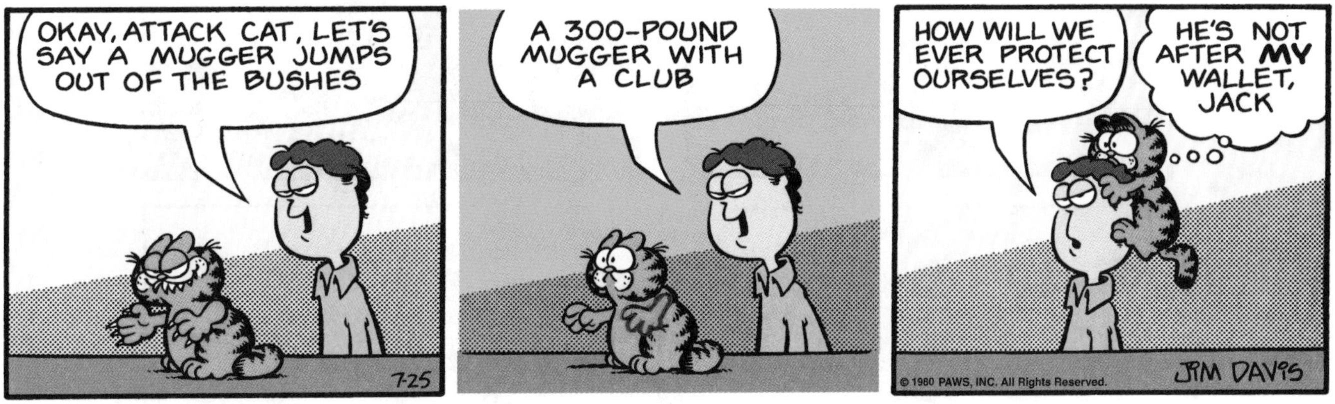
OKAY, ATTACK CAT, LET'S SAY A MUGGER JUMPS OUT OF THE BUSHES
7-25
A 300-POUND MUGGER WITH A CLUB
HOW WILL WE EVER PROTECT OURSELVES?
HE'S NOT AFTER MY WALLET, JACK
© 1980 PAWS, INC. All Rights Reserved.
JIM DAVIS

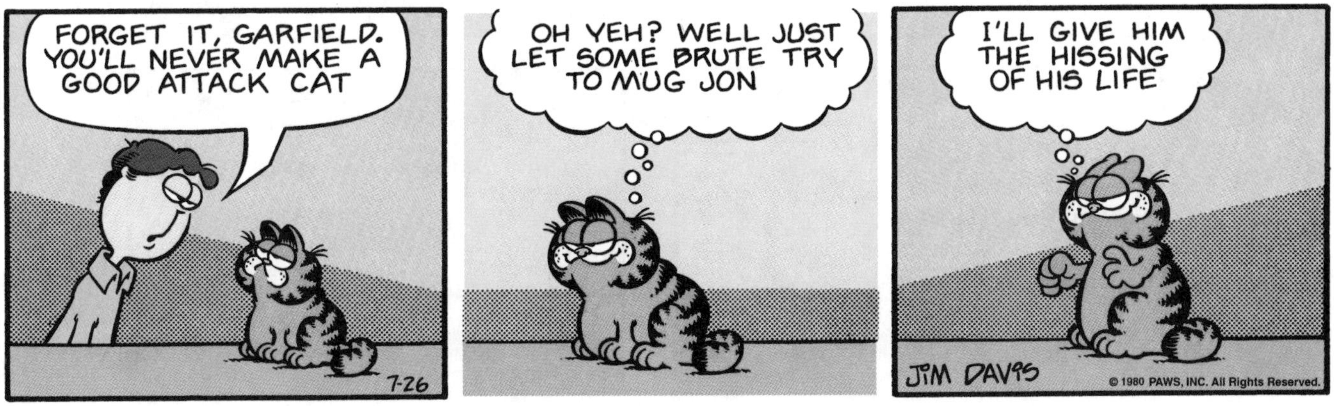
FORGET IT, GARFIELD. YOU'LL NEVER MAKE A GOOD ATTACK CAT
7-26
OH YEH? WELL JUST LET SOME BRUTE TRY TO MUG JON
I'LL GIVE HIM THE HISSING OF HIS LIFE
JIM DAVIS
© 1980 PAWS, INC. All Rights Reserved.

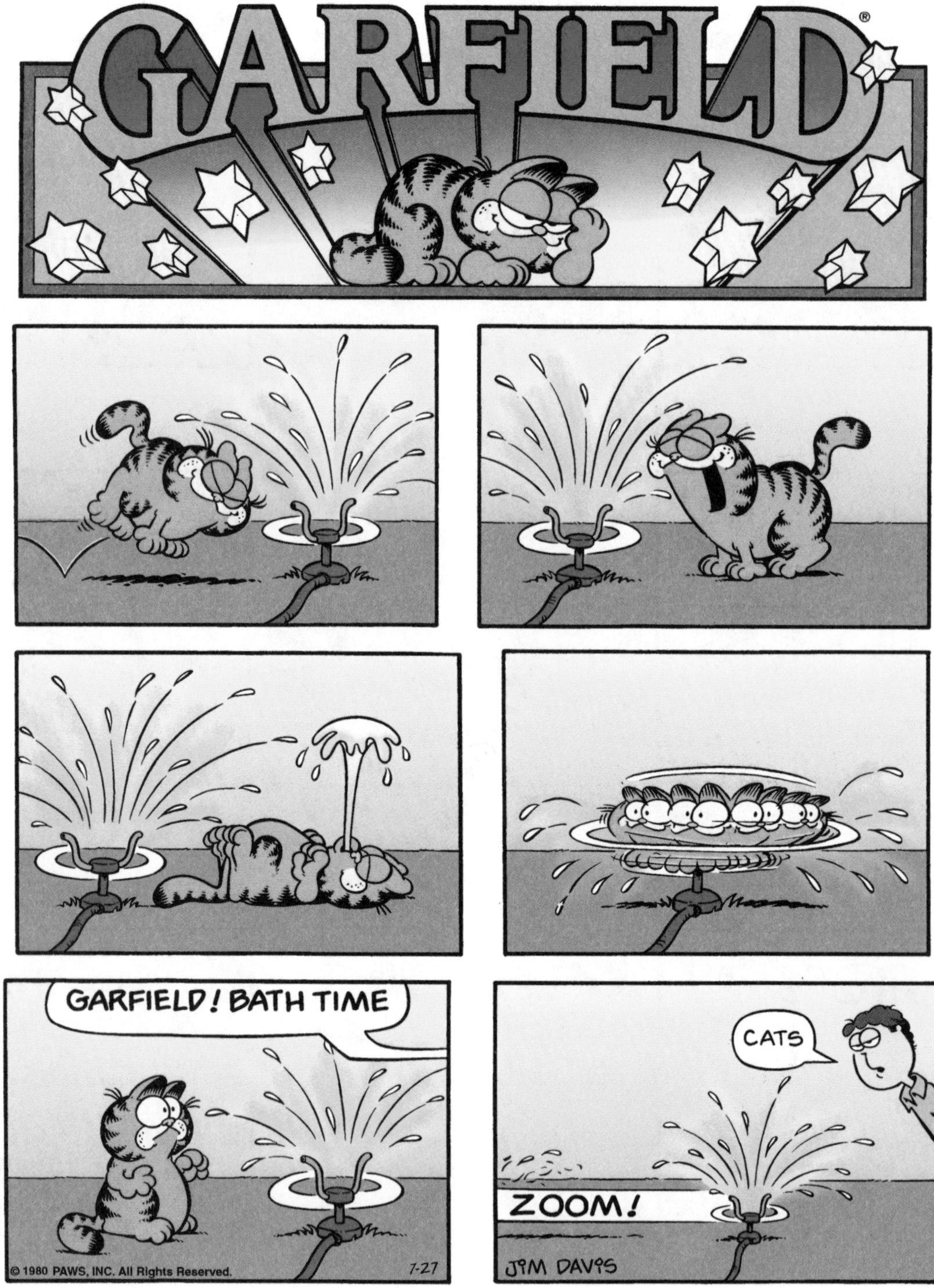
GARFIELD®
GARFIELD! BATH TIME
CATS
ZOOM!
© 1980 PAWS, INC. All Rights Reserved.
7-27
JIM DAVIS

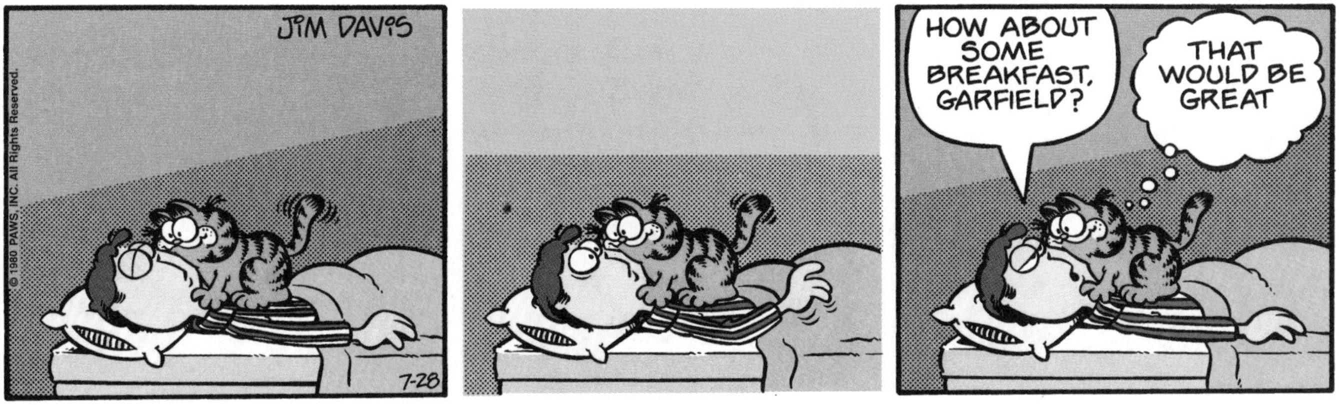
JIM DAVIS
© 1980 PAWS, INC. All Rights Reserved.
7-28
HOW ABOUT SOME BREAKFAST, GARFIELD?
THAT WOULD BE GREAT

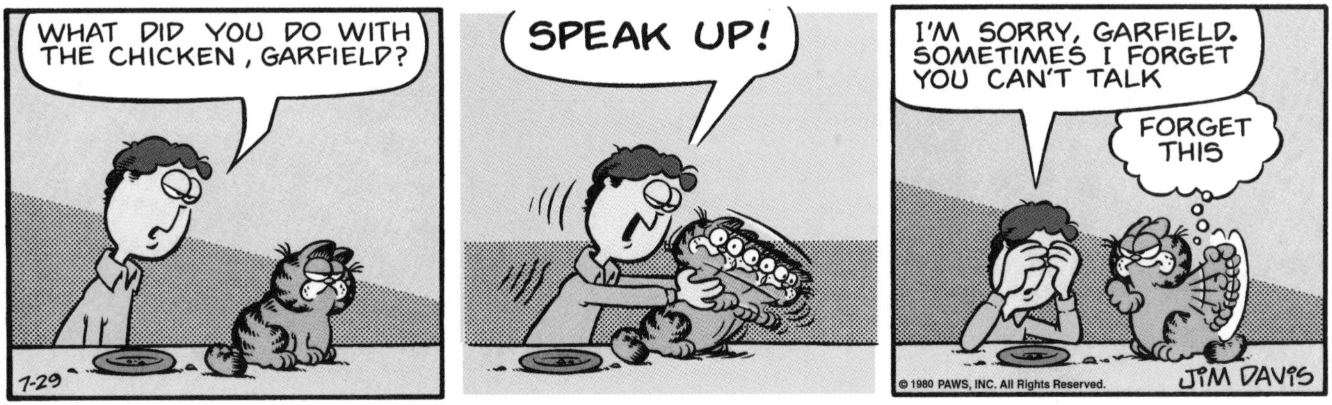
WHAT DID YOU DO WITH THE CHICKEN, GARFIELD?
7-29
SPEAK UP!
I'M SORRY, GARFIELD. SOMETIMES I FORGET YOU CAN'T TALK
FORGET THIS
© 1980 PAWS, INC. All Rights Reserved.
JIM DAVIS

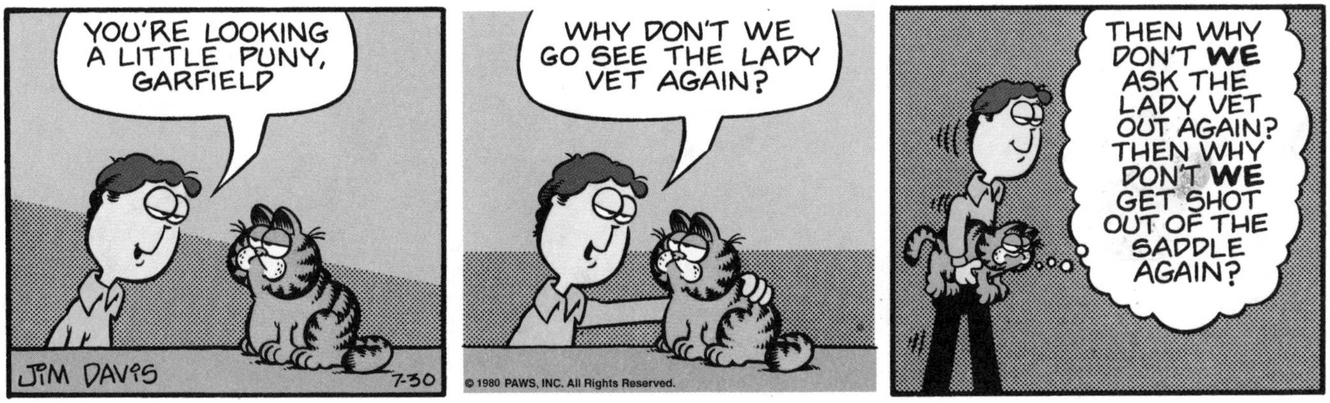
YOU'RE LOOKING A LITTLE PUNY, GARFIELD
JIM DAVIS
7-30
WHY DON'T WE GO SEE THE LADY VET AGAIN?
© 1980 PAWS, INC. All Rights Reserved.
THEN WHY DON'T **WE** ASK THE LADY VET OUT AGAIN? THEN WHY DON'T **WE** GET SHOT OUT OF THE SADDLE AGAIN?

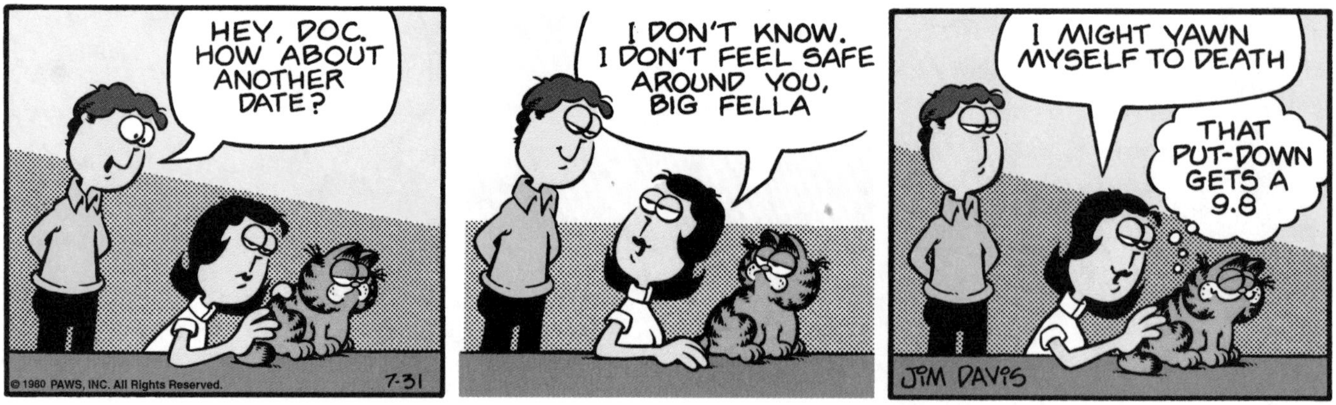
HEY, DOC. HOW ABOUT ANOTHER DATE?
I DON'T KNOW. I DON'T FEEL SAFE AROUND YOU, BIG FELLA
I MIGHT YAWN MYSELF TO DEATH
THAT PUT-DOWN GETS A 9.8
© 1980 PAWS, INC. All Rights Reserved.
7-31
JIM DAVIS

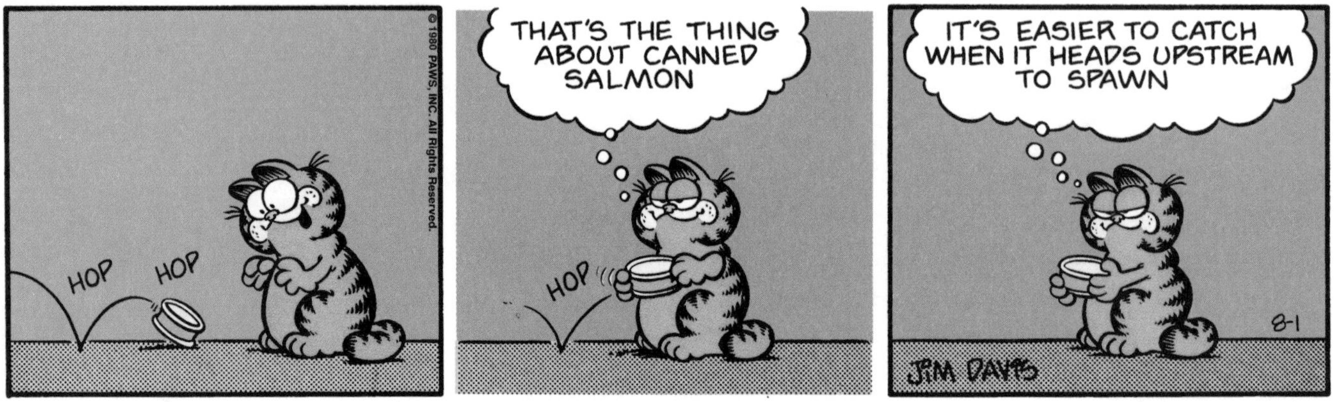
HOP
HOP
© 1980 PAWS, INC. All Rights Reserved.
THAT'S THE THING ABOUT CANNED SALMON
HOP
IT'S EASIER TO CATCH WHEN IT HEADS UPSTREAM TO SPAWN
8-1
JIM DAVIS

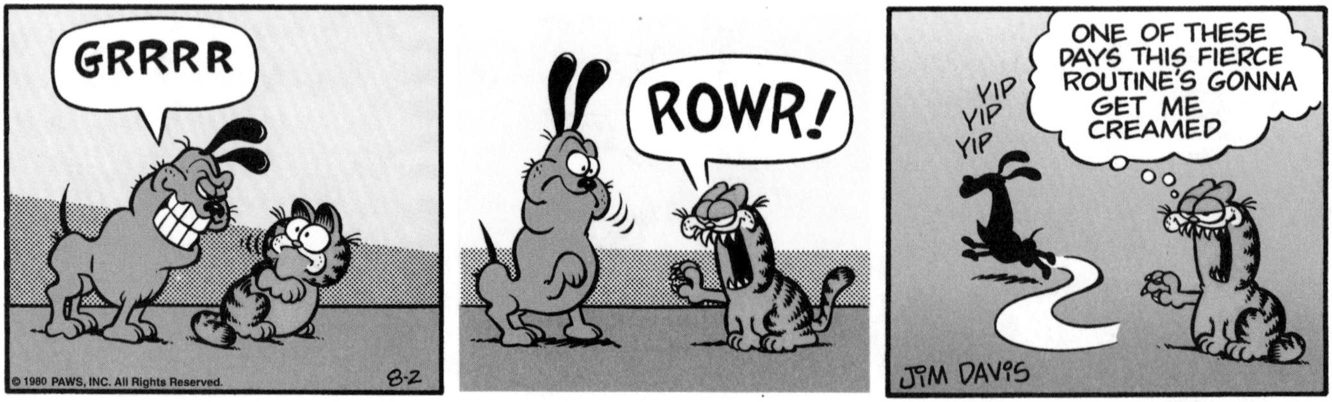
GRRRR
© 1980 PAWS, INC. All Rights Reserved.
8-2
ROWR!
YIP
YIP
YIP
ONE OF THESE DAYS THIS FIERCE ROUTINE'S GONNA GET ME CREAMED
JIM DAVIS

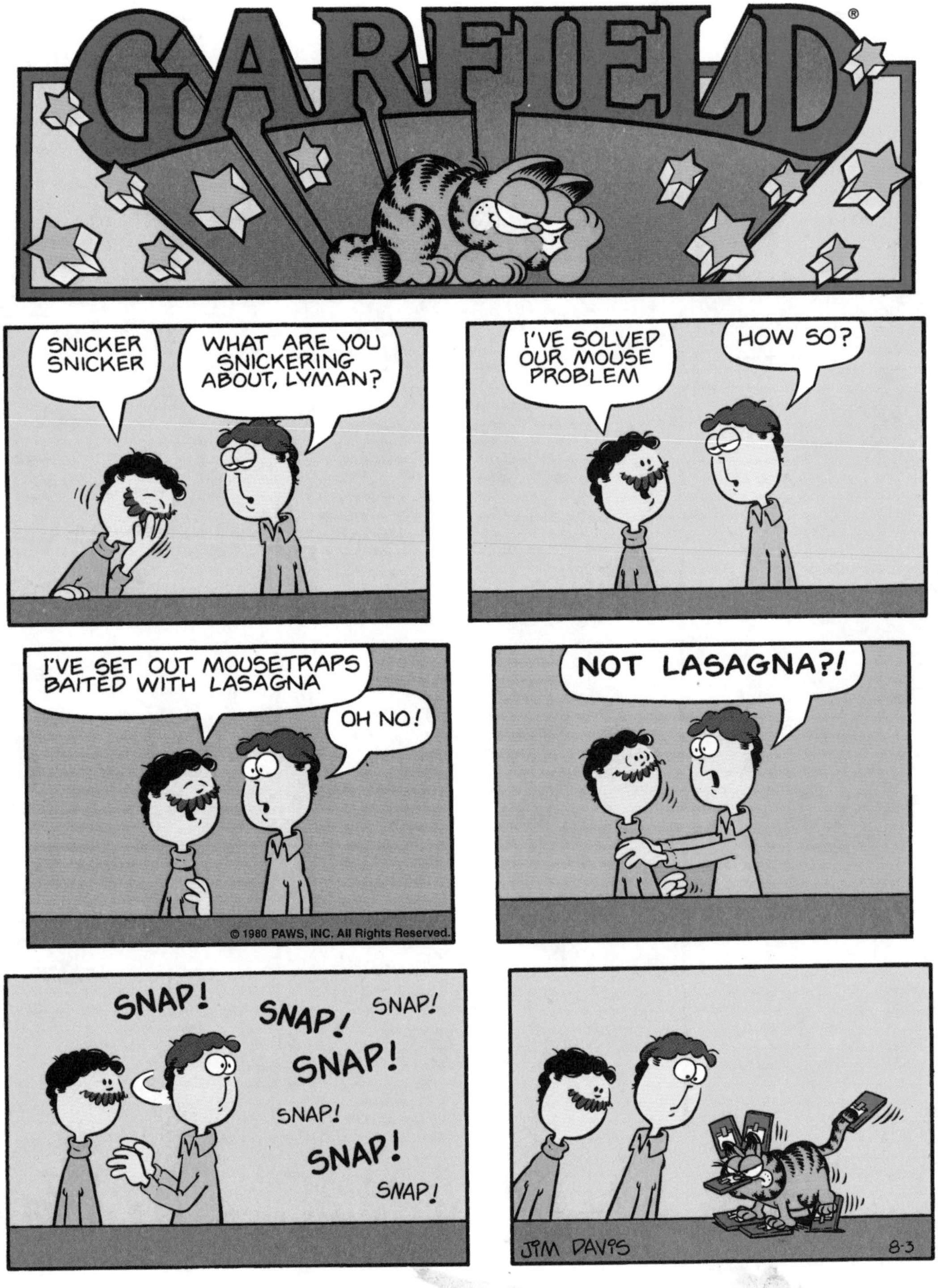
GARFIELD®
SNICKER SNICKER
WHAT ARE YOU SNICKERING ABOUT, LYMAN?
I'VE SOLVED OUR MOUSE PROBLEM
HOW SO?
I'VE SET OUT MOUSETRAPS BAITED WITH LASAGNA
OH NO!
NOT LASAGNA?!
SNAP!
SNAP!
SNAP!
SNAP!
SNAP!
SNAP!
SNAP!
JIM DAVIS
8-3

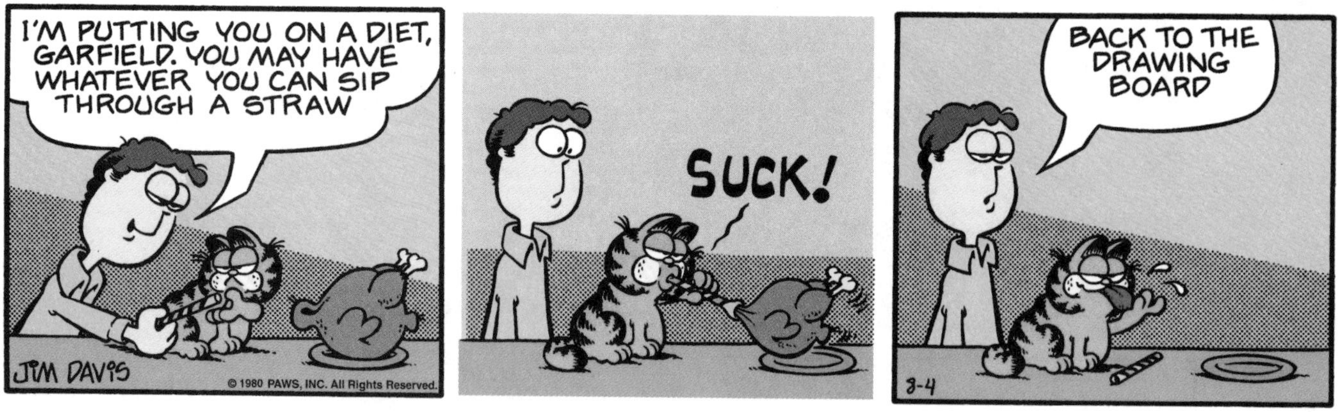
I'M PUTTING YOU ON A DIET, GARFIELD. YOU MAY HAVE WHATEVER YOU CAN SIP THROUGH A STRAW
JIM DAVIS
© 1980 PAWS, INC. All Rights Reserved.
SUCK!
BACK TO THE DRAWING BOARD
8-4

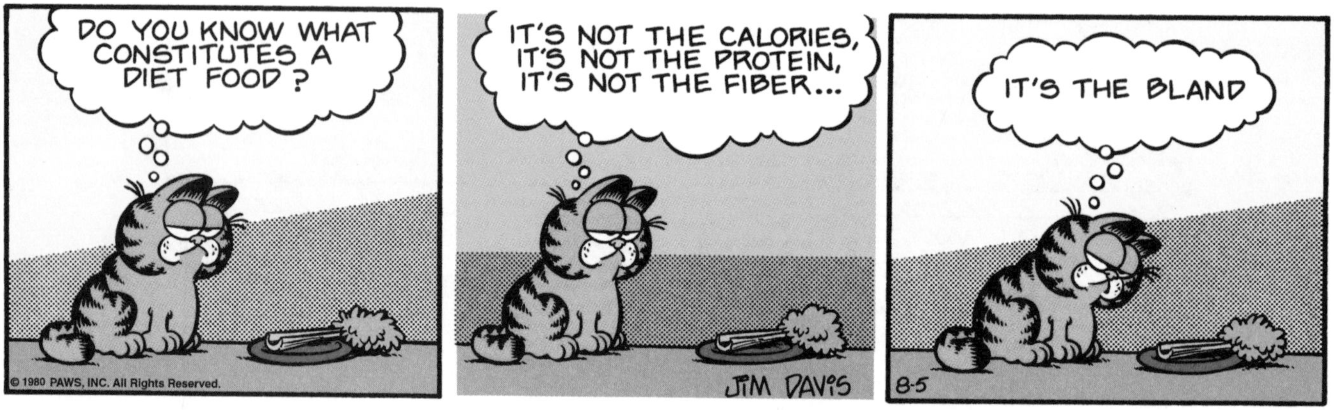
DO YOU KNOW WHAT CONSTITUTES A DIET FOOD ?
© 1980 PAWS, INC. All Rights Reserved.
IT'S NOT THE CALORIES, IT'S NOT THE PROTEIN, IT'S NOT THE FIBER...
JIM DAVIS
IT'S THE BLAND
8-5

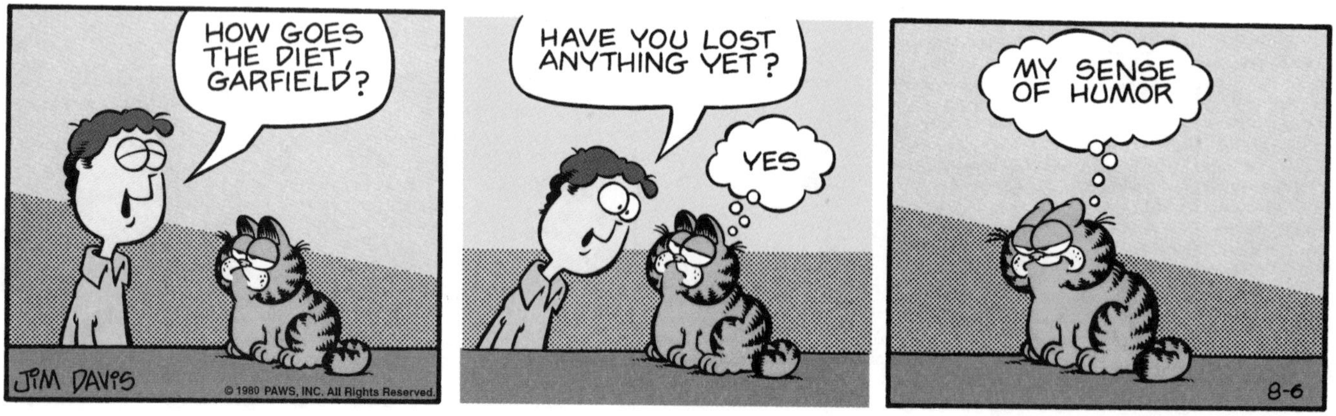
HOW GOES THE DIET, GARFIELD?
JIM DAVIS
© 1980 PAWS, INC. All Rights Reserved.
HAVE YOU LOST ANYTHING YET ?
YES
MY SENSE OF HUMOR
8-6

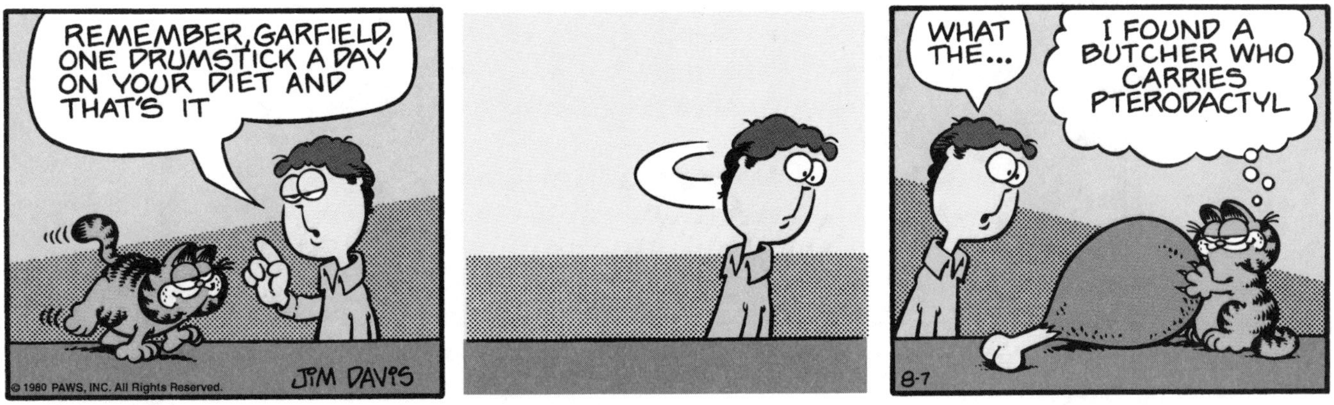
REMEMBER, GARFIELD, ONE DRUMSTICK A DAY ON YOUR DIET AND THAT'S IT
JIM DAVIS
© 1980 PAWS, INC. All Rights Reserved.
WHAT THE...
I FOUND A BUTCHER WHO CARRIES PTERODACTYL
8-7

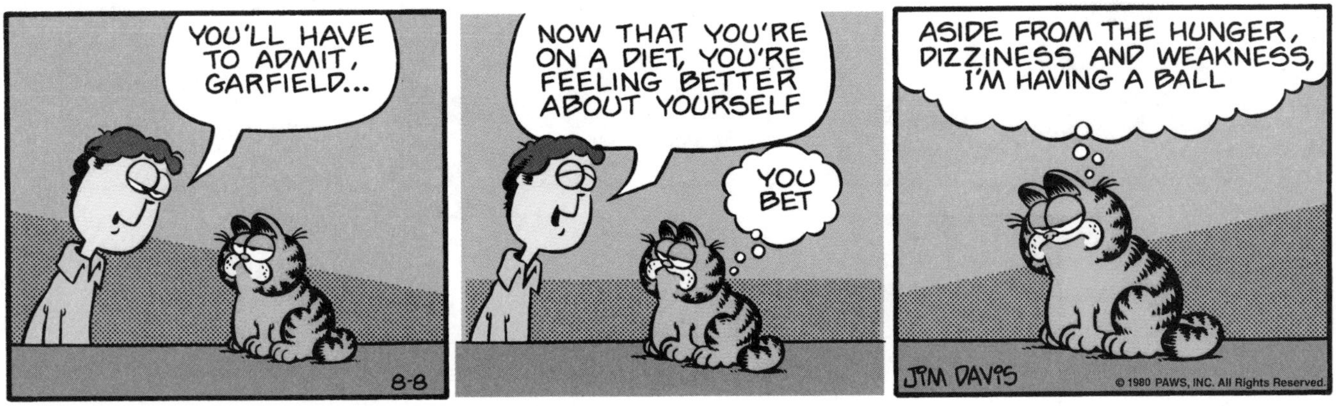
YOU'LL HAVE TO ADMIT, GARFIELD...
8-8
NOW THAT YOU'RE ON A DIET, YOU'RE FEELING BETTER ABOUT YOURSELF
YOU BET
ASIDE FROM THE HUNGER, DIZZINESS AND WEAKNESS, I'M HAVING A BALL
JIM DAVIS
© 1980 PAWS, INC. All Rights Reserved.

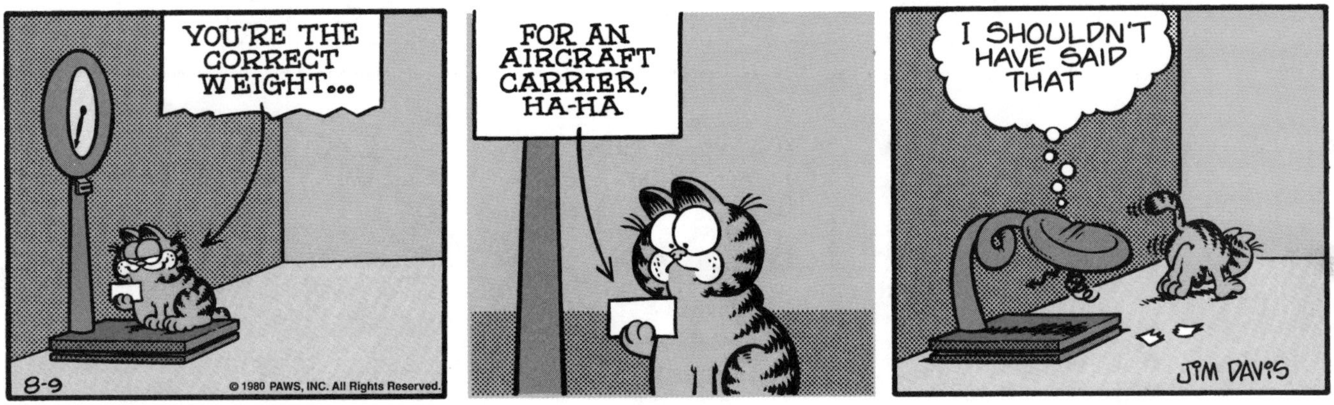
YOU'RE THE CORRECT WEIGHT...
8-9
© 1980 PAWS, INC. All Rights Reserved.
FOR AN AIRCRAFT CARRIER, HA-HA
I SHOULDN'T HAVE SAID THAT
JIM DAVIS

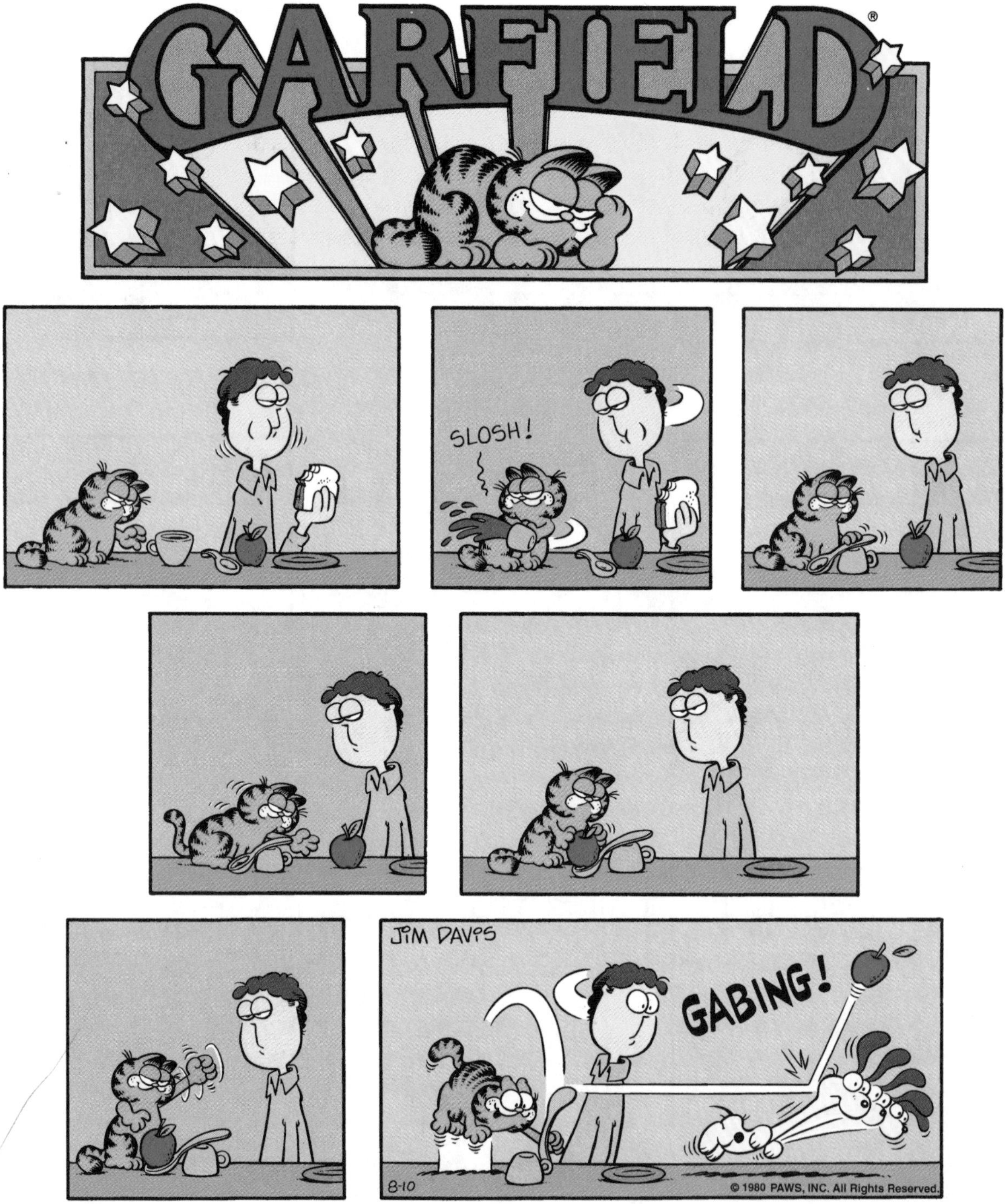
GARFIELD®
SLOSH!
JIM DAVIS
GABING!
8-10
© 1980 PAWS, INC. All Rights Reserved.

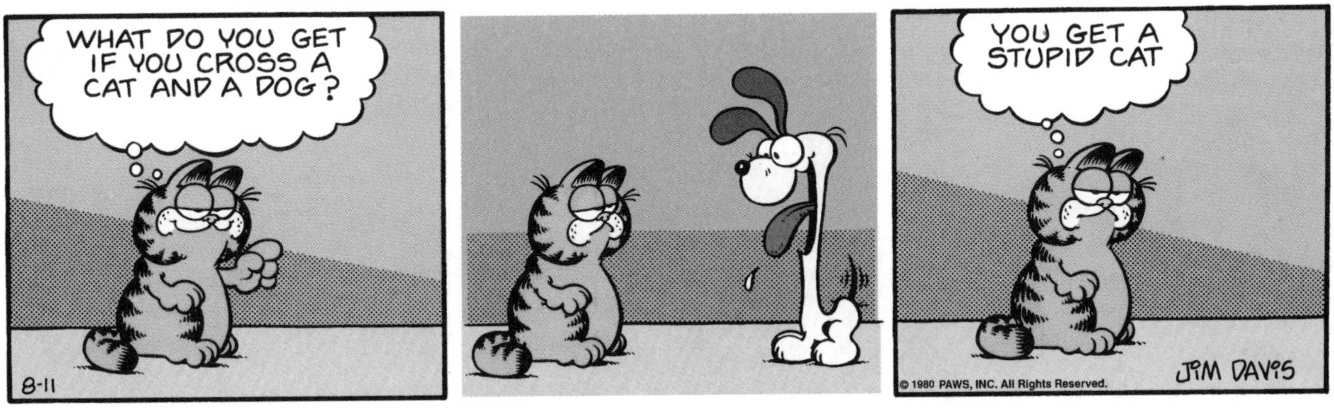
WHAT DO YOU GET IF YOU CROSS A CAT AND A DOG?
8-11
YOU GET A STUPID CAT
© 1980 PAWS, INC. All Rights Reserved.
JIM DAVIS

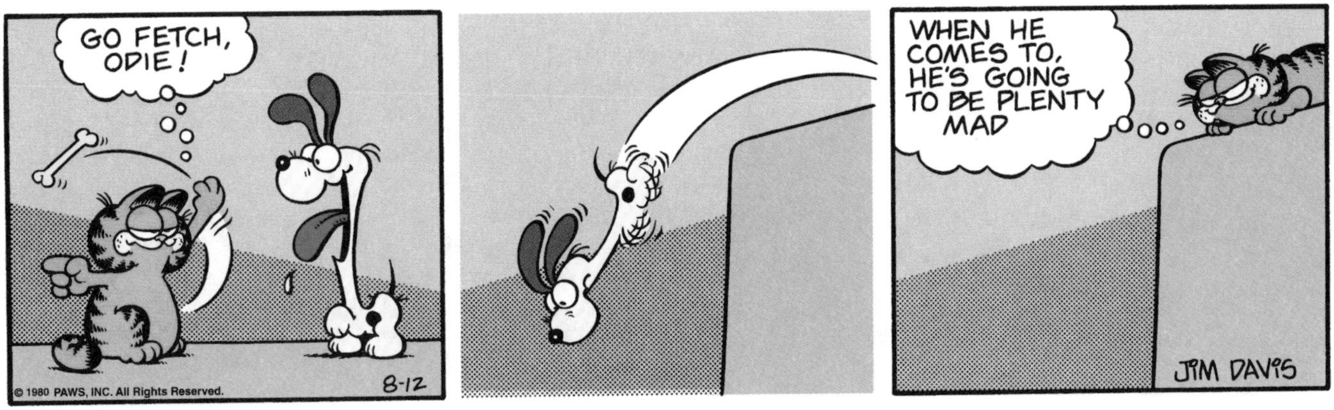
GO FETCH, ODIE!
© 1980 PAWS, INC. All Rights Reserved.
8-12
WHEN HE COMES TO, HE'S GOING TO BE PLENTY MAD
JIM DAVIS

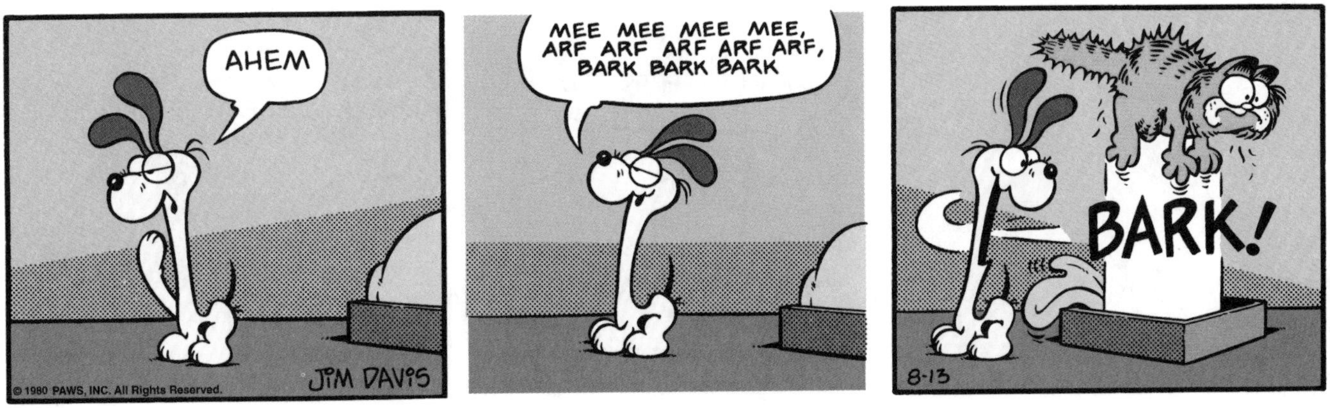
AHEM
© 1980 PAWS, INC. All Rights Reserved.
JIM DAVIS
MEE MEE MEE MEE, ARF ARF ARF ARF ARF, BARK BARK BARK
BARK!
8-13

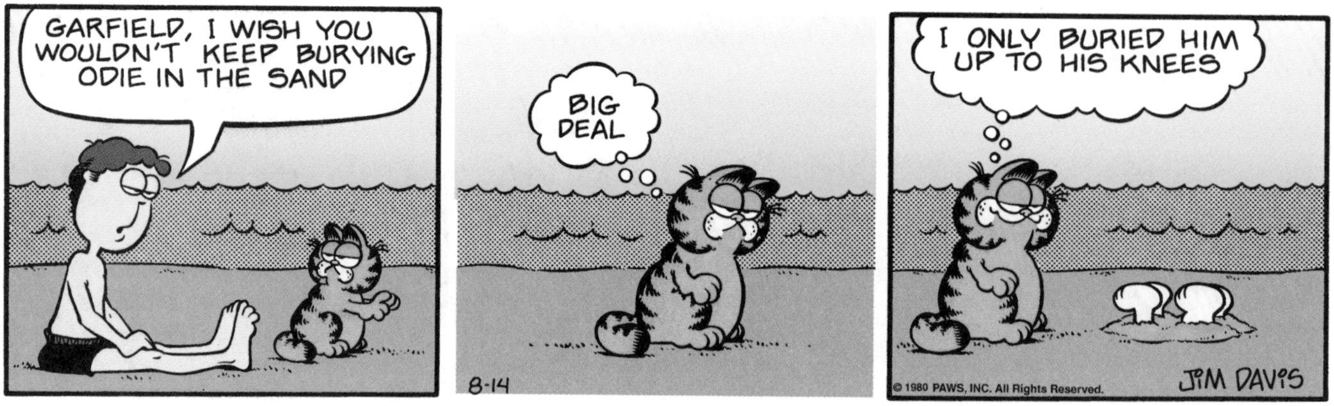
GARFIELD, I WISH YOU WOULDN'T KEEP BURYING ODIE IN THE SAND
BIG DEAL
I ONLY BURIED HIM UP TO HIS KNEES
8-14
© 1980 PAWS, INC. All Rights Reserved.
JIM DAVIS

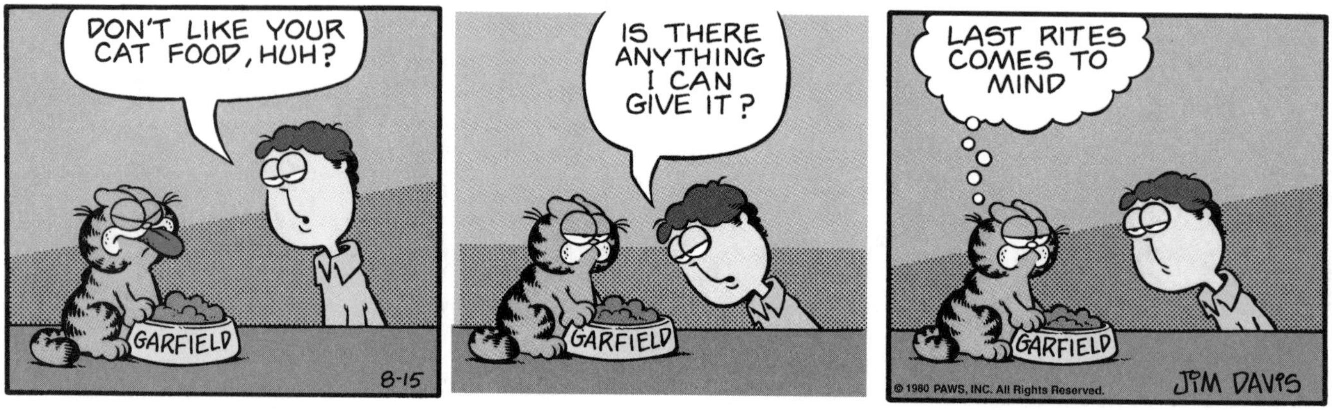
DON'T LIKE YOUR CAT FOOD, HUH?
GARFIELD
8-15
IS THERE ANYTHING I CAN GIVE IT?
GARFIELD
LAST RITES COMES TO MIND
GARFIELD
© 1980 PAWS, INC. All Rights Reserved.
JIM DAVIS

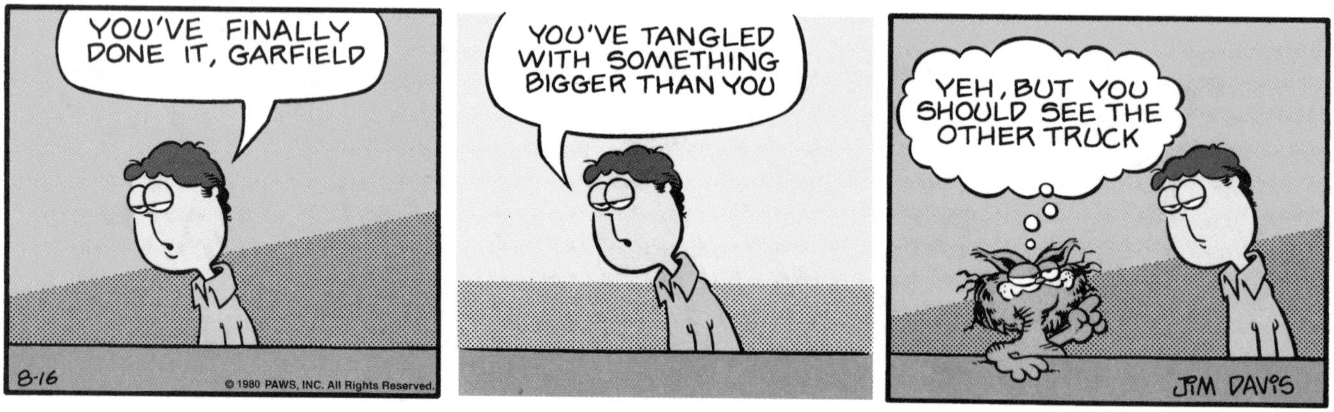
YOU'VE FINALLY DONE IT, GARFIELD
8-16
© 1980 PAWS, INC. All Rights Reserved.
YOU'VE TANGLED WITH SOMETHING BIGGER THAN YOU
YEH, BUT YOU SHOULD SEE THE OTHER TRUCK
JIM DAVIS

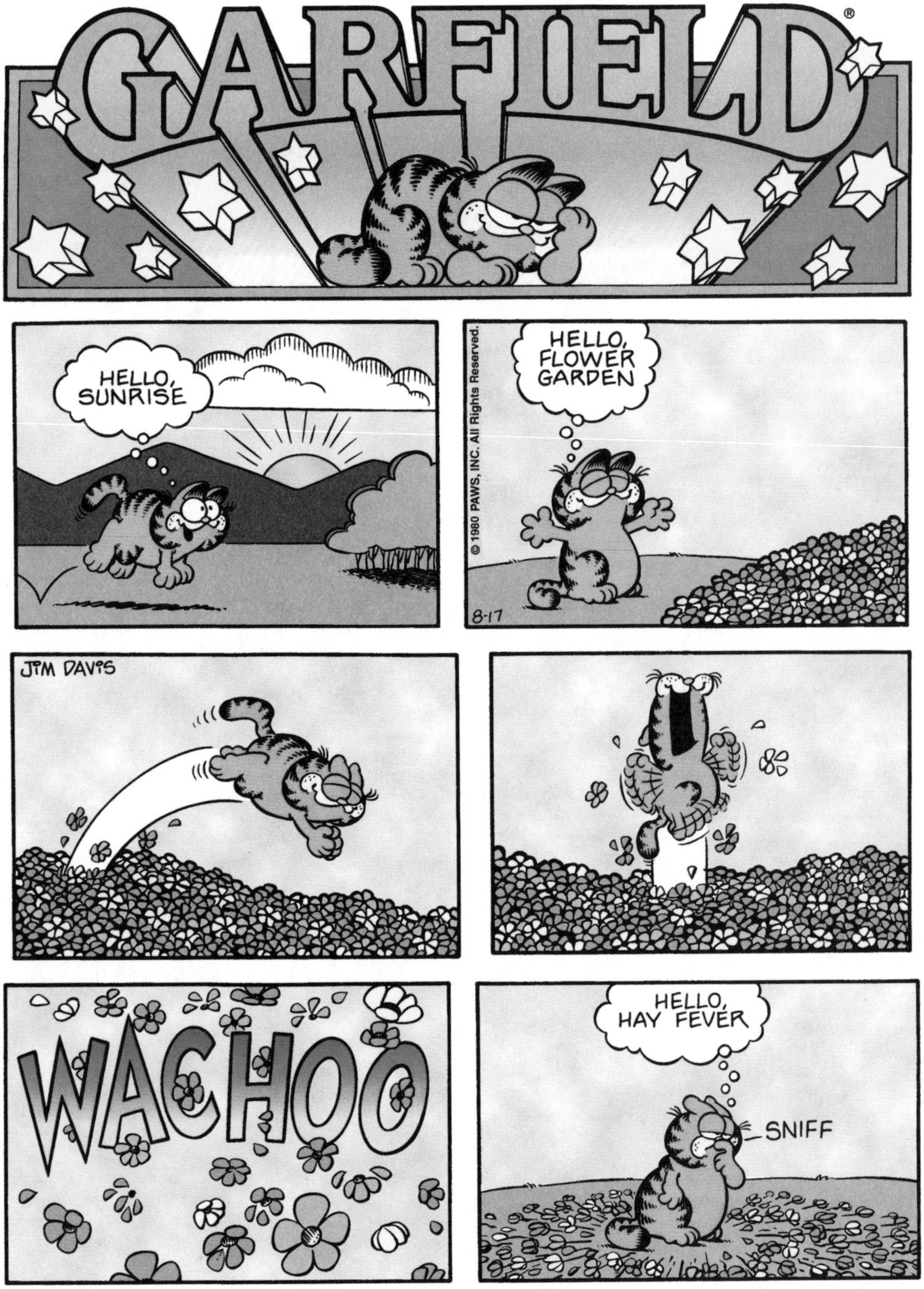
GARFIELD®
HELLO, SUNRISE
© 1980 PAWS, INC. All Rights Reserved.
HELLO, FLOWER GARDEN
8-17
JIM DAVIS
WACHOO
HELLO, HAY FEVER
SNIFF

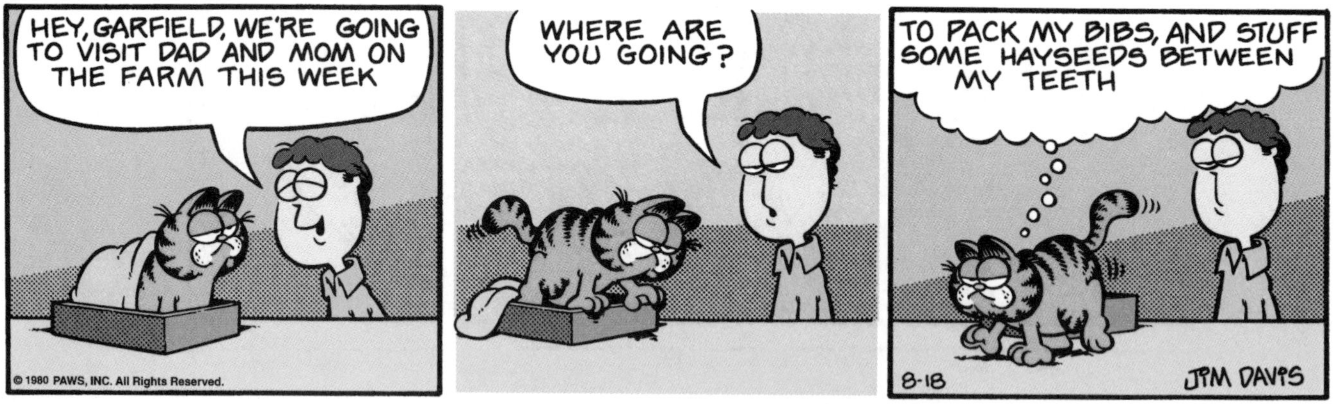
HEY, GARFIELD, WE'RE GOING TO VISIT DAD AND MOM ON THE FARM THIS WEEK
WHERE ARE YOU GOING?
TO PACK MY BIBS, AND STUFF SOME HAYSEEDS BETWEEN MY TEETH
© 1980 PAWS, INC. All Rights Reserved.
8-18
JIM DAVIS

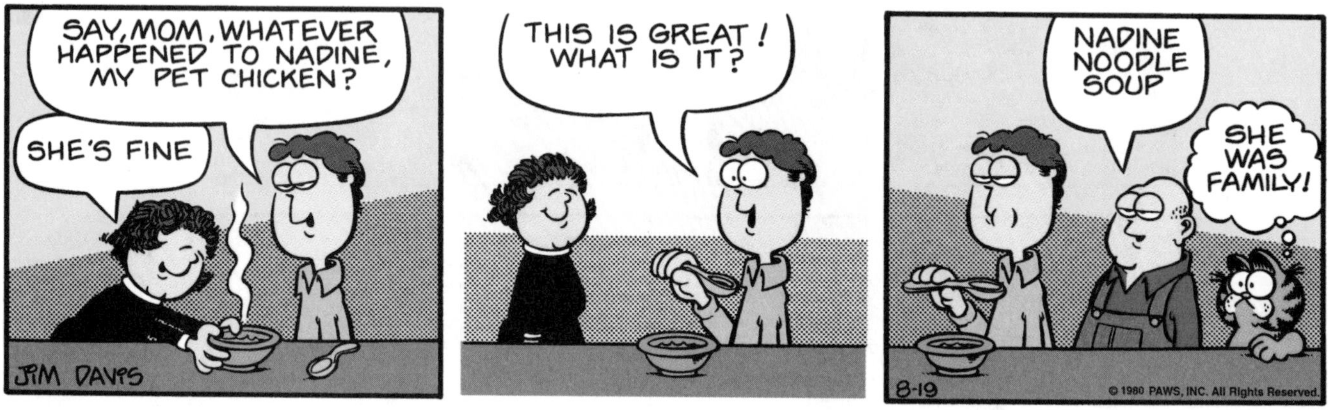
SAY, MOM, WHATEVER HAPPENED TO NADINE, MY PET CHICKEN?
SHE'S FINE
JIM DAVIS
THIS IS GREAT! WHAT IS IT?
NADINE NOODLE SOUP
SHE WAS FAMILY!
8-19
© 1980 PAWS, INC. All Rights Reserved.

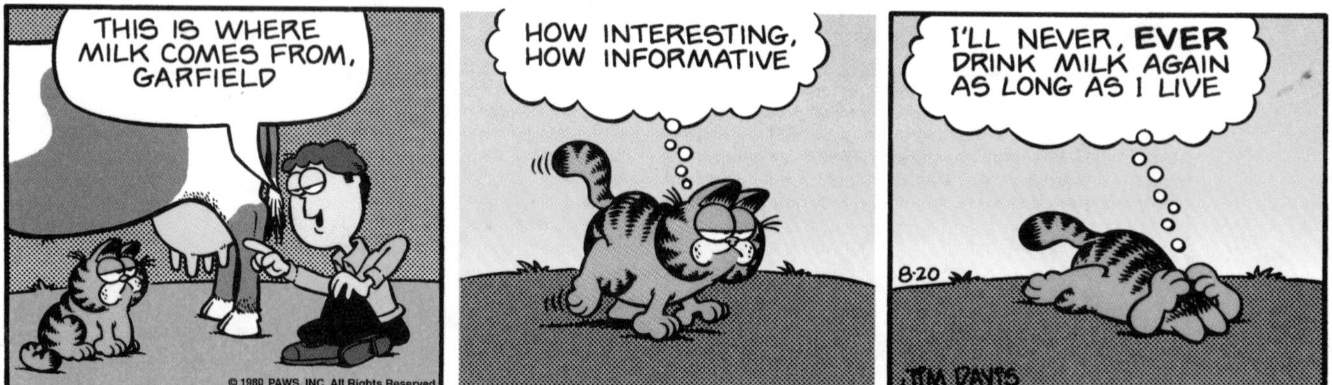
THIS IS WHERE MILK COMES FROM, GARFIELD
© 1980 PAWS, INC. All Rights Reserved.
HOW INTERESTING, HOW INFORMATIVE
I'LL NEVER, **EVER** DRINK MILK AGAIN AS LONG AS I LIVE
8-20
JIM DAVIS

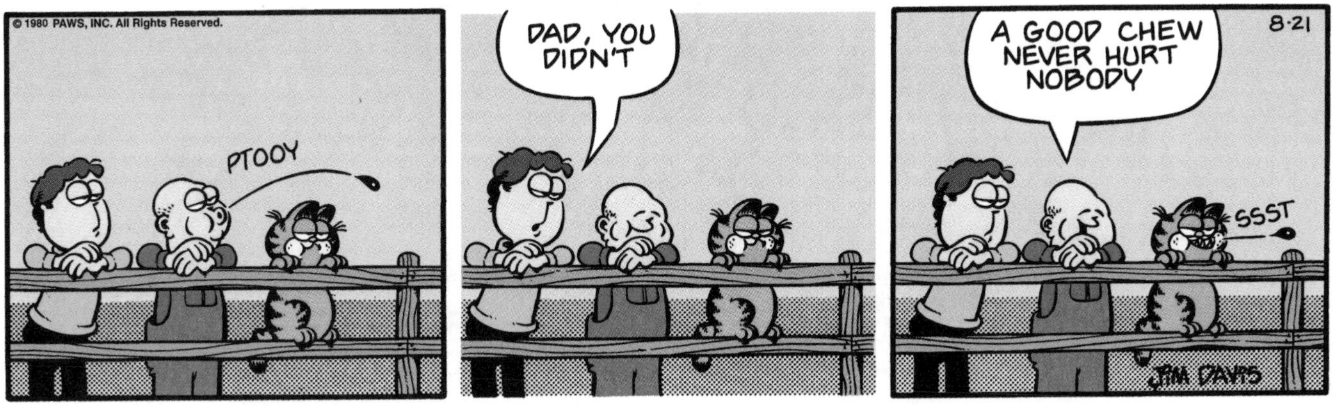
© 1980 PAWS, INC. All Rights Reserved.
PTOOY
DAD, YOU DIDN'T
A GOOD CHEW NEVER HURT NOBODY
8-21
SSST
JIM DAVIS

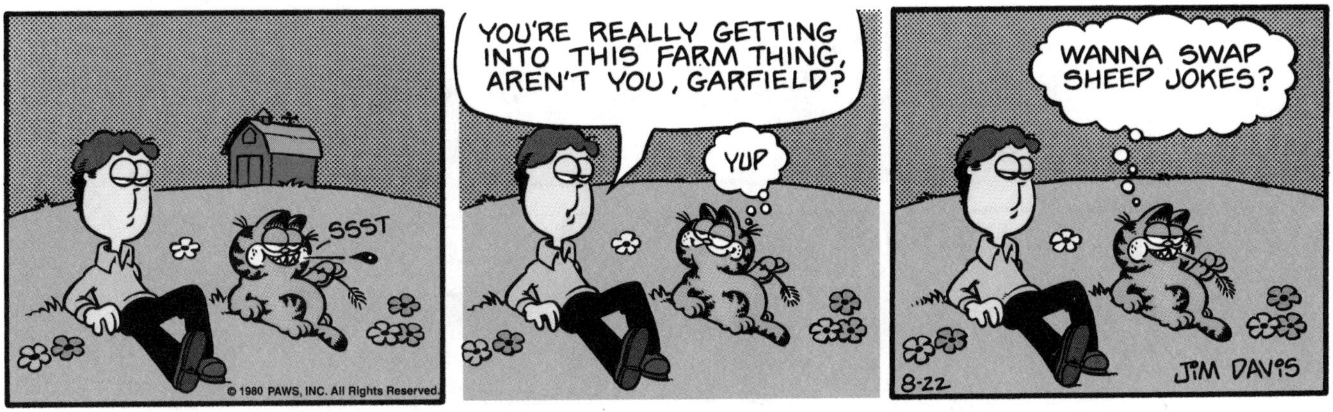
SSST
© 1980 PAWS, INC. All Rights Reserved.
YOU'RE REALLY GETTING INTO THIS FARM THING, AREN'T YOU, GARFIELD?
YUP
WANNA SWAP SHEEP JOKES?
8-22
JIM DAVIS

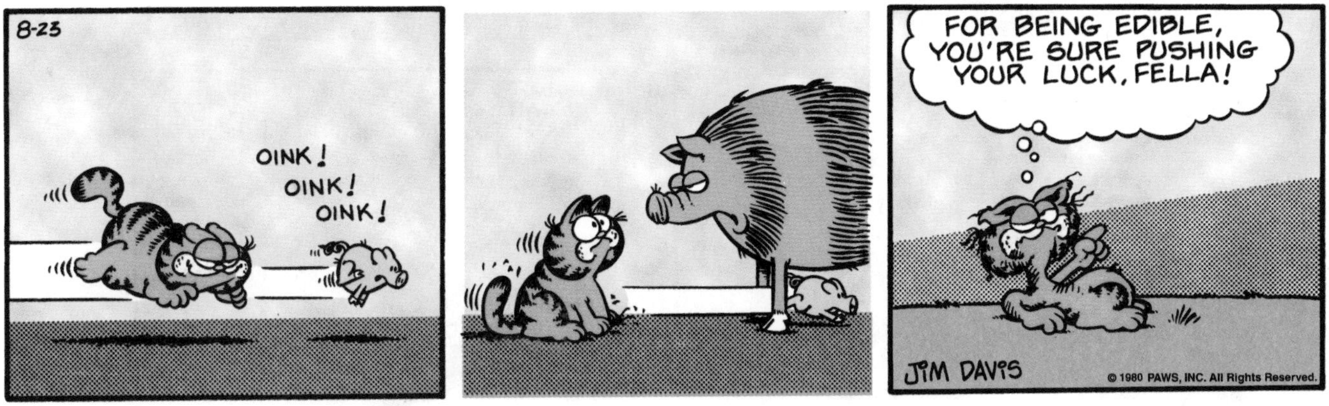
8-23
OINK!
OINK!
OINK!
FOR BEING EDIBLE, YOU'RE SURE PUSHING YOUR LUCK, FELLA!
JIM DAVIS
© 1980 PAWS, INC. All Rights Reserved.

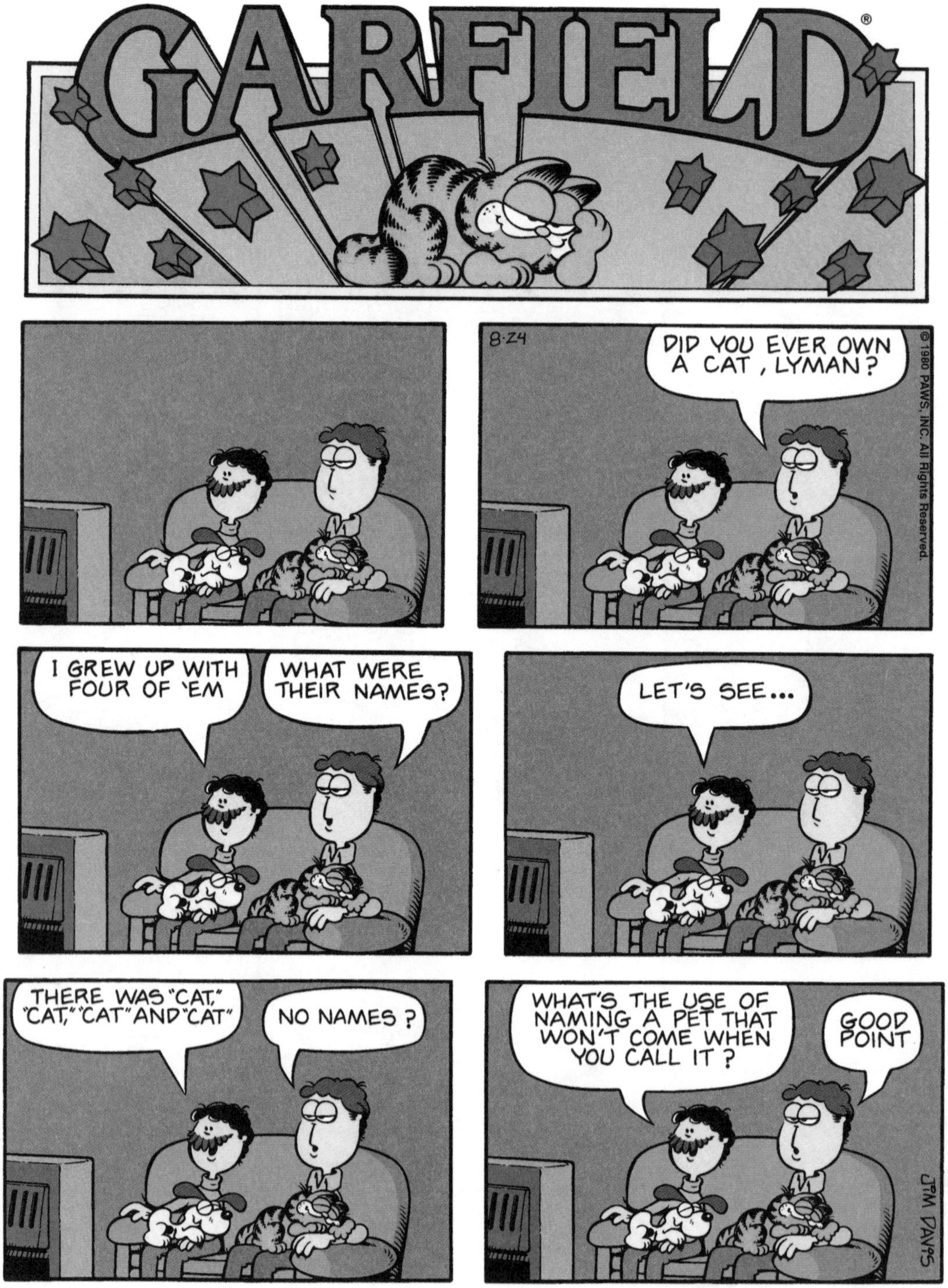
GARFIELD®
8·24
DID YOU EVER OWN A CAT, LYMAN?
© 1980 PAWS, INC. All Rights Reserved.
I GREW UP WITH FOUR OF 'EM
WHAT WERE THEIR NAMES?
LET'S SEE...
THERE WAS "CAT," "CAT," "CAT" AND "CAT"
NO NAMES?
WHAT'S THE USE OF NAMING A PET THAT WON'T COME WHEN YOU CALL IT?
GOOD POINT
JIM DAVIS

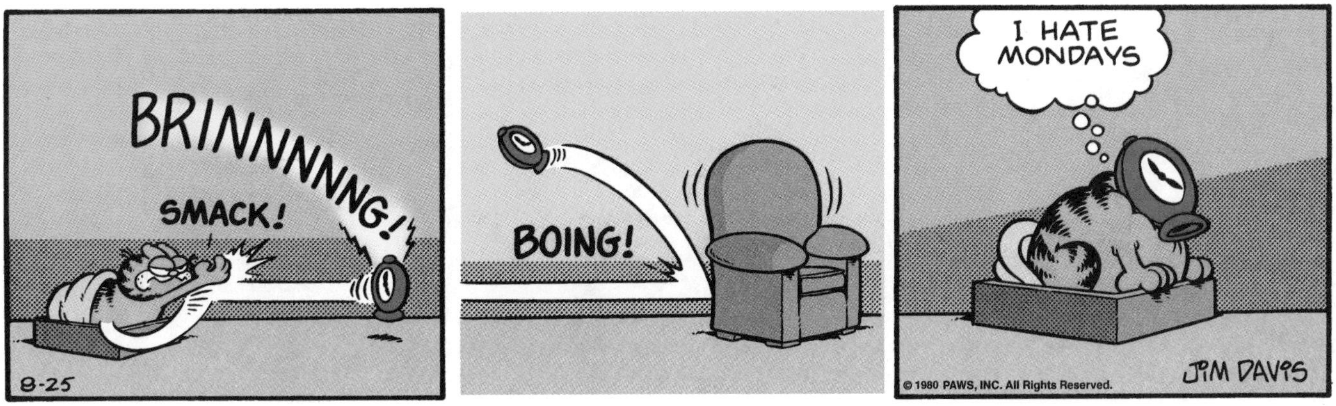
BRINNNNNNG!
SMACK!
8-25
BOING!
I HATE MONDAYS
© 1980 PAWS, INC. All Rights Reserved.
JIM DAVIS

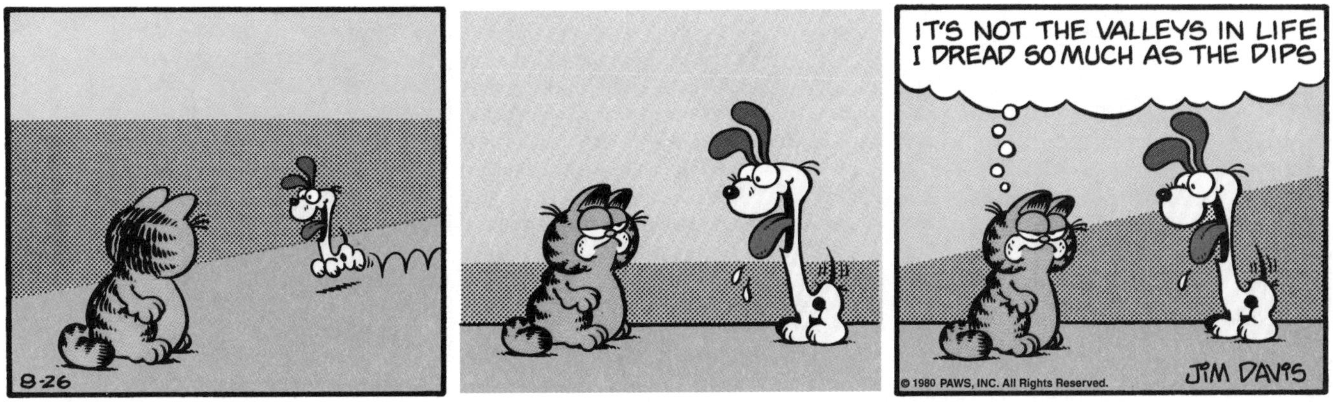
8-26
IT'S NOT THE VALLEYS IN LIFE I DREAD SO MUCH AS THE DIPS
© 1980 PAWS, INC. All Rights Reserved.
JIM DAVIS

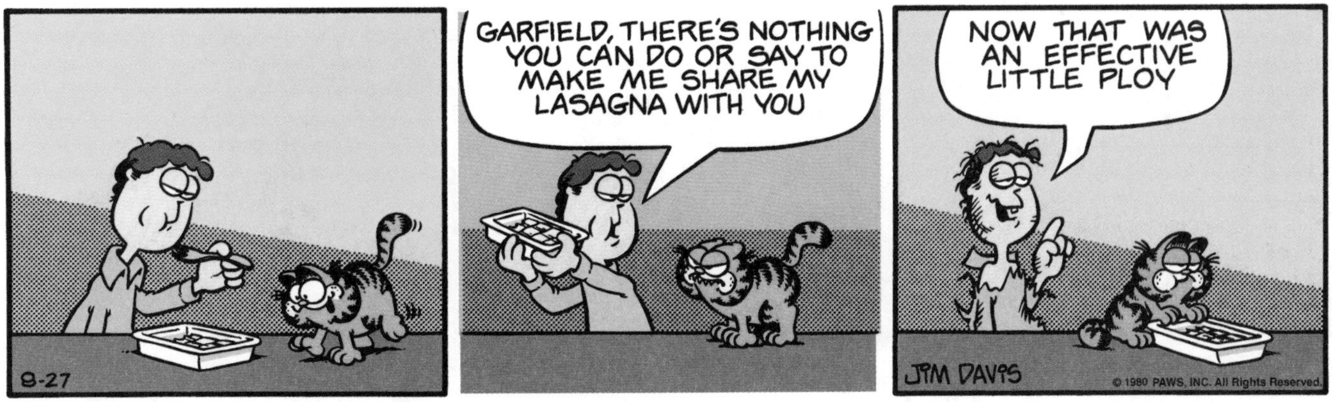
8-27
GARFIELD, THERE'S NOTHING YOU CAN DO OR SAY TO MAKE ME SHARE MY LASAGNA WITH YOU
NOW THAT WAS AN EFFECTIVE LITTLE PLOY
JIM DAVIS
© 1980 PAWS, INC. All Rights Reserved.

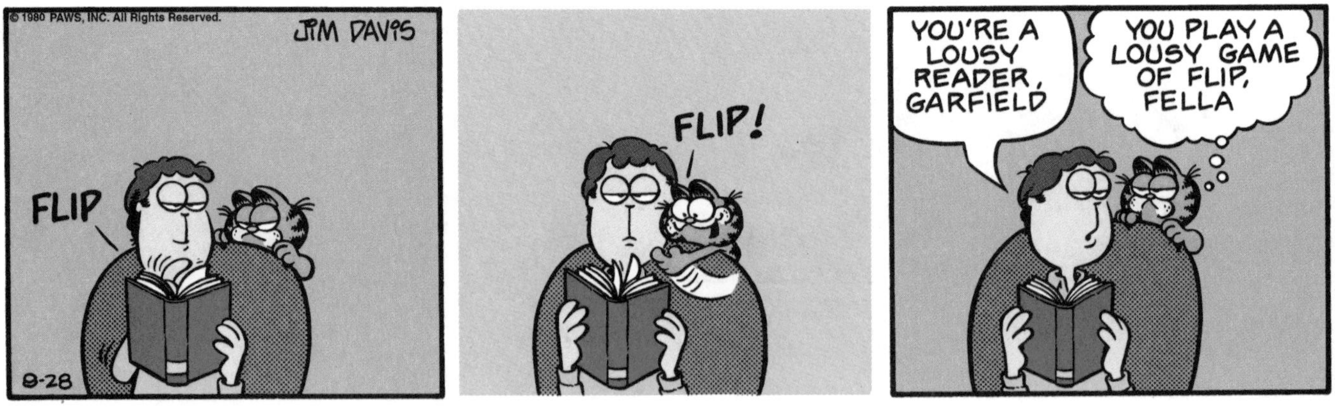
© 1980 PAWS, INC. All Rights Reserved.
JIM DAVIS
FLIP
8-28
FLIP!
YOU'RE A LOUSY READER, GARFIELD
YOU PLAY A LOUSY GAME OF FLIP, FELLA

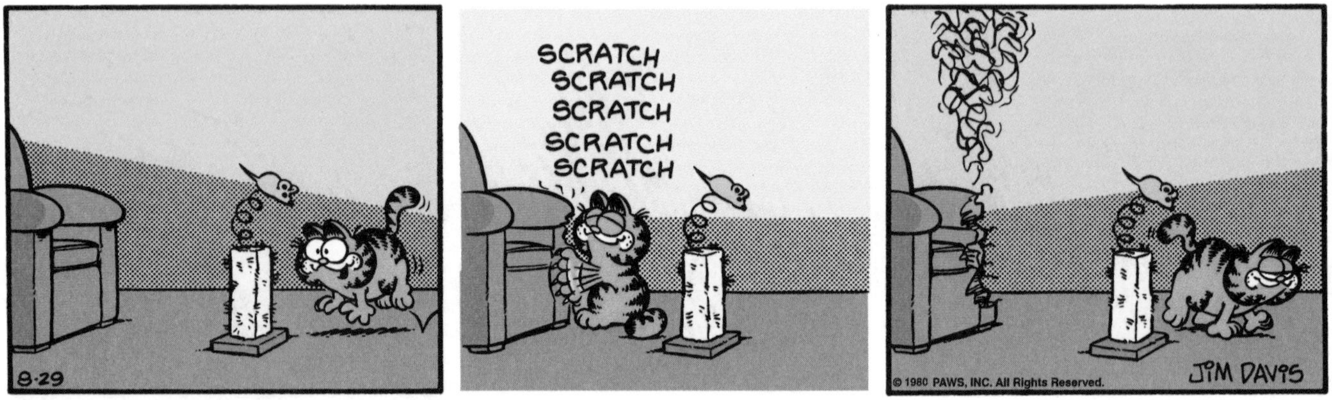
8-29
SCRATCH
SCRATCH
SCRATCH
SCRATCH
SCRATCH
© 1980 PAWS, INC. All Rights Reserved.
JIM DAVIS

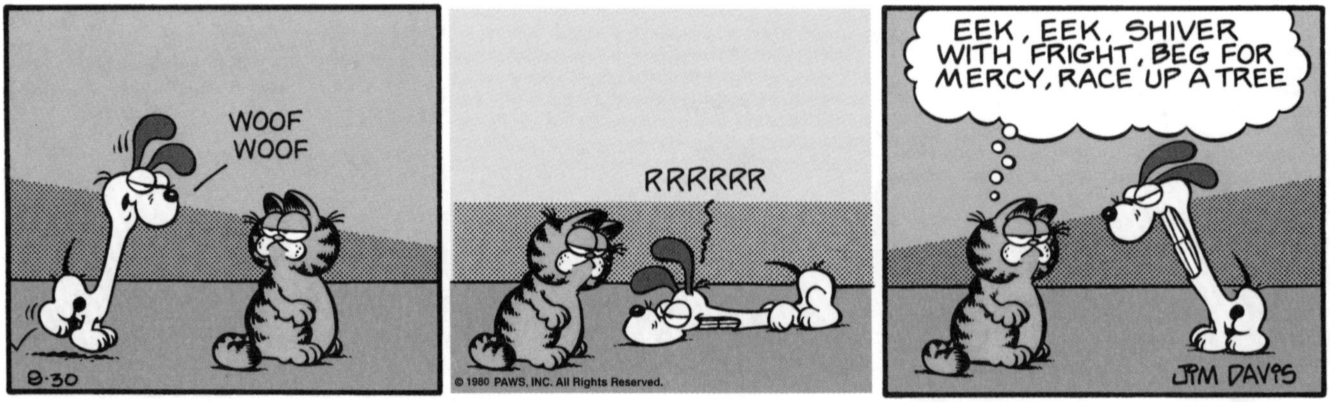
WOOF WOOF
8-30
RRRRRR
© 1980 PAWS, INC. All Rights Reserved.
EEK, EEK, SHIVER WITH FRIGHT, BEG FOR MERCY, RACE UP A TREE
JIM DAVIS

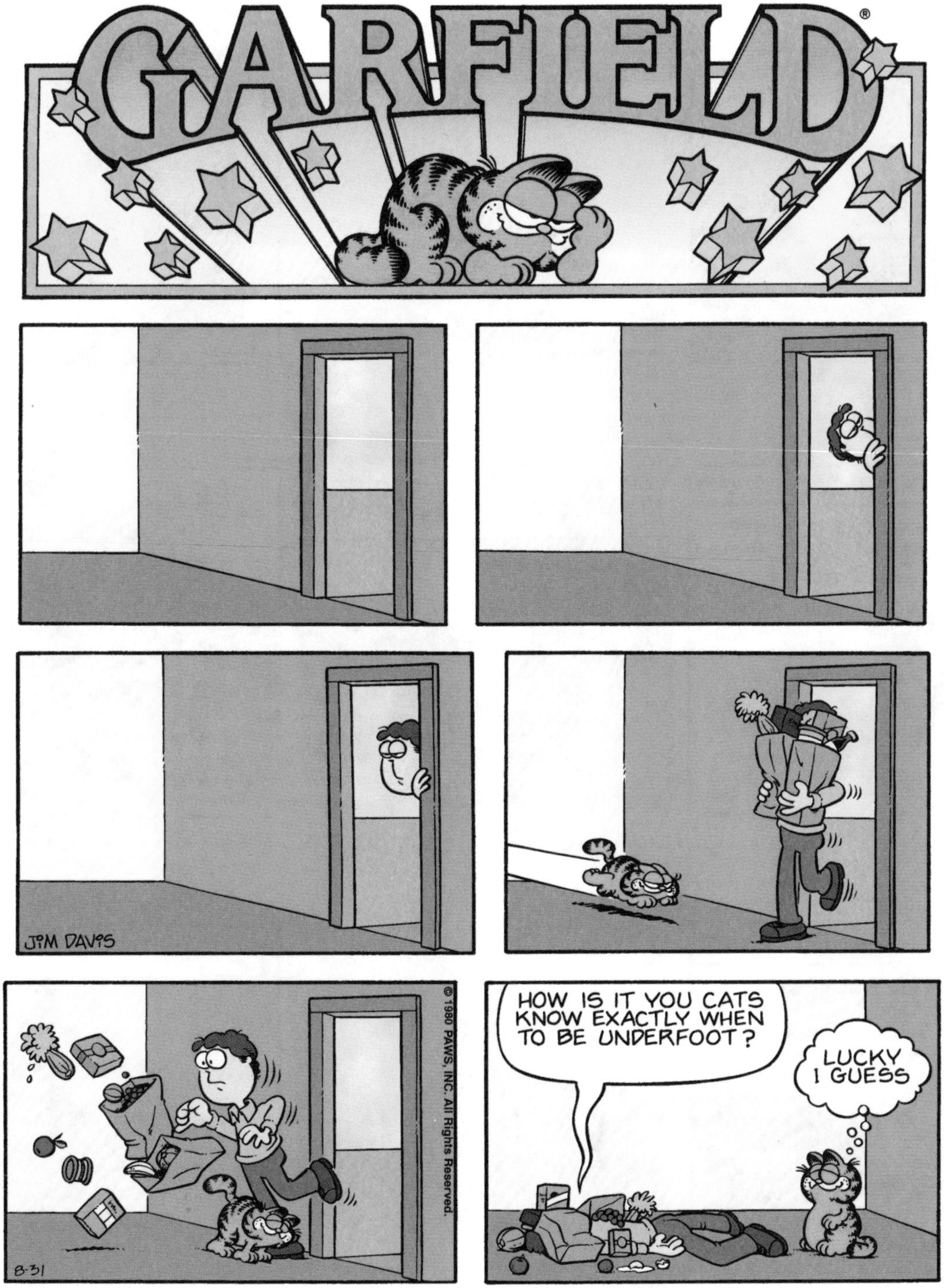
GARFIELD®
JIM DAVIS
© 1980 PAWS, INC. All Rights Reserved.
8-31
HOW IS IT YOU CATS KNOW EXACTLY WHEN TO BE UNDERFOOT?
LUCKY I GUESS

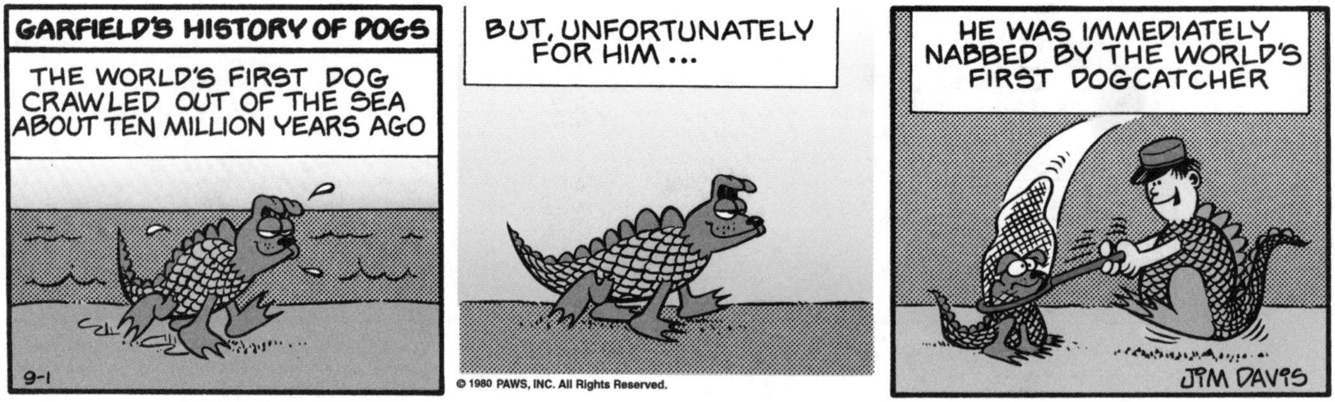
GARFIELD'S HISTORY OF DOGS
THE WORLD'S FIRST DOG CRAWLED OUT OF THE SEA ABOUT TEN MILLION YEARS AGO
9-1
BUT, UNFORTUNATELY FOR HIM ...
© 1980 PAWS, INC. All Rights Reserved.
HE WAS IMMEDIATELY NABBED BY THE WORLD'S FIRST DOGCATCHER
JIM DAVIS

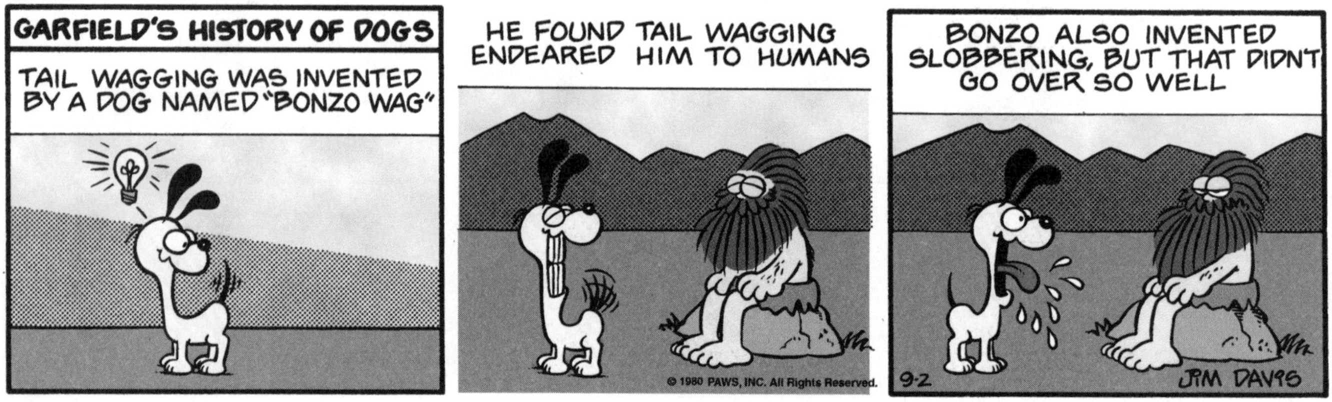
GARFIELD'S HISTORY OF DOGS
TAIL WAGGING WAS INVENTED BY A DOG NAMED "BONZO WAG"
HE FOUND TAIL WAGGING ENDEARED HIM TO HUMANS
© 1980 PAWS, INC. All Rights Reserved.
BONZO ALSO INVENTED SLOBBERING, BUT THAT DIDN'T GO OVER SO WELL
9-2
JIM DAVIS

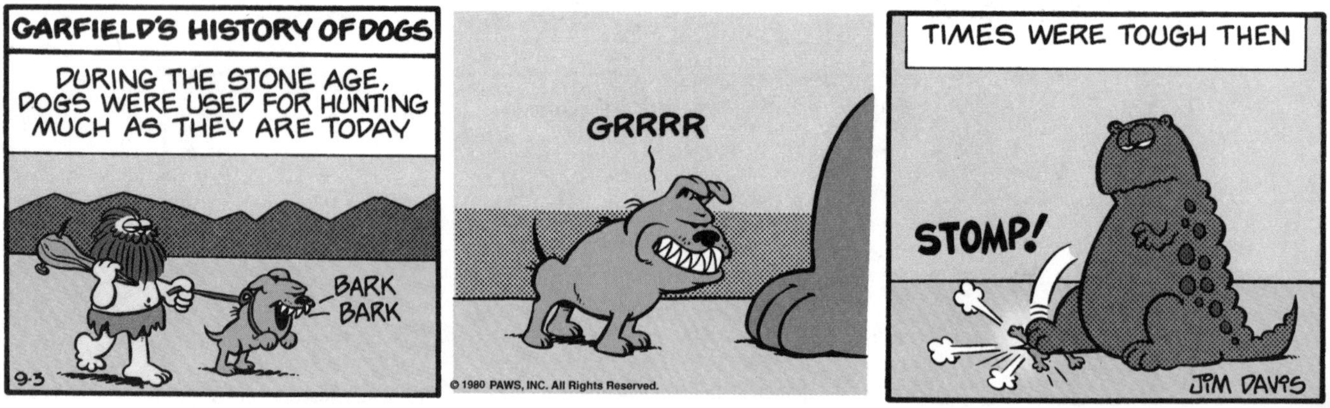
GARFIELD'S HISTORY OF DOGS
DURING THE STONE AGE, DOGS WERE USED FOR HUNTING MUCH AS THEY ARE TODAY
BARK BARK
9-3
GRRRR
© 1980 PAWS, INC. All Rights Reserved.
TIMES WERE TOUGH THEN
STOMP!
JIM DAVIS

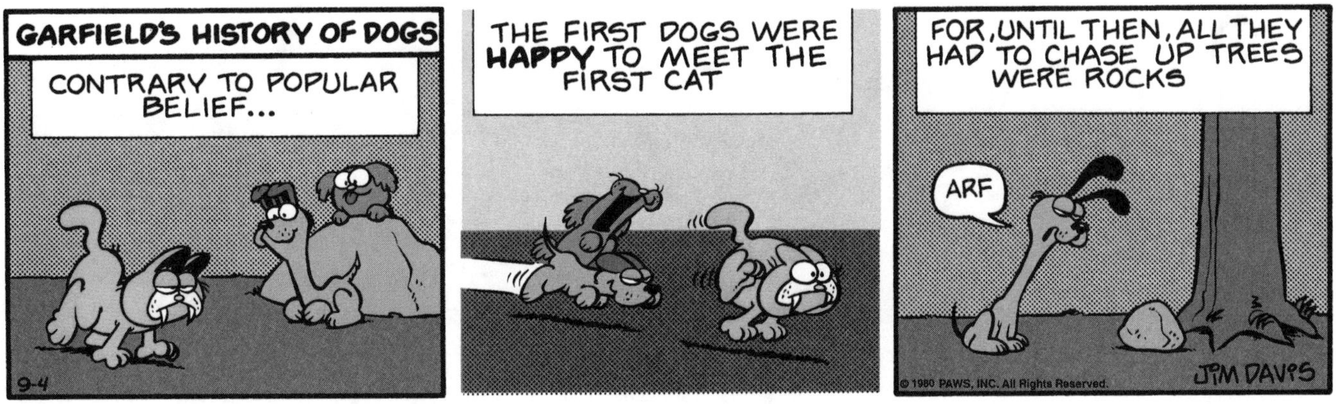
GARFIELD'S HISTORY OF DOGS
CONTRARY TO POPULAR BELIEF...
9-4
THE FIRST DOGS WERE HAPPY TO MEET THE FIRST CAT
FOR, UNTIL THEN, ALL THEY HAD TO CHASE UP TREES WERE ROCKS
ARF
© 1980 PAWS, INC. All Rights Reserved.
JIM DAVIS

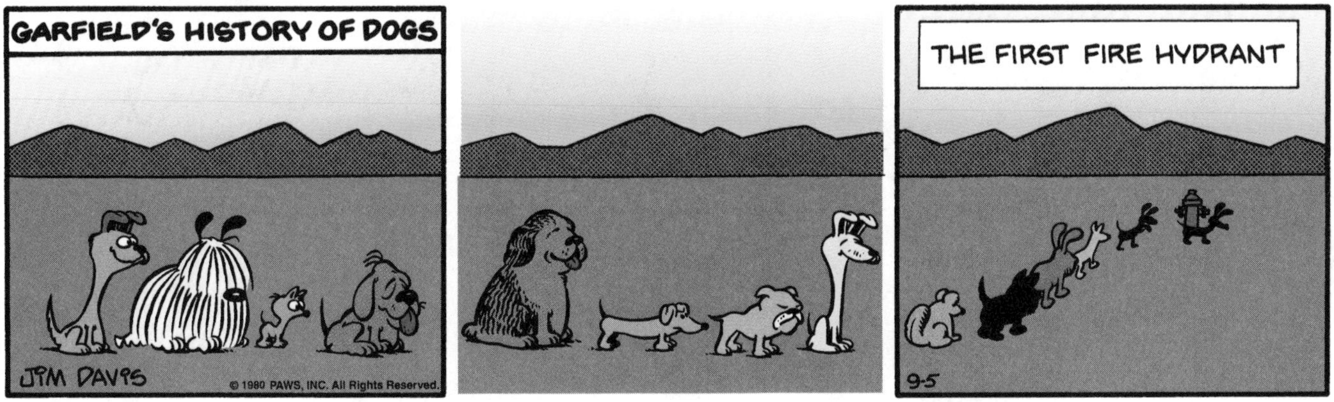
GARFIELD'S HISTORY OF DOGS
JIM DAVIS
© 1980 PAWS, INC. All Rights Reserved.
THE FIRST FIRE HYDRANT
9-5

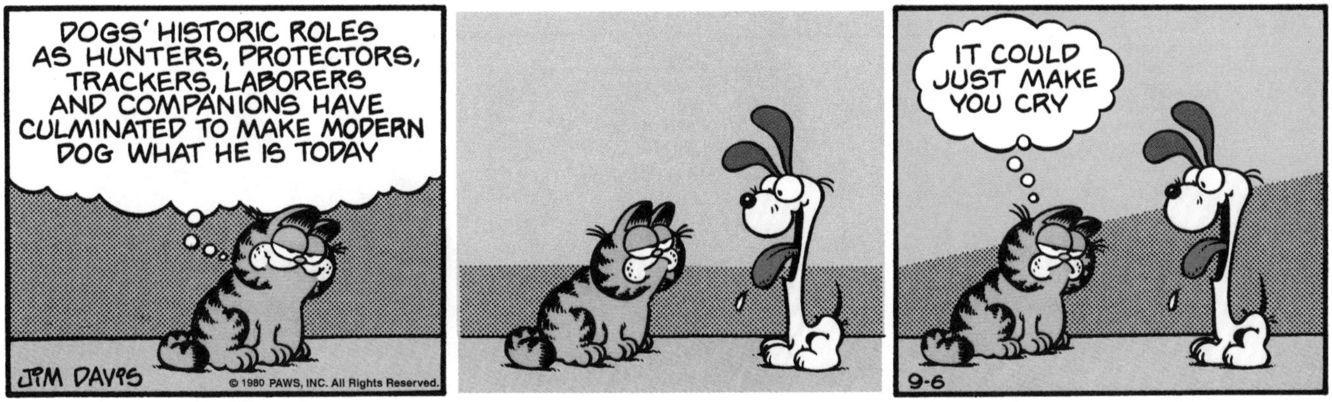
DOGS' HISTORIC ROLES AS HUNTERS, PROTECTORS, TRACKERS, LABORERS AND COMPANIONS HAVE CULMINATED TO MAKE MODERN DOG WHAT HE IS TODAY
JIM DAVIS
© 1980 PAWS, INC. All Rights Reserved.
IT COULD JUST MAKE YOU CRY
9-6

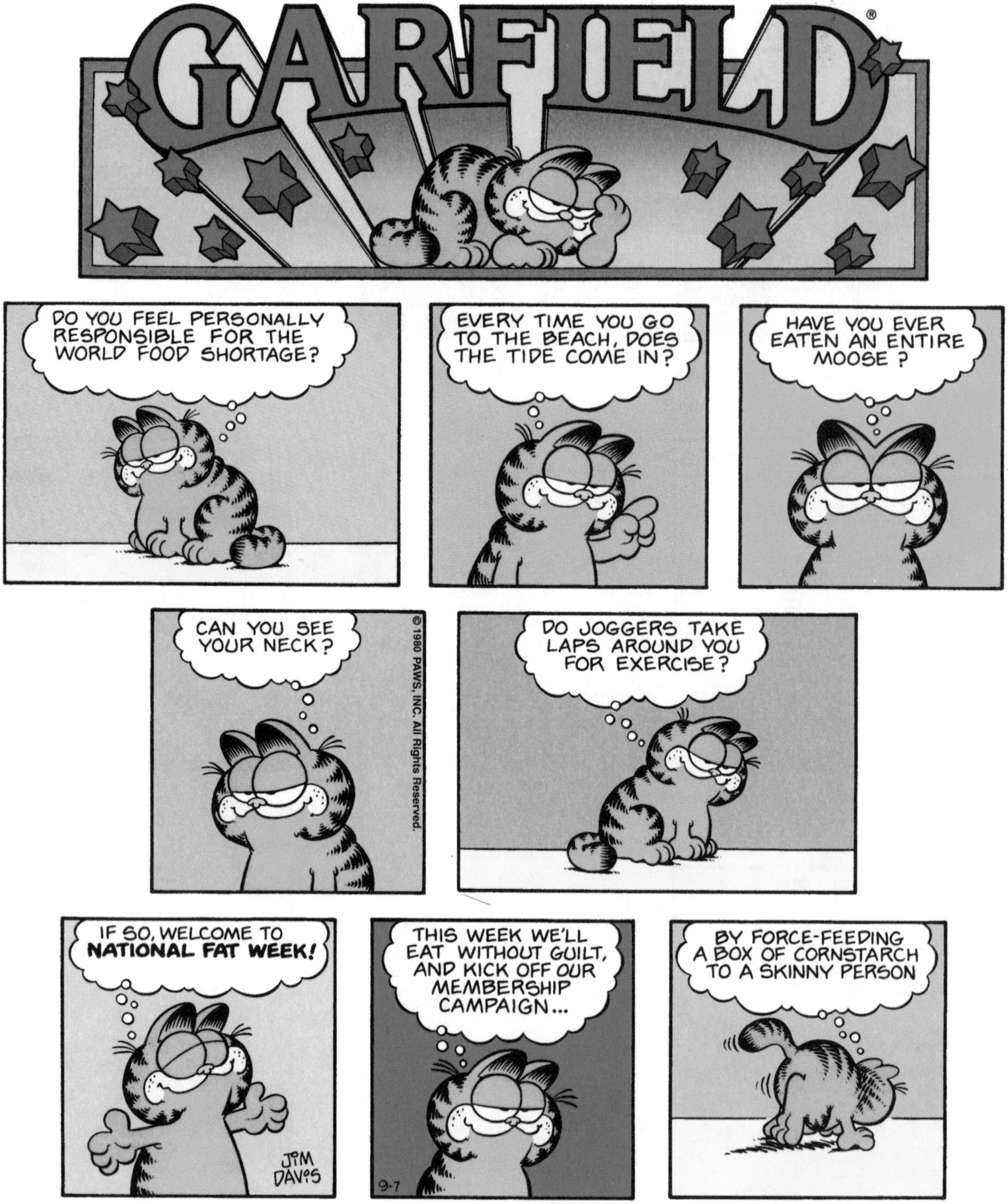
GARFIELD
DO YOU FEEL PERSONALLY RESPONSIBLE FOR THE WORLD FOOD SHORTAGE?
EVERY TIME YOU GO TO THE BEACH, DOES THE TIDE COME IN?
HAVE YOU EVER EATEN AN ENTIRE MOOSE ?
CAN YOU SEE YOUR NECK?
DO JOGGERS TAKE LAPS AROUND YOU FOR EXERCISE?
IF SO, WELCOME TO **NATIONAL FAT WEEK!**
JIM DAVIS
THIS WEEK WE'LL EAT WITHOUT GUILT, AND KICK OFF OUR MEMBERSHIP CAMPAIGN...
9-7
BY FORCE-FEEDING A BOX OF CORNSTARCH TO A SKINNY PERSON

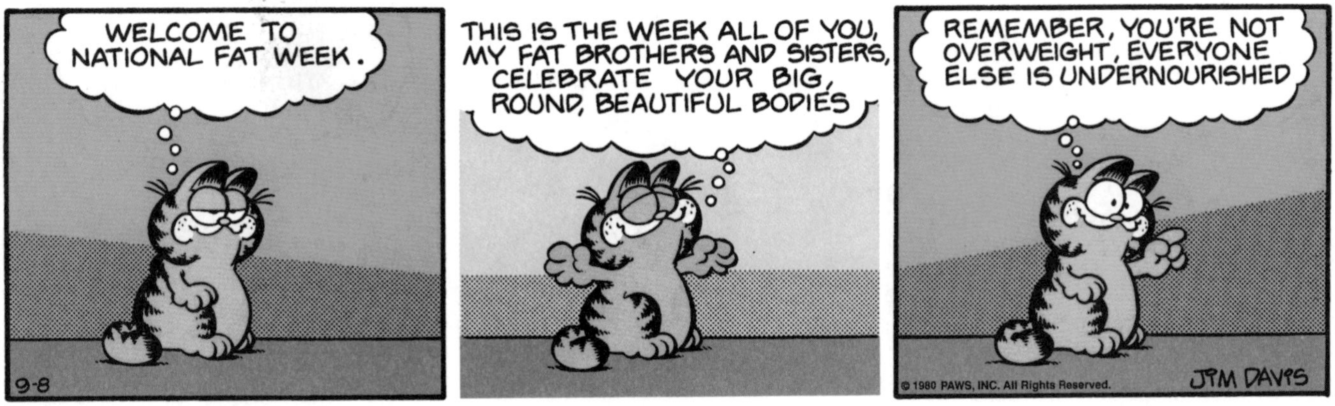
WELCOME TO NATIONAL FAT WEEK.
9-8
THIS IS THE WEEK ALL OF YOU, MY FAT BROTHERS AND SISTERS, CELEBRATE YOUR BIG, ROUND, BEAUTIFUL BODIES
REMEMBER, YOU'RE NOT OVERWEIGHT, EVERYONE ELSE IS UNDERNOURISHED
© 1980 PAWS, INC. All Rights Reserved.
JIM DAVIS

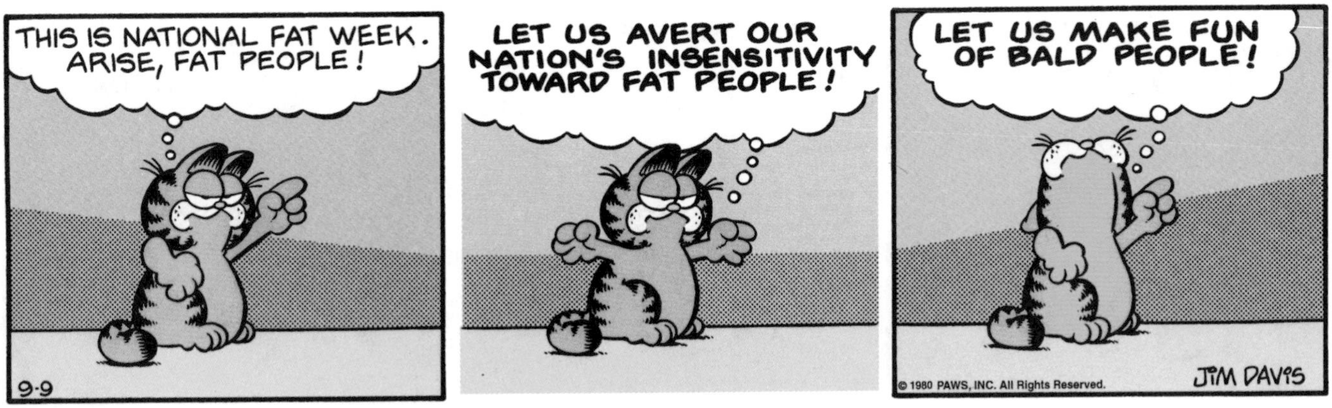
THIS IS NATIONAL FAT WEEK. ARISE, FAT PEOPLE!
9-9
LET US AVERT OUR NATION'S INSENSITIVITY TOWARD FAT PEOPLE!
LET US MAKE FUN OF BALD PEOPLE!
© 1980 PAWS, INC. All Rights Reserved.
JIM DAVIS

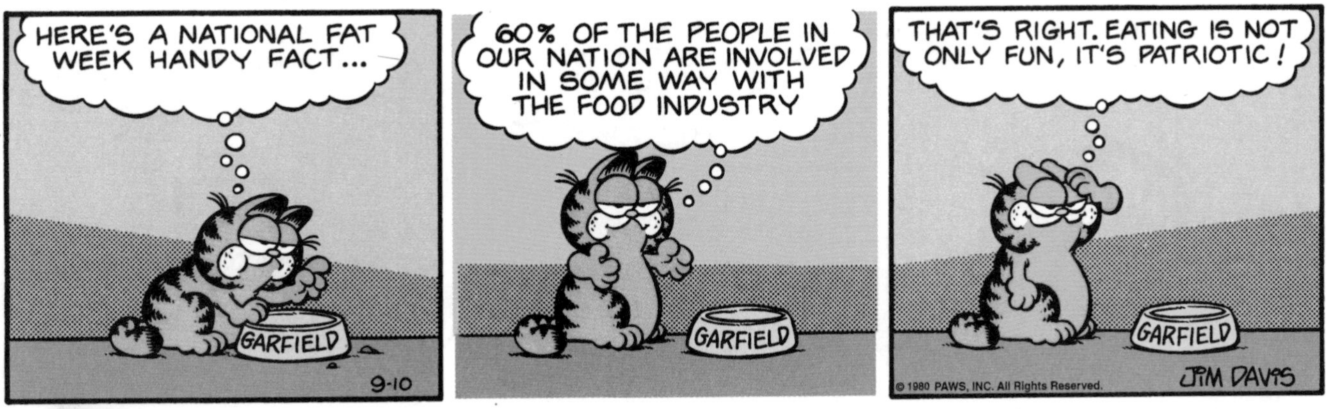
HERE'S A NATIONAL FAT WEEK HANDY FACT...
GARFIELD
9-10
60% OF THE PEOPLE IN OUR NATION ARE INVOLVED IN SOME WAY WITH THE FOOD INDUSTRY
GARFIELD
THAT'S RIGHT. EATING IS NOT ONLY FUN, IT'S PATRIOTIC!
GARFIELD
© 1980 PAWS, INC. All Rights Reserved.
JIM DAVIS

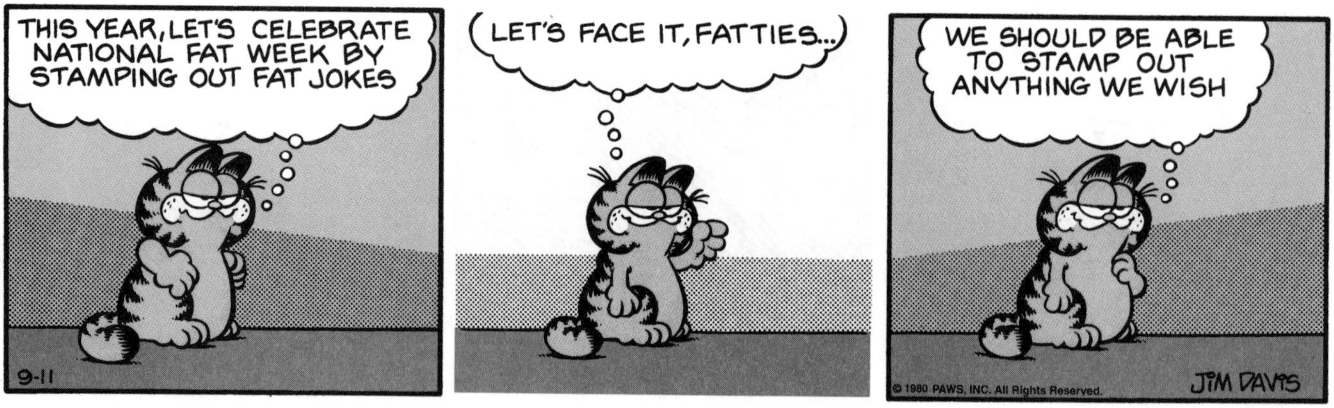
THIS YEAR, LET'S CELEBRATE NATIONAL FAT WEEK BY STAMPING OUT FAT JOKES
9-11
LET'S FACE IT, FATTIES...
WE SHOULD BE ABLE TO STAMP OUT ANYTHING WE WISH
© 1980 PAWS, INC. All Rights Reserved.
JIM DAVIS

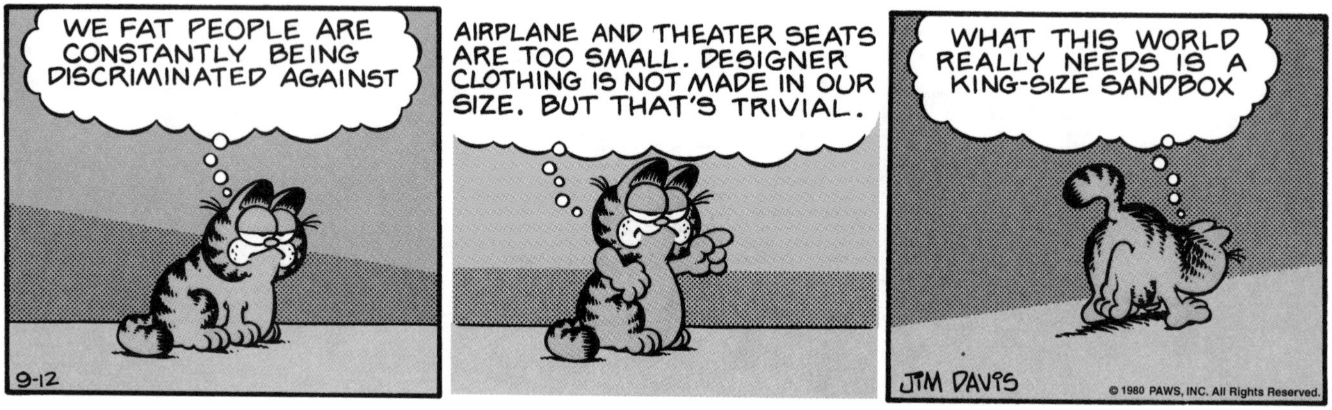
WE FAT PEOPLE ARE CONSTANTLY BEING DISCRIMINATED AGAINST
9-12
AIRPLANE AND THEATER SEATS ARE TOO SMALL. DESIGNER CLOTHING IS NOT MADE IN OUR SIZE. BUT THAT'S TRIVIAL.
WHAT THIS WORLD REALLY NEEDS IS A KING-SIZE SANDBOX
JIM DAVIS
© 1980 PAWS, INC. All Rights Reserved.

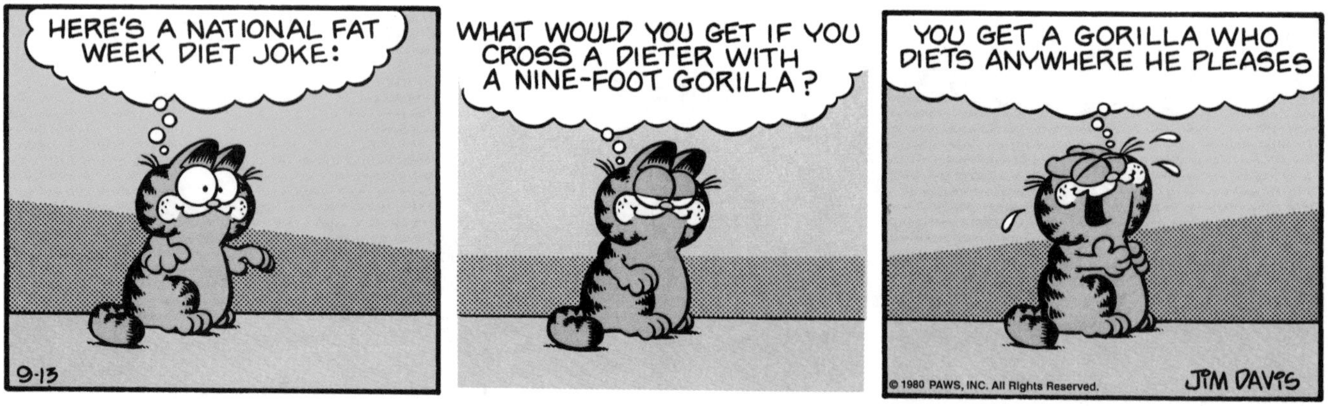
HERE'S A NATIONAL FAT WEEK DIET JOKE:
9-13
WHAT WOULD YOU GET IF YOU CROSS A DIETER WITH A NINE-FOOT GORILLA?
YOU GET A GORILLA WHO DIETS ANYWHERE HE PLEASES
© 1980 PAWS, INC. All Rights Reserved.
JIM DAVIS

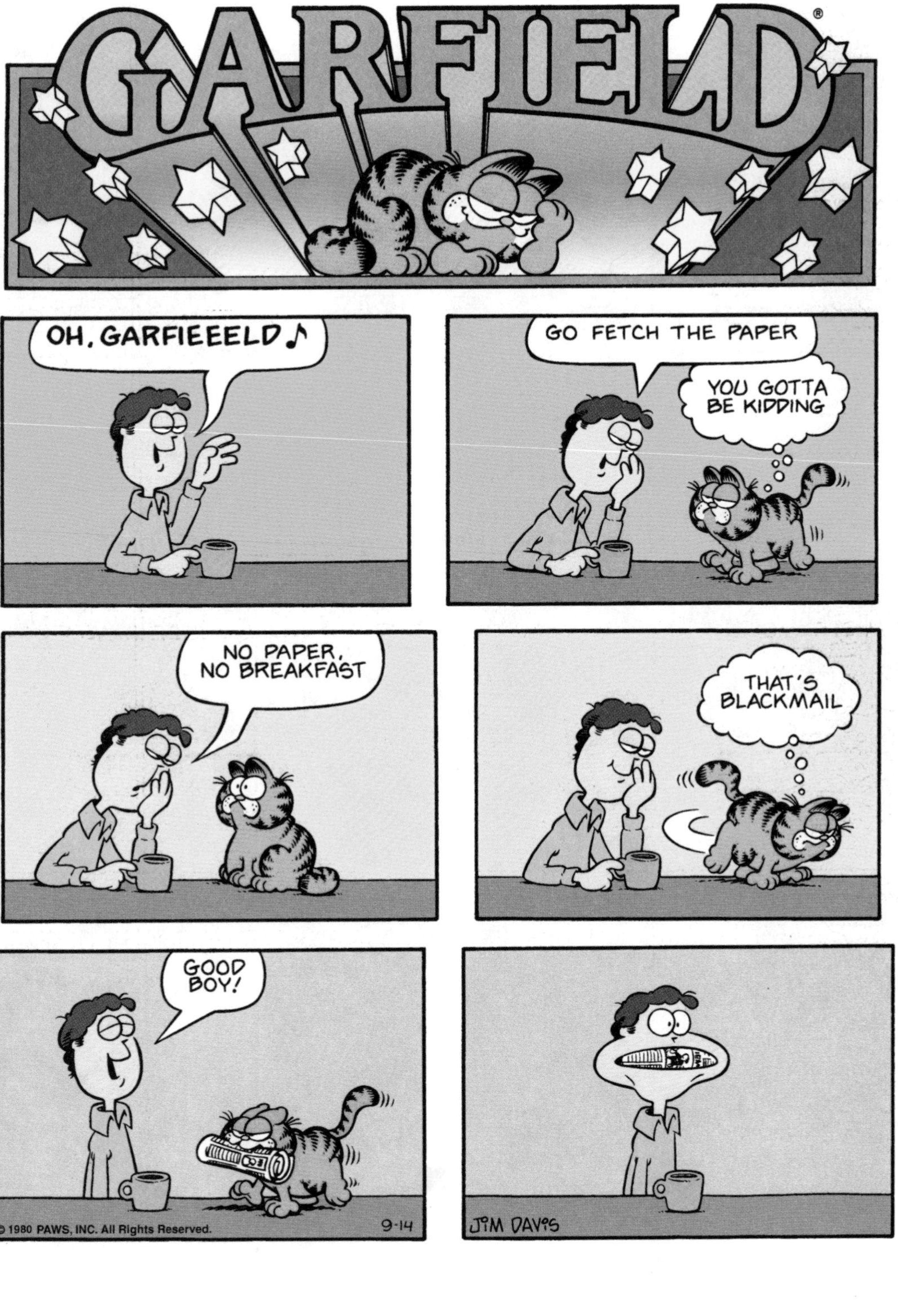
GARFIELD
OH, GARFIEEELD ♪
GO FETCH THE PAPER
YOU GOTTA BE KIDDING
NO PAPER, NO BREAKFAST
THAT'S BLACKMAIL
GOOD BOY!
© 1980 PAWS, INC. All Rights Reserved.
9-14
JIM DAVIS

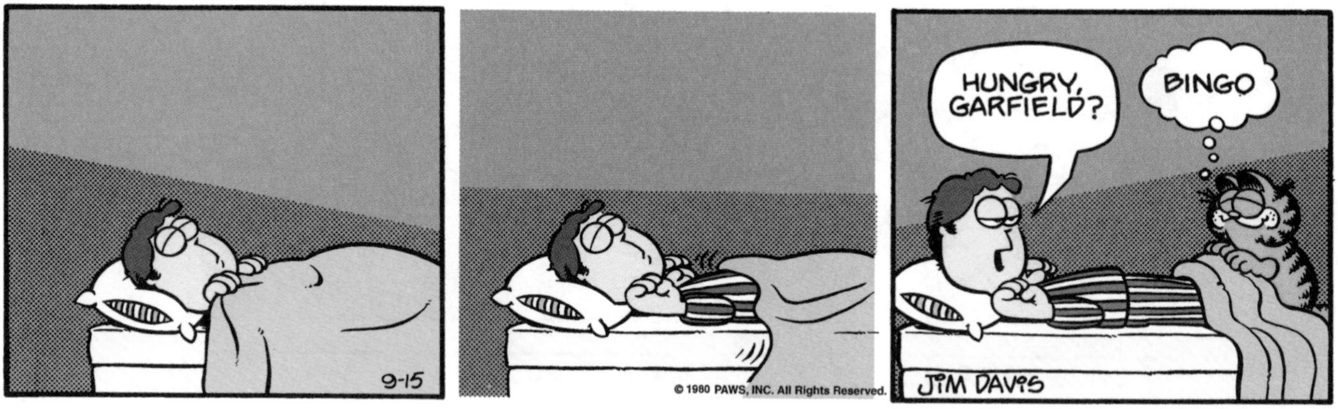
HUNGRY, GARFIELD?
BINGO
9-15
© 1980 PAWS, INC. All Rights Reserved.
JIM DAVIS

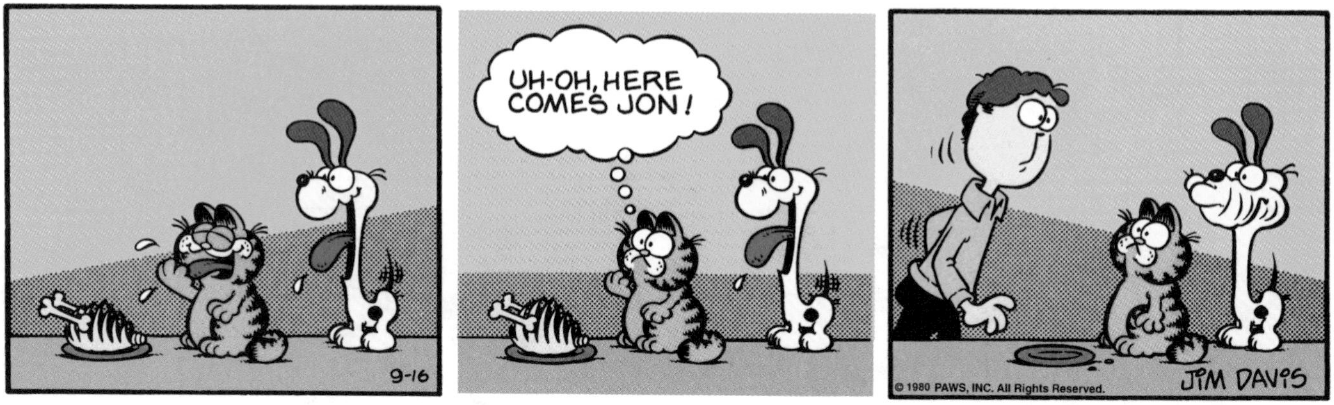
9-16
UH-OH, HERE COMES JON!
© 1980 PAWS, INC. All Rights Reserved.
JIM DAVIS

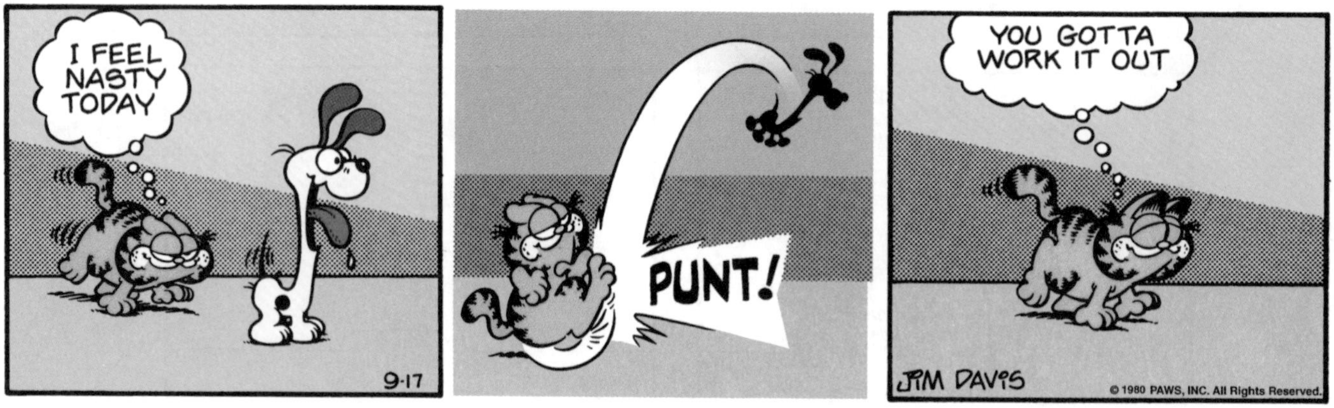
I FEEL NASTY TODAY
9-17
PUNT!
YOU GOTTA WORK IT OUT
JIM DAVIS
© 1980 PAWS, INC. All Rights Reserved.

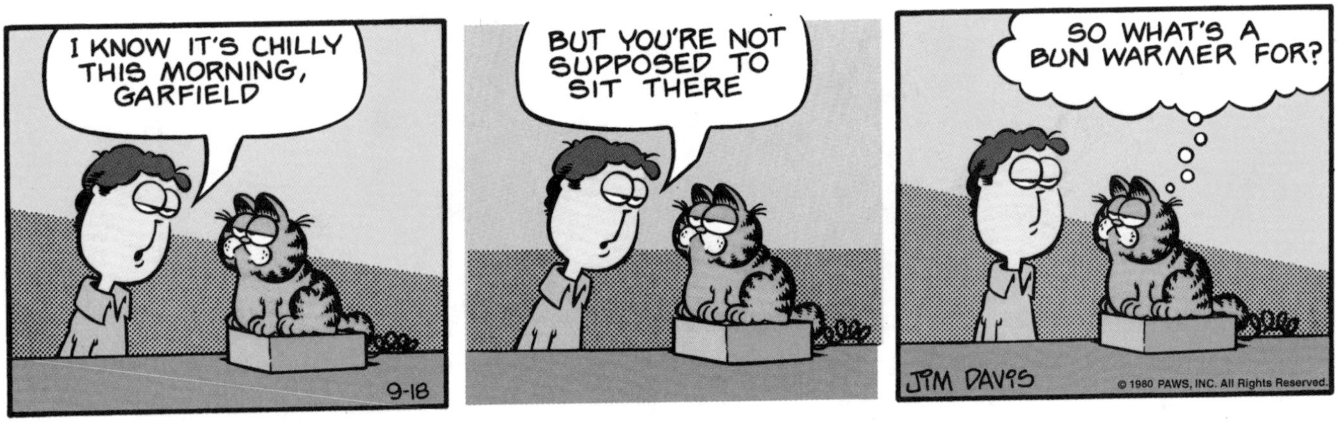
I KNOW IT'S CHILLY THIS MORNING, GARFIELD
9-18
BUT YOU'RE NOT SUPPOSED TO SIT THERE
SO WHAT'S A BUN WARMER FOR?
JIM DAVIS
© 1980 PAWS, INC. All Rights Reserved.

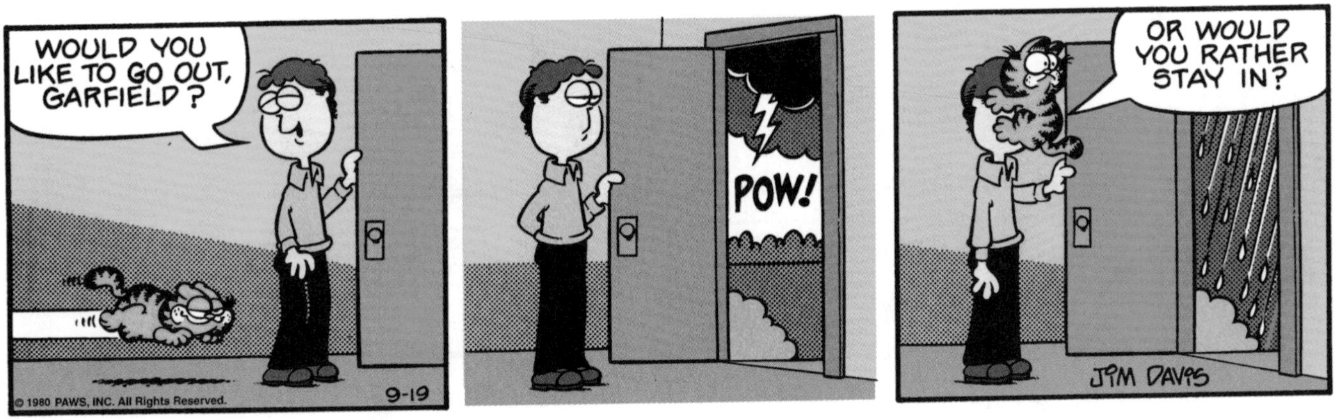
WOULD YOU LIKE TO GO OUT, GARFIELD?
© 1980 PAWS, INC. All Rights Reserved.
9-19
POW!
OR WOULD YOU RATHER STAY IN?
JIM DAVIS

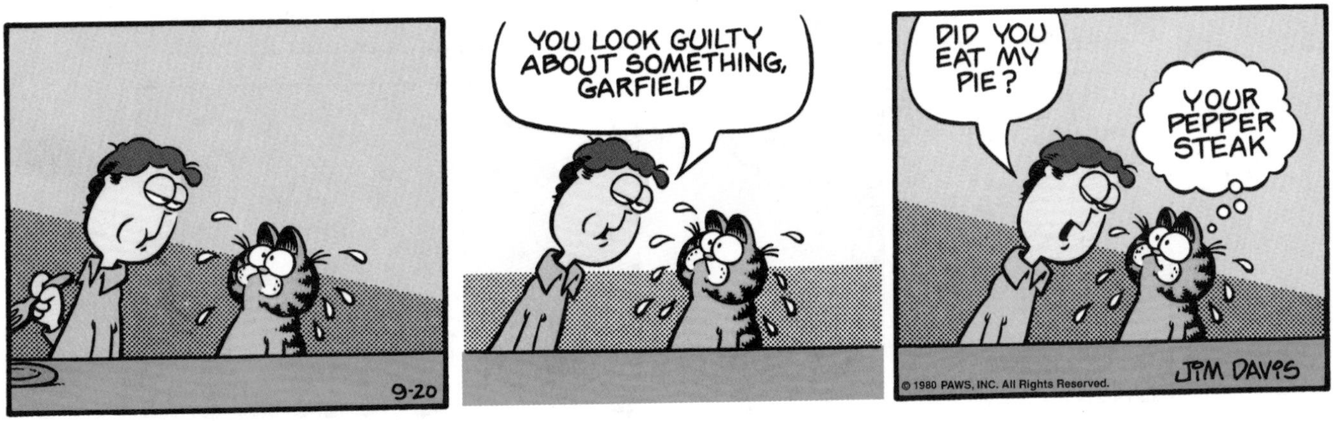
9-20
YOU LOOK GUILTY ABOUT SOMETHING, GARFIELD
DID YOU EAT MY PIE?
YOUR PEPPER STEAK
© 1980 PAWS, INC. All Rights Reserved.
JIM DAVIS

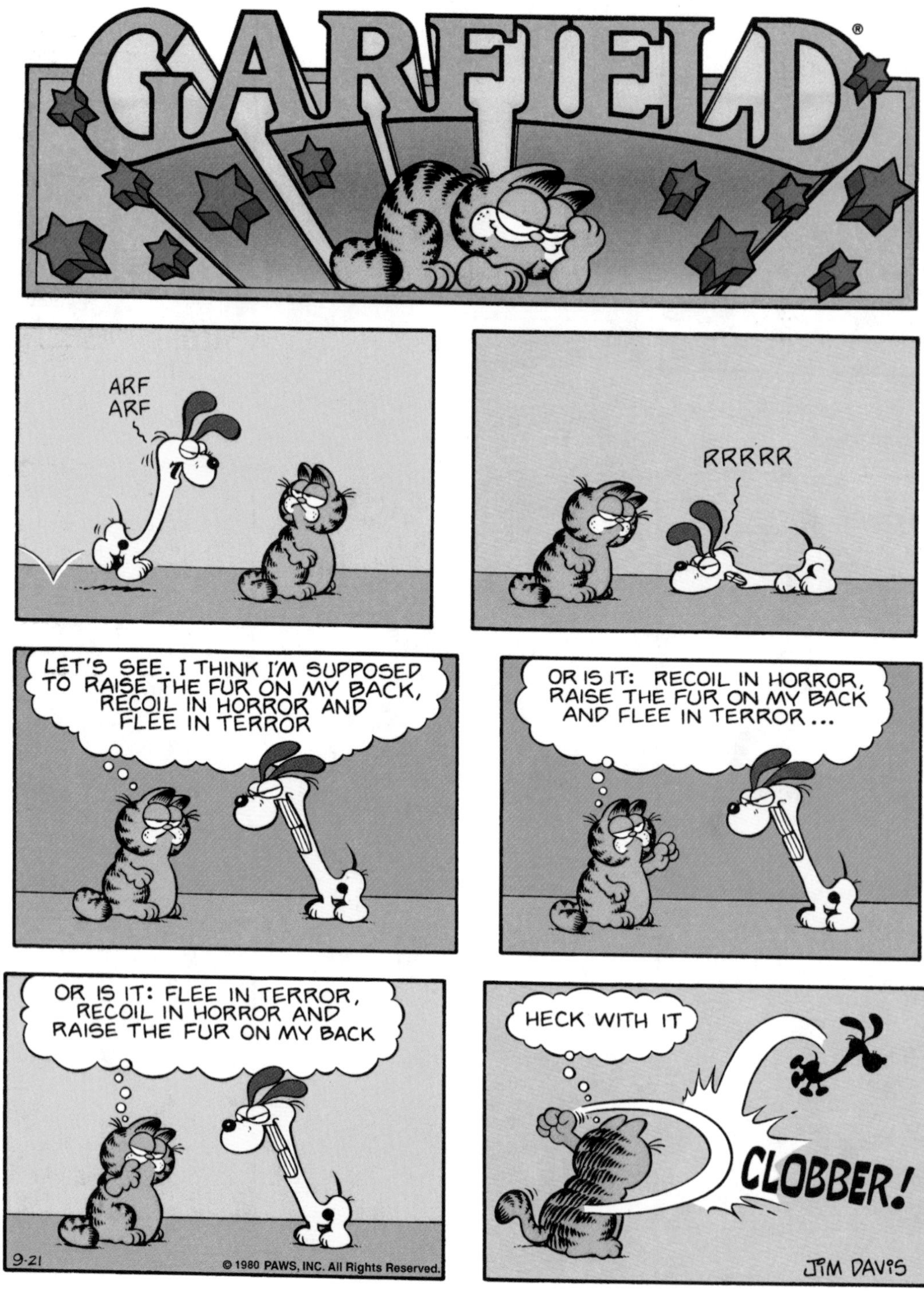
GARFIELD®
ARF ARF
RRRRR
LET'S SEE. I THINK I'M SUPPOSED TO RAISE THE FUR ON MY BACK, RECOIL IN HORROR AND FLEE IN TERROR
OR IS IT: RECOIL IN HORROR, RAISE THE FUR ON MY BACK AND FLEE IN TERROR...
OR IS IT: FLEE IN TERROR, RECOIL IN HORROR AND RAISE THE FUR ON MY BACK
HECK WITH IT
CLOBBER!
9-21
© 1980 PAWS, INC. All Rights Reserved.
JIM DAVIS

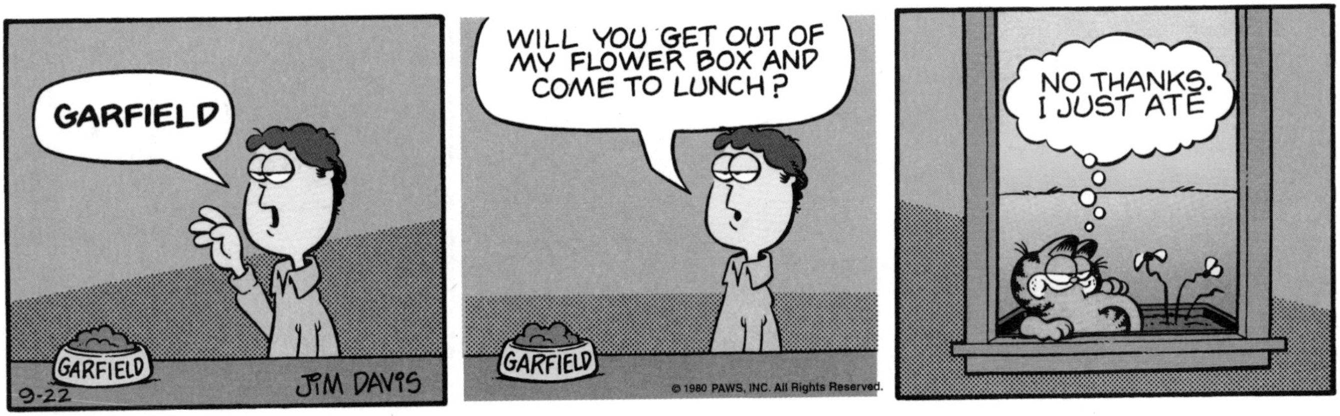
GARFIELD
GARFIELD
9-22
JIM DAVIS
WILL YOU GET OUT OF MY FLOWER BOX AND COME TO LUNCH?
GARFIELD
© 1980 PAWS, INC. All Rights Reserved.
NO THANKS. I JUST ATE

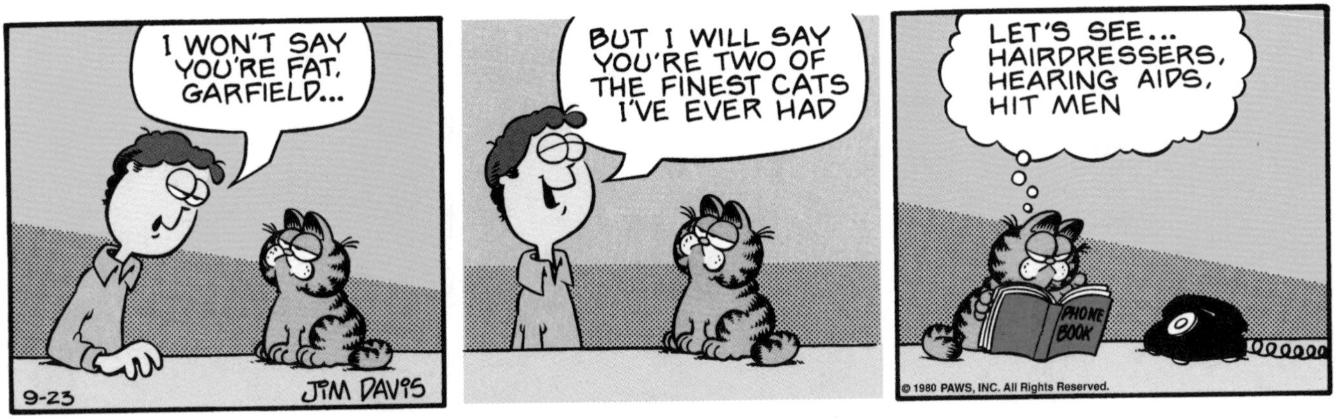
I WON'T SAY YOU'RE FAT, GARFIELD...
9-23
JIM DAVIS
BUT I WILL SAY YOU'RE TWO OF THE FINEST CATS I'VE EVER HAD
LET'S SEE... HAIRDRESSERS, HEARING AIDS, HIT MEN
PHONE BOOK
© 1980 PAWS, INC. All Rights Reserved.

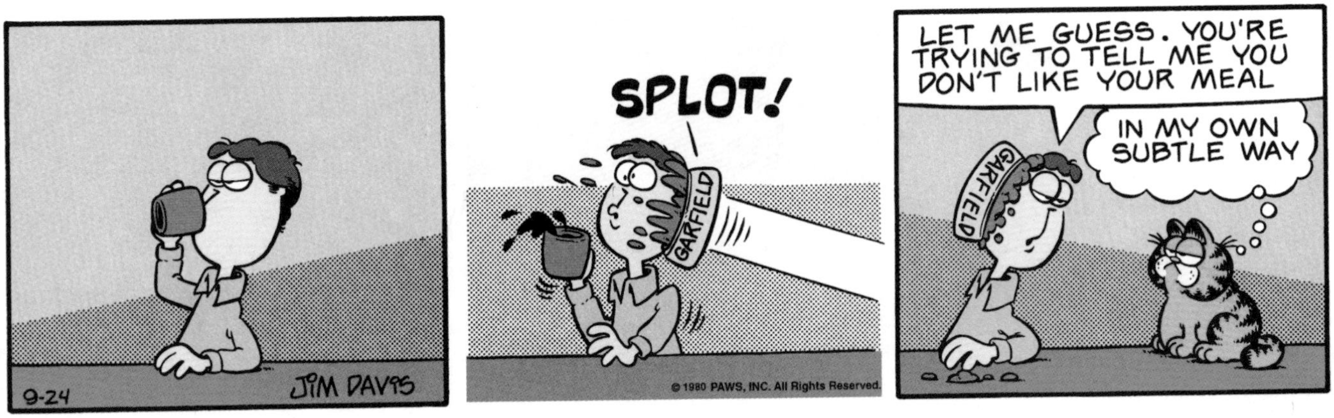
9-24
JIM DAVIS
SPLOT!
GARFIELD
© 1980 PAWS, INC. All Rights Reserved.
LET ME GUESS. YOU'RE TRYING TO TELL ME YOU DON'T LIKE YOUR MEAL
GARFIELD
IN MY OWN SUBTLE WAY

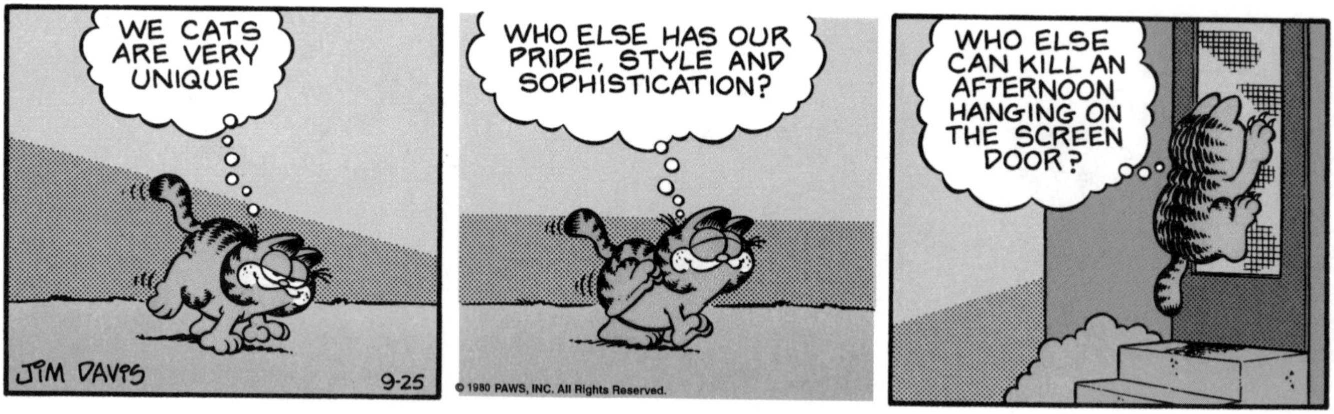
WE CATS ARE VERY UNIQUE
JIM DAVIS
9-25
WHO ELSE HAS OUR PRIDE, STYLE AND SOPHISTICATION?
© 1980 PAWS, INC. All Rights Reserved.
WHO ELSE CAN KILL AN AFTERNOON HANGING ON THE SCREEN DOOR?

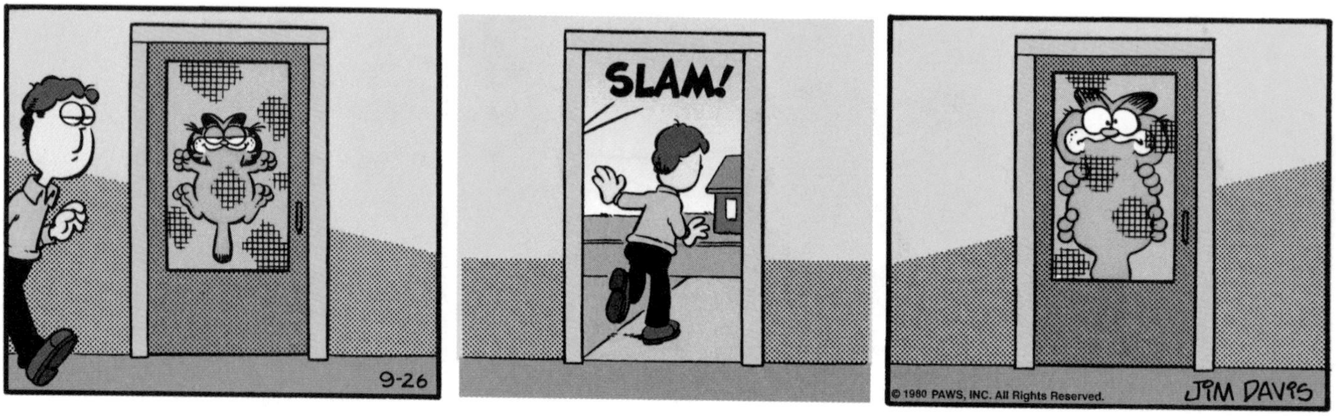
9-26
SLAM!
© 1980 PAWS, INC. All Rights Reserved.
JIM DAVIS

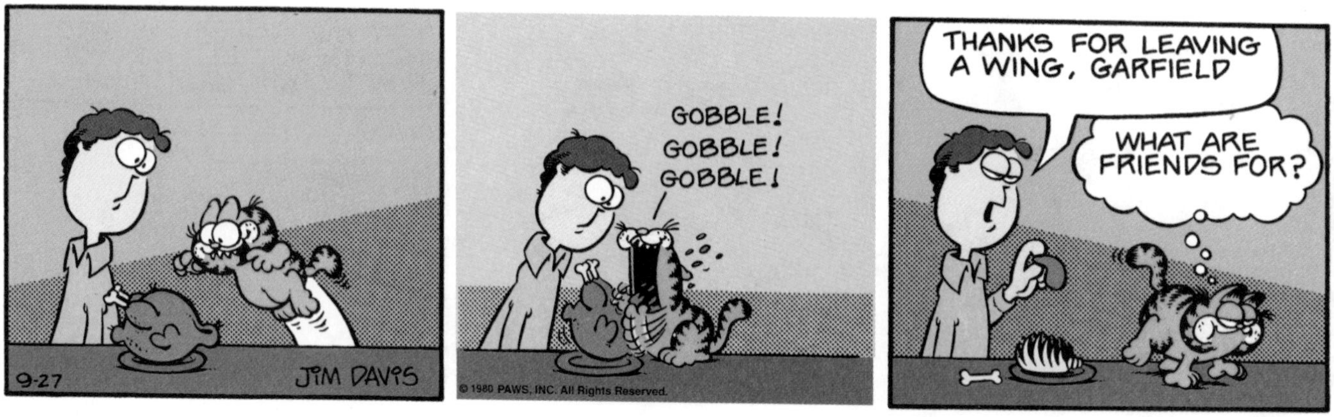
9-27
JIM DAVIS
GOBBLE! GOBBLE! GOBBLE!
© 1980 PAWS, INC. All Rights Reserved.
THANKS FOR LEAVING A WING, GARFIELD
WHAT ARE FRIENDS FOR?

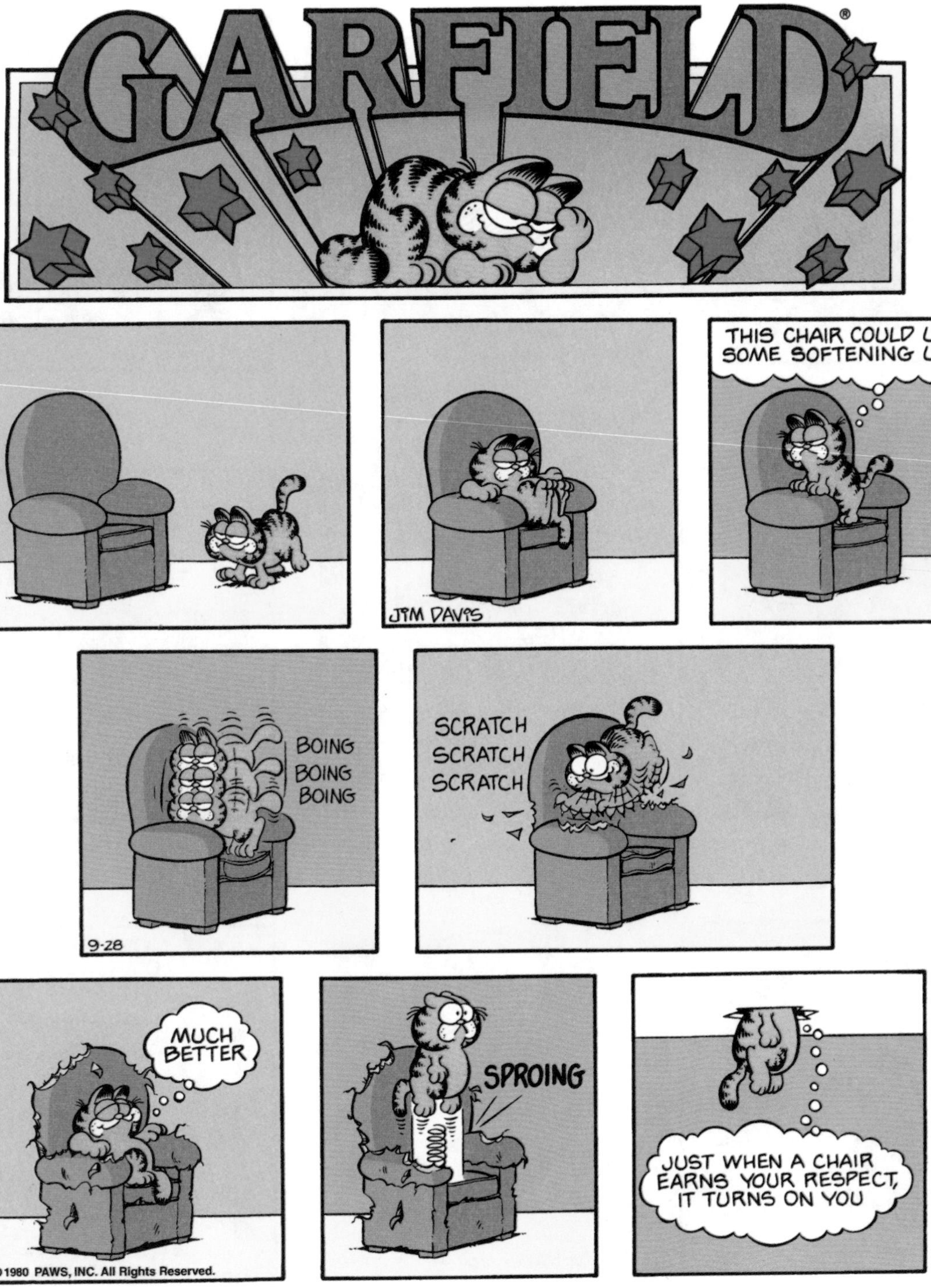
GARFIELD
JIM DAVIS
THIS CHAIR COULD USE SOME SOFTENING UP
BOING
BOING
BOING
9-28
SCRATCH
SCRATCH
SCRATCH
MUCH BETTER
SPROING
JUST WHEN A CHAIR EARNS YOUR RESPECT, IT TURNS ON YOU
©1980 PAWS, INC. All Rights Reserved.

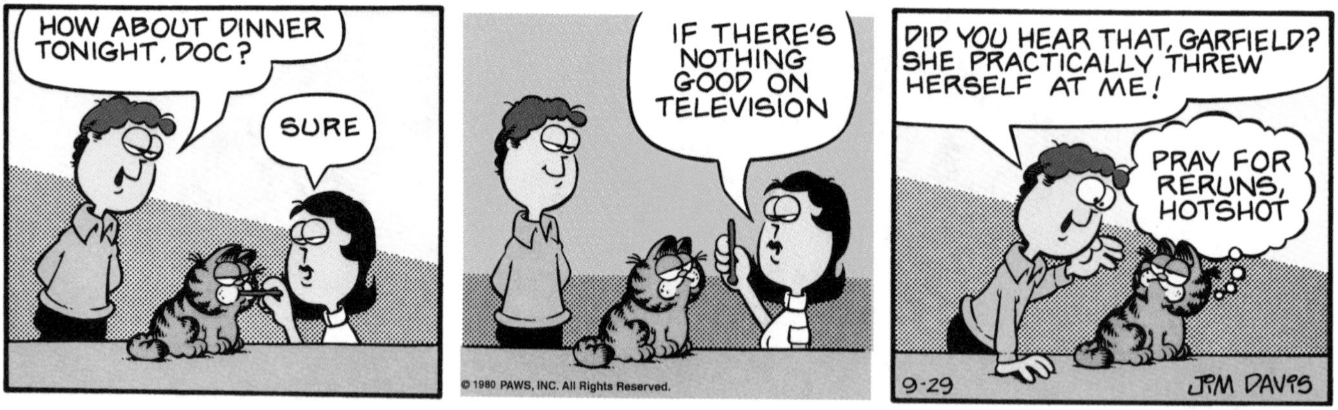
HOW ABOUT DINNER TONIGHT, DOC?
SURE
IF THERE'S NOTHING GOOD ON TELEVISION
© 1980 PAWS, INC. All Rights Reserved.
DID YOU HEAR THAT, GARFIELD? SHE PRACTICALLY THREW HERSELF AT ME!
PRAY FOR RERUNS, HOTSHOT
9-29
JIM DAVIS

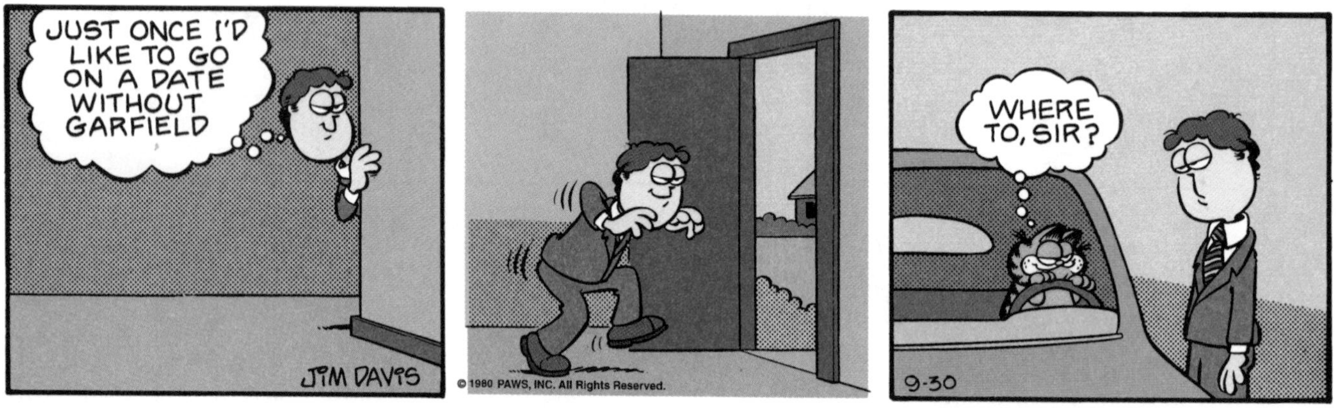
JUST ONCE I'D LIKE TO GO ON A DATE WITHOUT GARFIELD
JIM DAVIS
© 1980 PAWS, INC. All Rights Reserved.
WHERE TO, SIR?
9-30

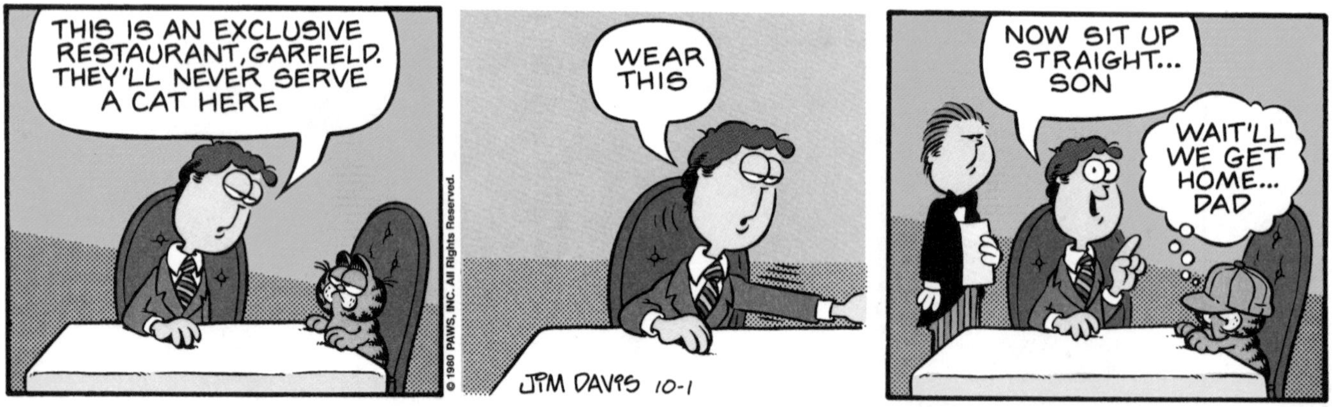
THIS IS AN EXCLUSIVE RESTAURANT, GARFIELD. THEY'LL NEVER SERVE A CAT HERE
© 1980 PAWS, INC. All Rights Reserved.
WEAR THIS
JIM DAVIS 10-1
NOW SIT UP STRAIGHT... SON
WAIT'LL WE GET HOME... DAD

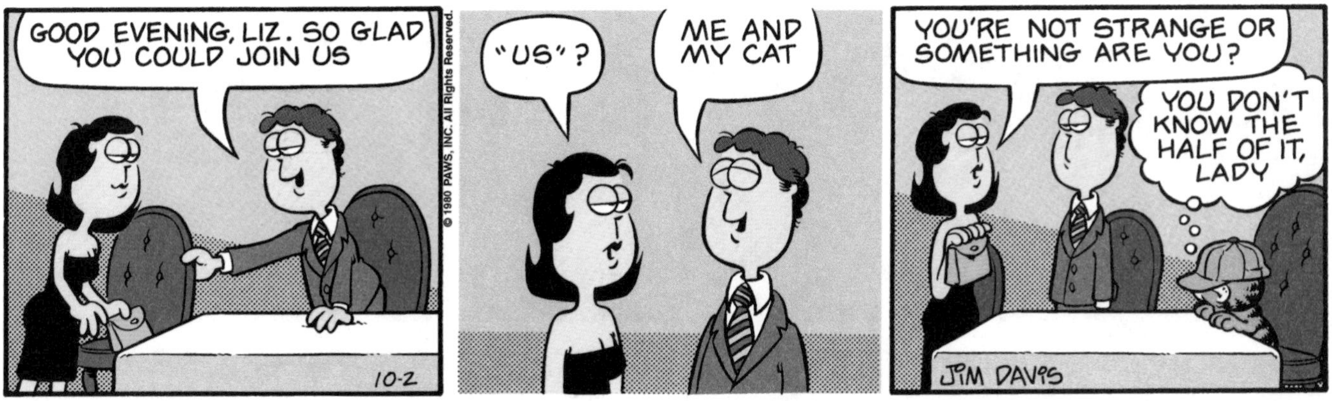
GOOD EVENING, LIZ. SO GLAD YOU COULD JOIN US
10-2
© 1980 PAWS, INC. All Rights Reserved.
"US"?
ME AND MY CAT
YOU'RE NOT STRANGE OR SOMETHING ARE YOU?
YOU DON'T KNOW THE HALF OF IT, LADY
JIM DAVIS

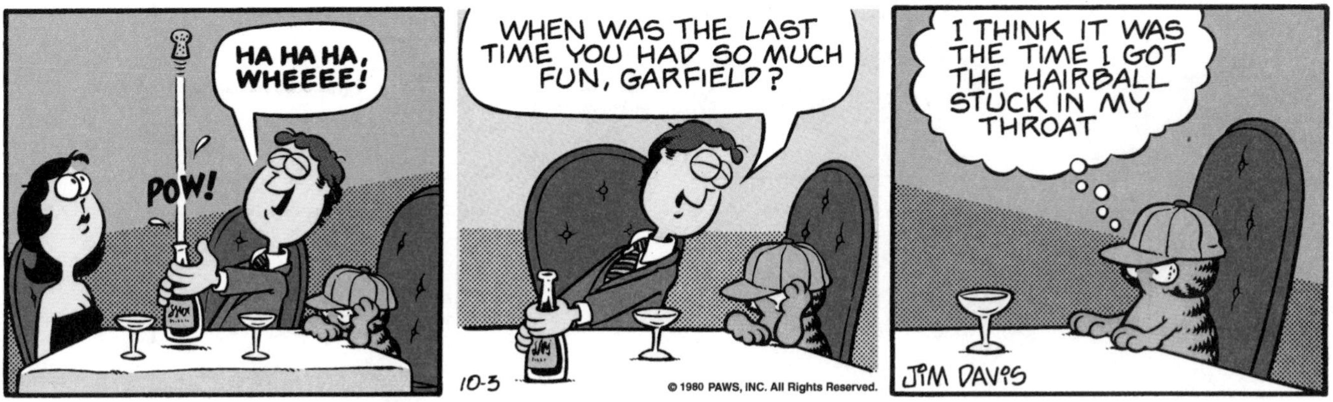
HA HA HA, WHEEEE!
POW!
WHEN WAS THE LAST TIME YOU HAD SO MUCH FUN, GARFIELD?
10-3
© 1980 PAWS, INC. All Rights Reserved.
I THINK IT WAS THE TIME I GOT THE HAIRBALL STUCK IN MY THROAT
JIM DAVIS

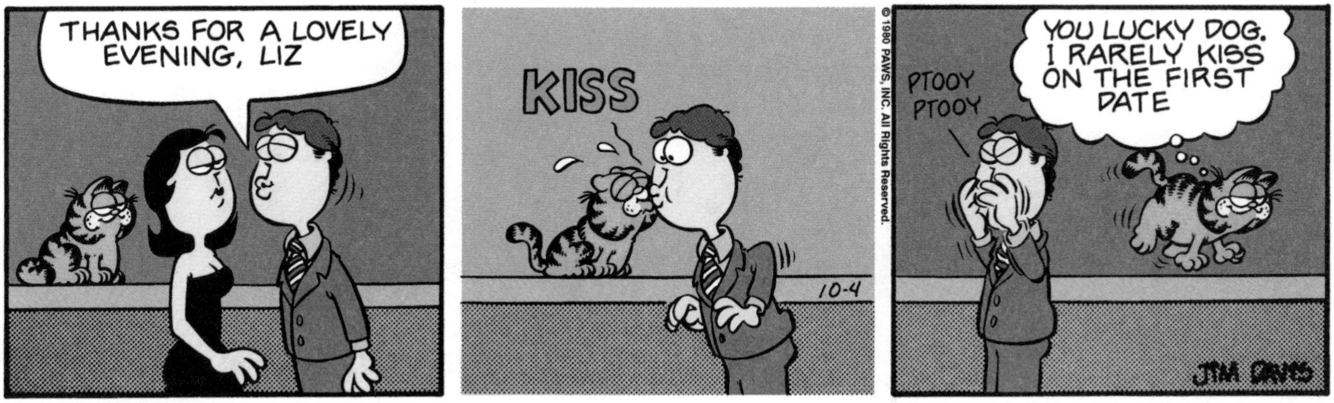
THANKS FOR A LOVELY EVENING, LIZ
KISS
10-4
© 1980 PAWS, INC. All Rights Reserved.
PTOOY PTOOY
YOU LUCKY DOG. I RARELY KISS ON THE FIRST DATE
JIM DAVIS

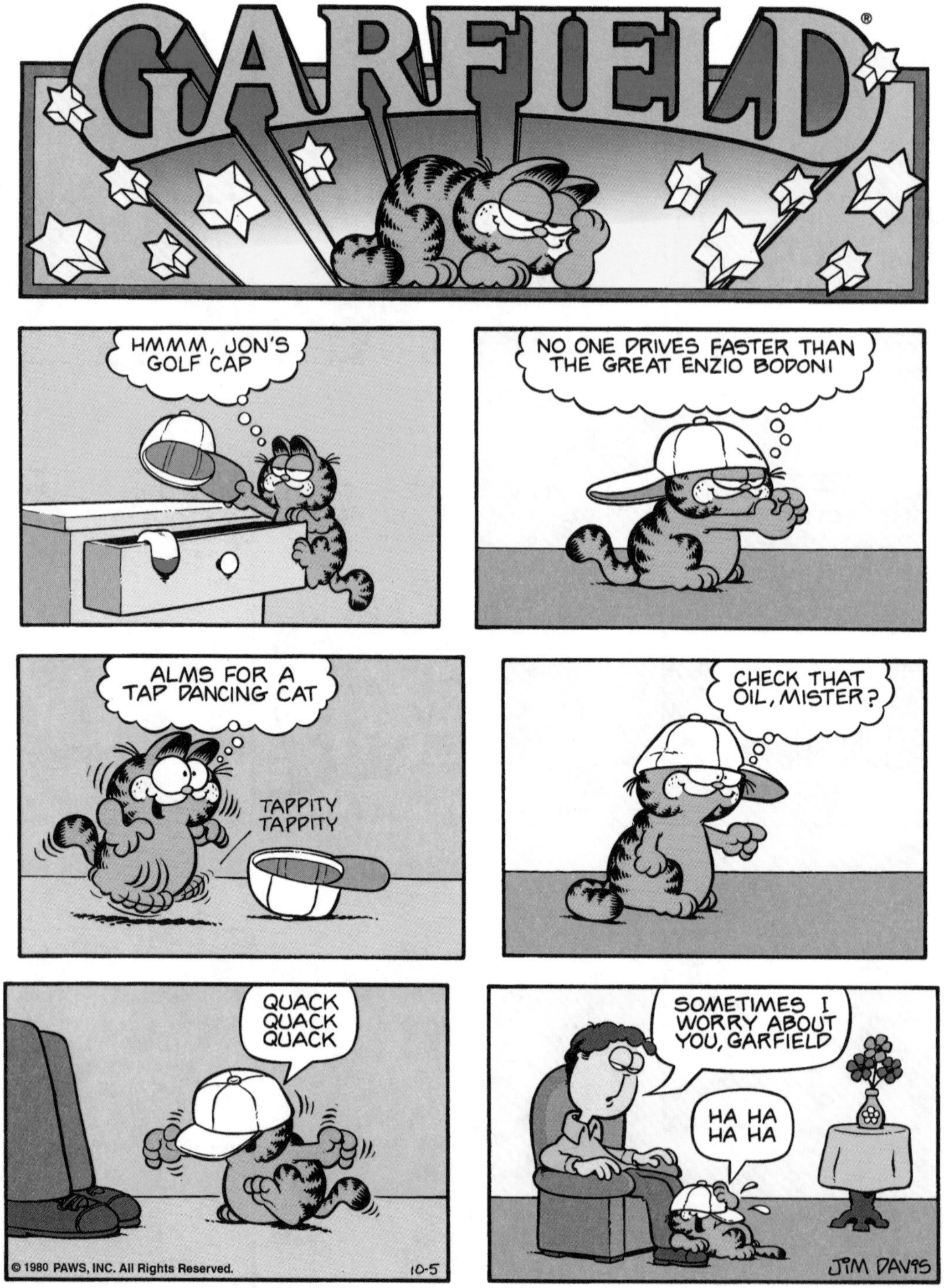
GARFIELD
HMMM, JON'S GOLF CAP
NO ONE DRIVES FASTER THAN THE GREAT ENZIO BODONI
ALMS FOR A TAP DANCING CAT
TAPPITY TAPPITY
CHECK THAT OIL, MISTER?
QUACK QUACK QUACK
© 1980 PAWS, INC. All Rights Reserved.
10-5
SOMETIMES I WORRY ABOUT YOU, GARFIELD
HA HA HA HA
JIM DAVIS

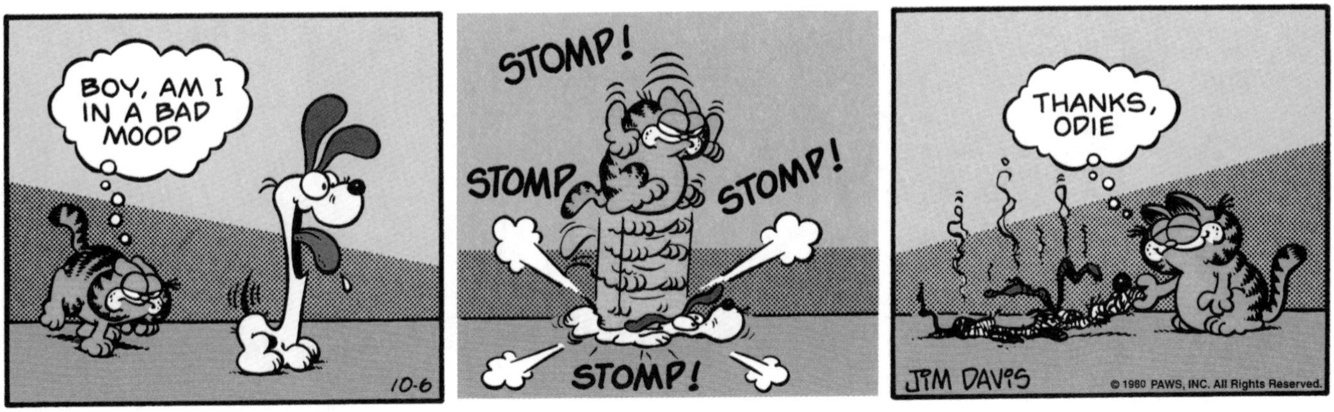
BOY, AM I IN A BAD MOOD
10-6
STOMP!
STOMP
STOMP!
STOMP!
THANKS, ODIE
JIM DAVIS
© 1980 PAWS, INC. All Rights Reserved.

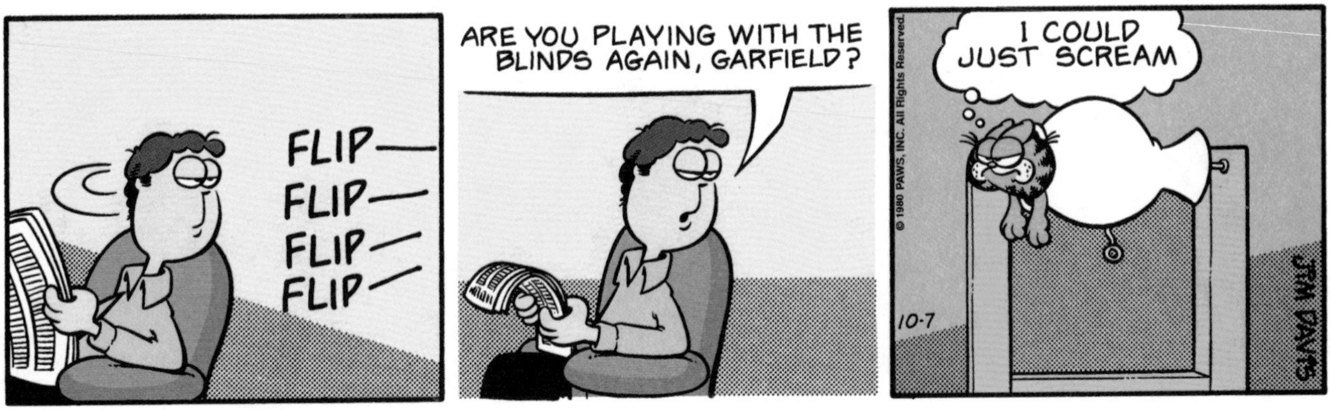
FLIP—
FLIP—
FLIP—
FLIP—
ARE YOU PLAYING WITH THE BLINDS AGAIN, GARFIELD?
© 1980 PAWS, INC. All Rights Reserved.
I COULD JUST SCREAM
10-7
JIM DAVIS

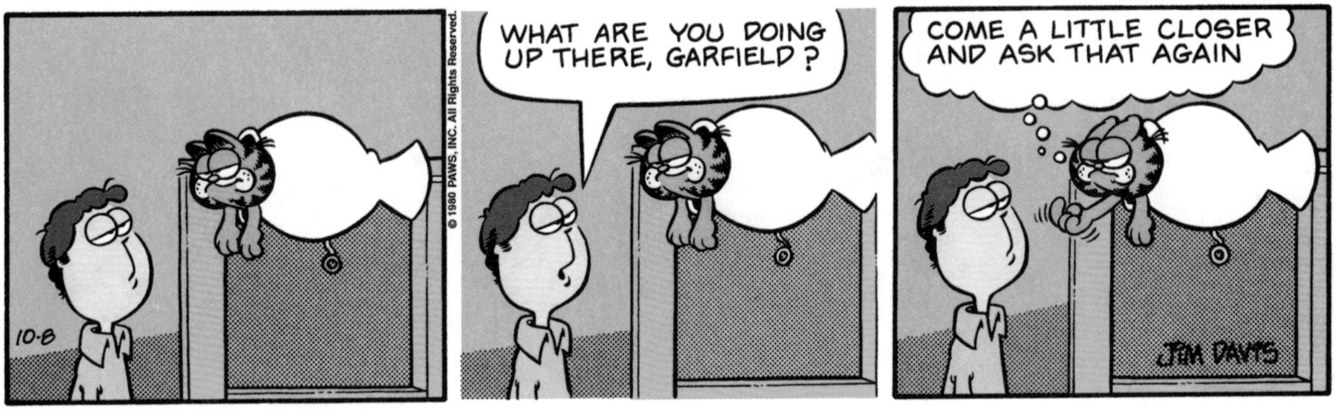
10-8
© 1980 PAWS, INC. All Rights Reserved.
WHAT ARE YOU DOING UP THERE, GARFIELD?
COME A LITTLE CLOSER AND ASK THAT AGAIN
JIM DAVIS

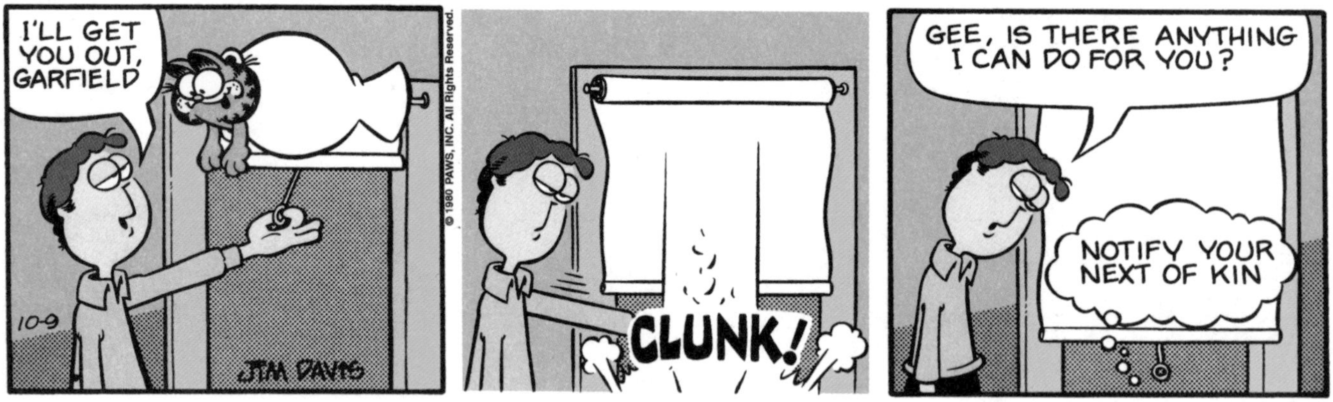
I'LL GET YOU OUT, GARFIELD
10-9
JIM DAVIS
© 1980 PAWS, INC. All Rights Reserved.
CLUNK!
GEE, IS THERE ANYTHING I CAN DO FOR YOU?
NOTIFY YOUR NEXT OF KIN

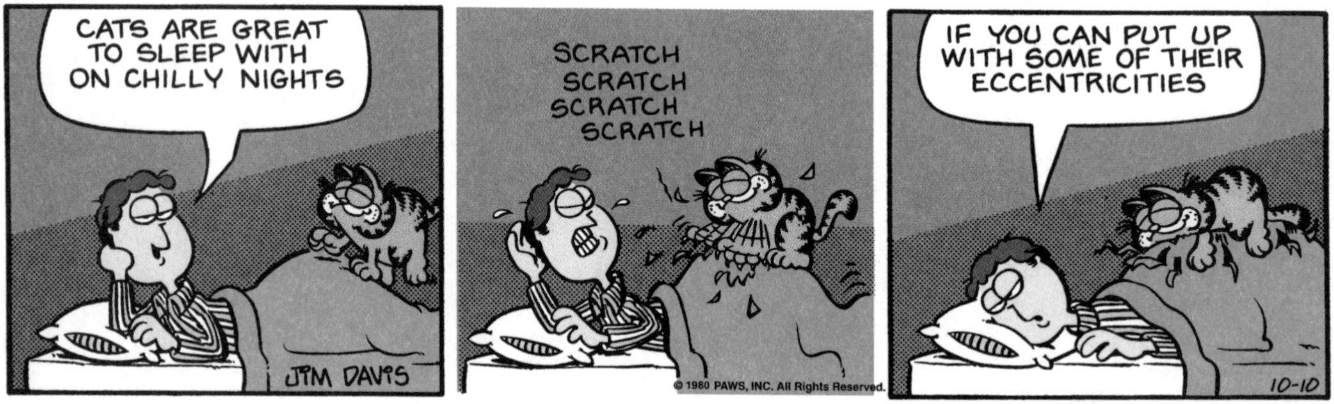
CATS ARE GREAT TO SLEEP WITH ON CHILLY NIGHTS
JIM DAVIS
SCRATCH SCRATCH SCRATCH SCRATCH SCRATCH
© 1980 PAWS, INC. All Rights Reserved.
IF YOU CAN PUT UP WITH SOME OF THEIR ECCENTRICITIES
10-10

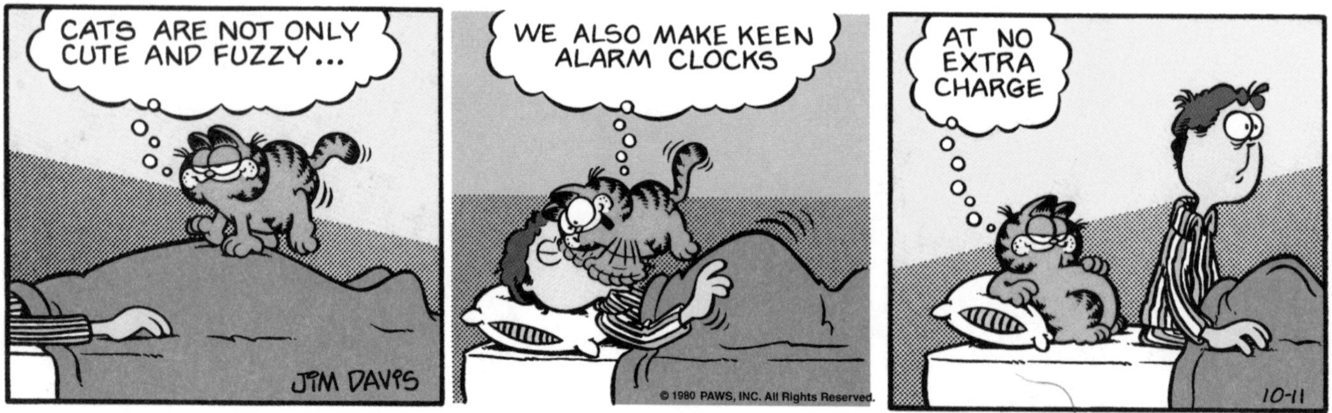
CATS ARE NOT ONLY CUTE AND FUZZY...
JIM DAVIS
WE ALSO MAKE KEEN ALARM CLOCKS
© 1980 PAWS, INC. All Rights Reserved.
AT NO EXTRA CHARGE
10-11

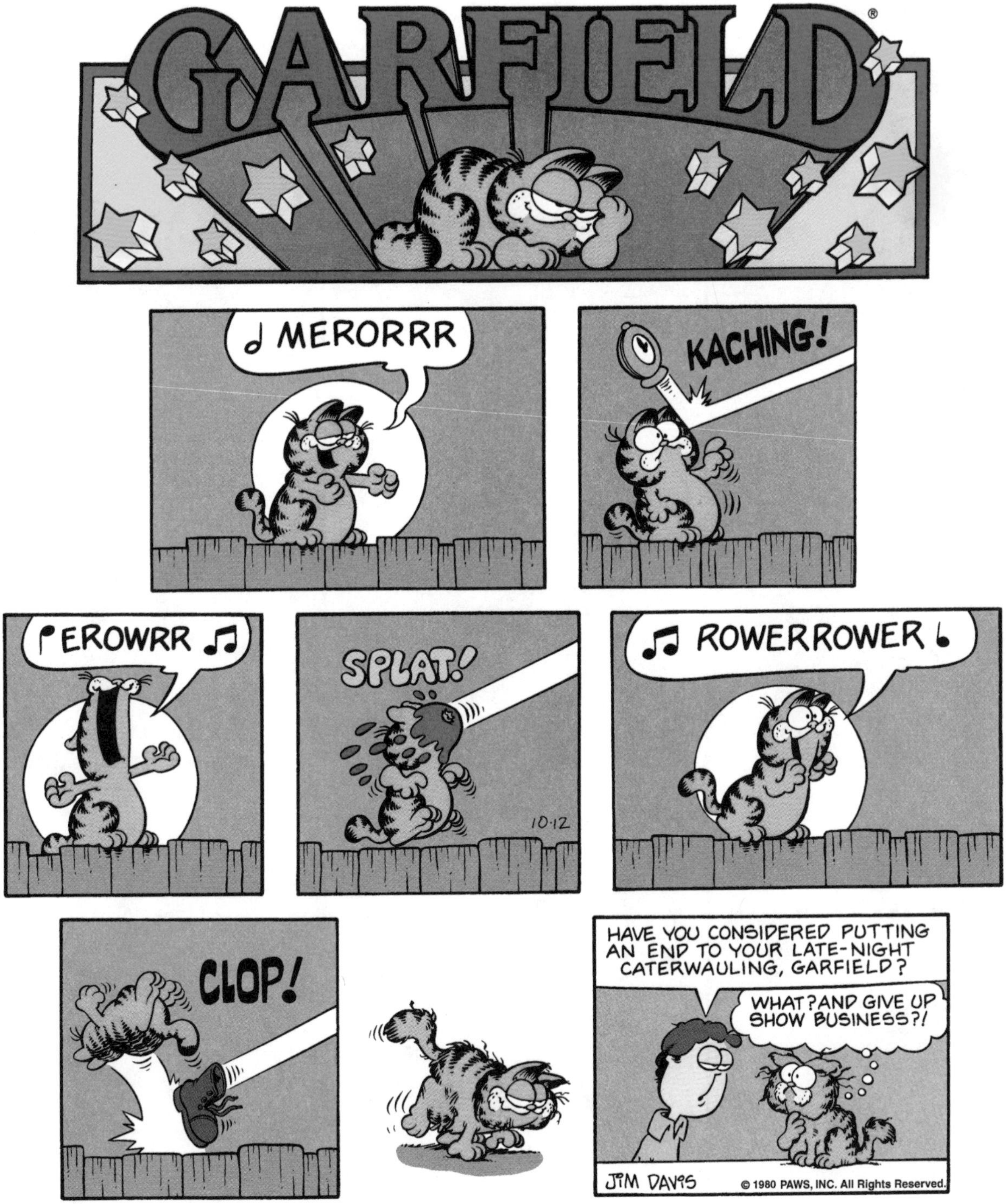
GARFIELD®
MERORRR
KACHING!
EROWRR
SPLAT!
ROWERROWER
CLOP!
HAVE YOU CONSIDERED PUTTING AN END TO YOUR LATE-NIGHT CATERWAULING, GARFIELD?
WHAT? AND GIVE UP SHOW BUSINESS?!
JIM DAVIS
© 1980 PAWS, INC. All Rights Reserved.

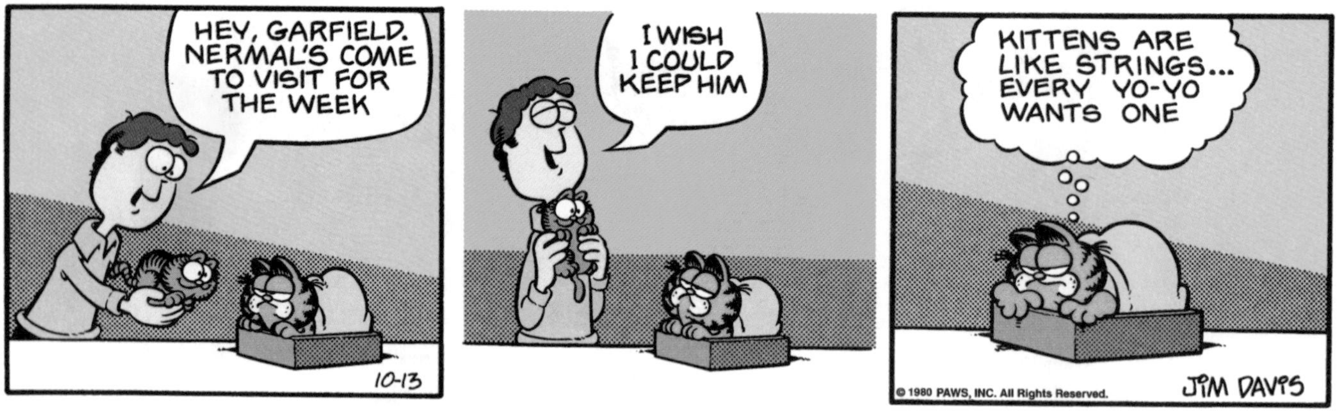
HEY, GARFIELD. NERMAL'S COME TO VISIT FOR THE WEEK
10-13
I WISH I COULD KEEP HIM
KITTENS ARE LIKE STRINGS... EVERY YO-YO WANTS ONE
© 1980 PAWS, INC. All Rights Reserved.
JIM DAVIS

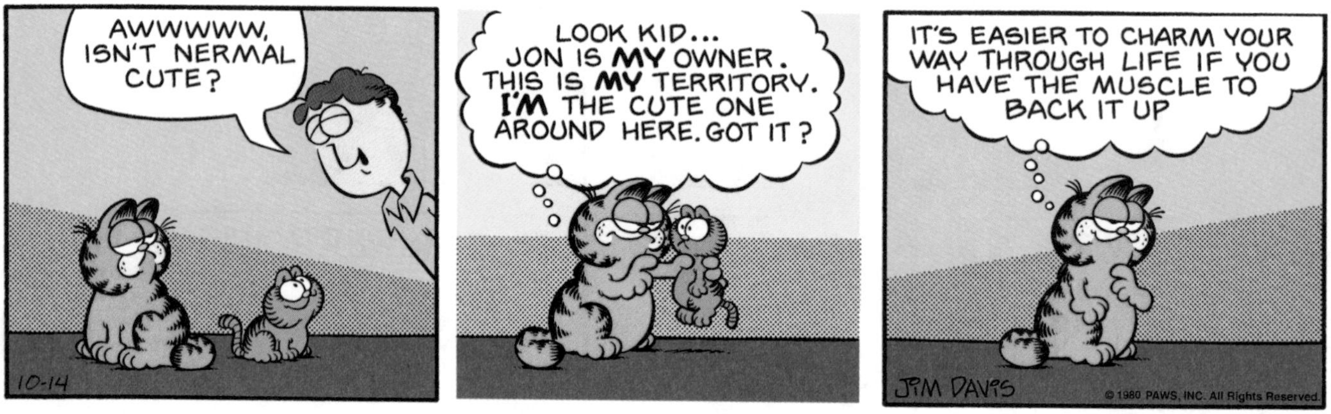
AWWWWW, ISN'T NERMAL CUTE?
10-14
LOOK KID... JON IS MY OWNER. THIS IS MY TERRITORY. I'M THE CUTE ONE AROUND HERE. GOT IT?
IT'S EASIER TO CHARM YOUR WAY THROUGH LIFE IF YOU HAVE THE MUSCLE TO BACK IT UP
JIM DAVIS
© 1980 PAWS, INC. All Rights Reserved.

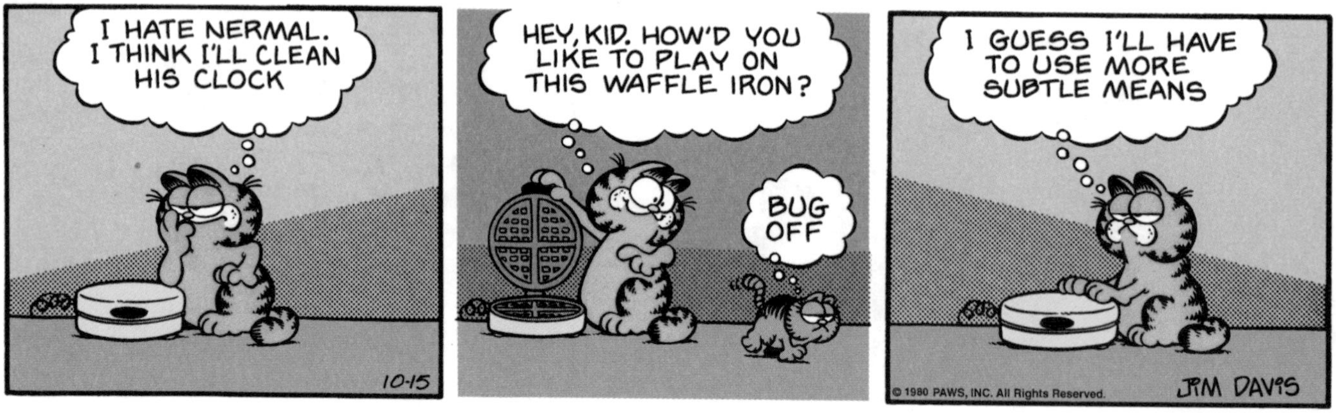
I HATE NERMAL. I THINK I'LL CLEAN HIS CLOCK
10-15
HEY, KID. HOW'D YOU LIKE TO PLAY ON THIS WAFFLE IRON?
BUG OFF
I GUESS I'LL HAVE TO USE MORE SUBTLE MEANS
© 1980 PAWS, INC. All Rights Reserved.
JIM DAVIS

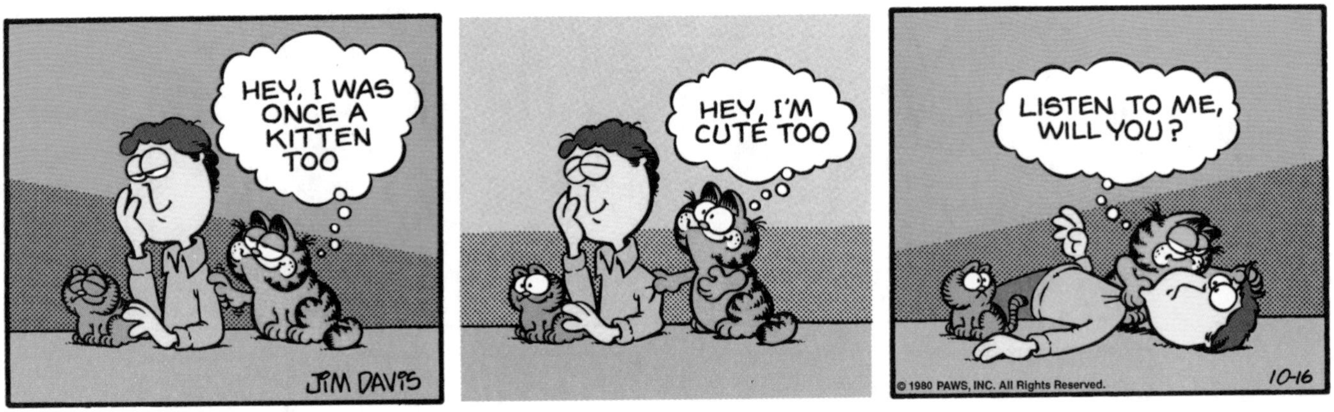
HEY, I WAS ONCE A KITTEN TOO
JIM DAVIS
HEY, I'M CUTE TOO
LISTEN TO ME, WILL YOU?
© 1980 PAWS, INC. All Rights Reserved.
10-16

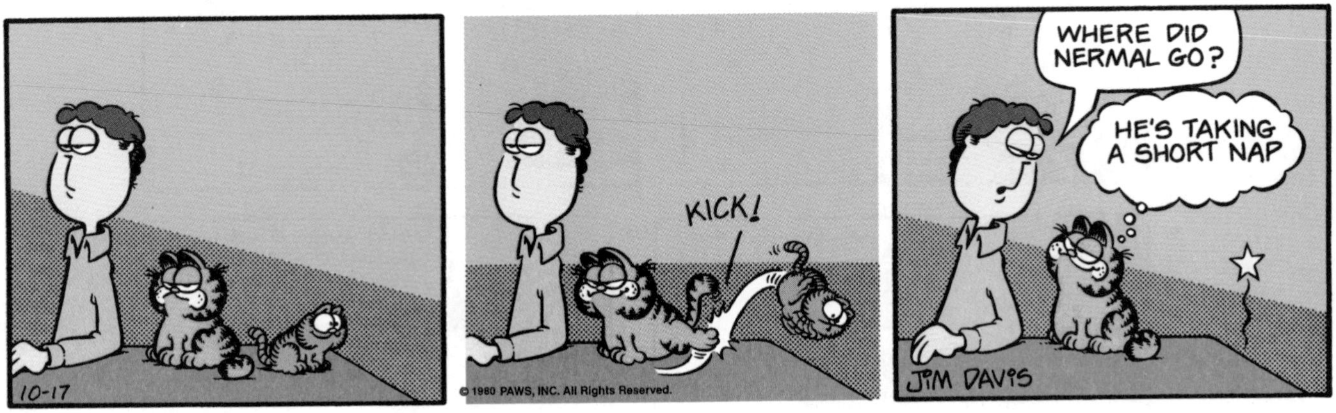
10-17
KICK!
© 1980 PAWS, INC. All Rights Reserved.
WHERE DID NERMAL GO?
HE'S TAKING A SHORT NAP
JIM DAVIS

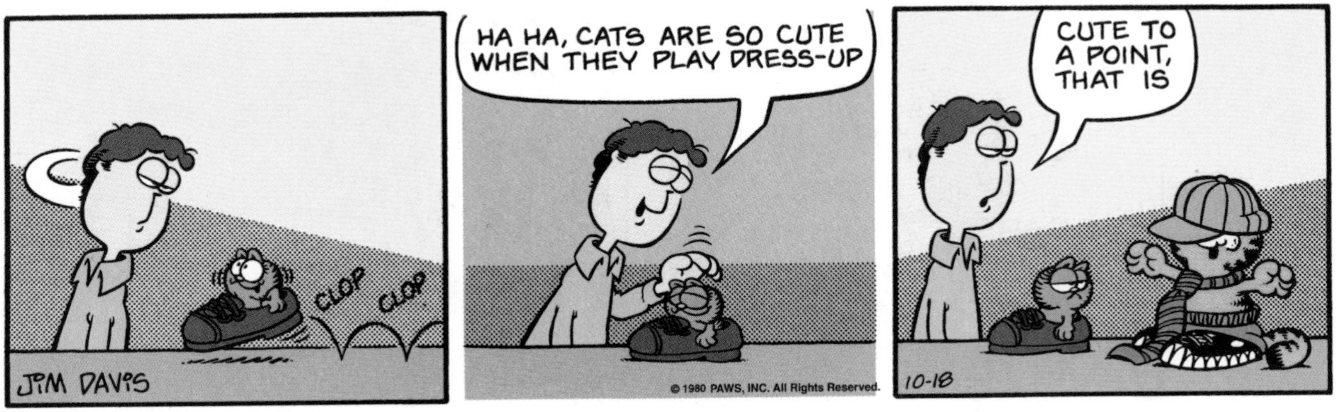
CLOP
CLOP
JIM DAVIS
HA HA, CATS ARE SO CUTE WHEN THEY PLAY DRESS-UP
© 1980 PAWS, INC. All Rights Reserved.
CUTE TO A POINT, THAT IS
10-18

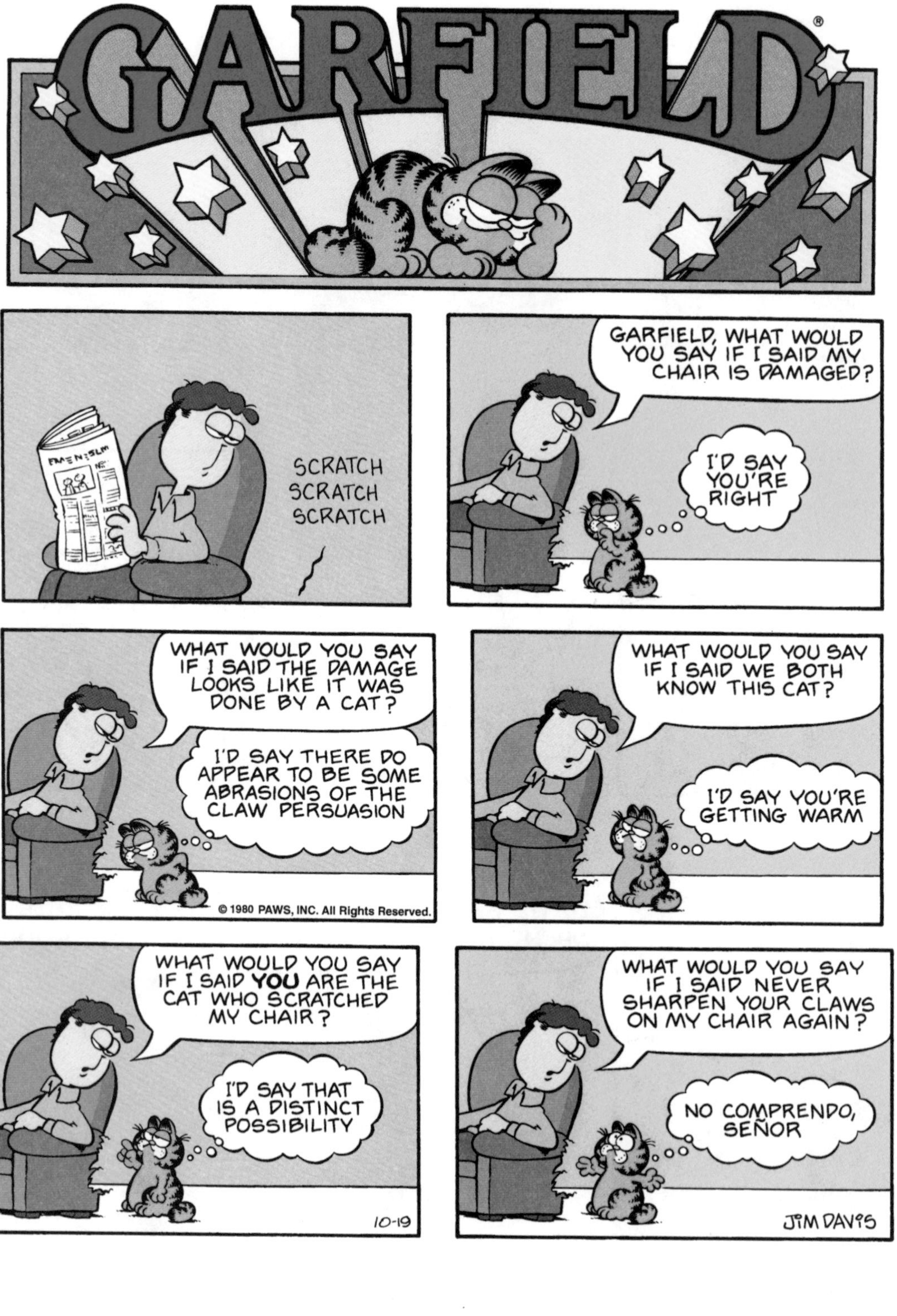
GARFIELD®
SCRATCH SCRATCH SCRATCH
GARFIELD, WHAT WOULD YOU SAY IF I SAID MY CHAIR IS DAMAGED?
I'D SAY YOU'RE RIGHT
WHAT WOULD YOU SAY IF I SAID THE DAMAGE LOOKS LIKE IT WAS DONE BY A CAT?
I'D SAY THERE DO APPEAR TO BE SOME ABRASIONS OF THE CLAW PERSUASION
© 1980 PAWS, INC. All Rights Reserved.
WHAT WOULD YOU SAY IF I SAID WE BOTH KNOW THIS CAT?
I'D SAY YOU'RE GETTING WARM
WHAT WOULD YOU SAY IF I SAID **YOU** ARE THE CAT WHO SCRATCHED MY CHAIR?
I'D SAY THAT IS A DISTINCT POSSIBILITY
10-19
WHAT WOULD YOU SAY IF I SAID NEVER SHARPEN YOUR CLAWS ON MY CHAIR AGAIN?
NO COMPRENDO, SEÑOR
JIM DAVIS

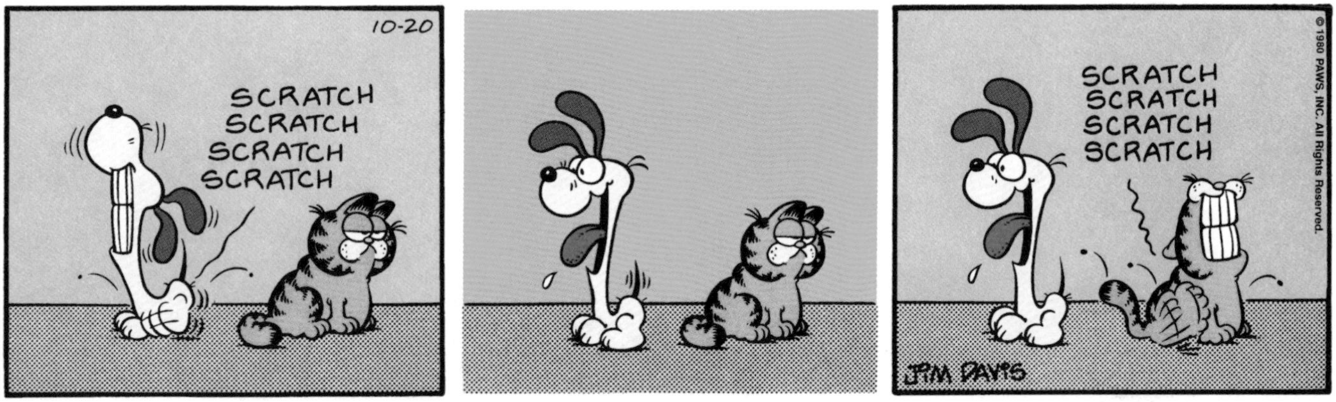
10-20
SCRATCH SCRATCH SCRATCH SCRATCH
SCRATCH SCRATCH SCRATCH SCRATCH
© 1980 PAWS, INC. All Rights Reserved.
JIM DAVIS

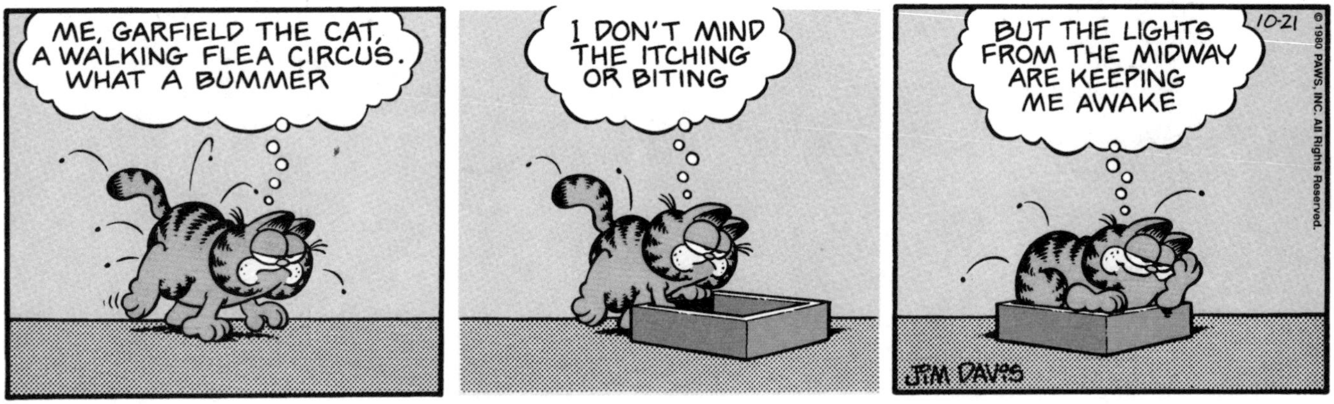
ME, GARFIELD THE CAT, A WALKING FLEA CIRCUS. WHAT A BUMMER
I DON'T MIND THE ITCHING OR BITING
10-21
BUT THE LIGHTS FROM THE MIDWAY ARE KEEPING ME AWAKE
© 1980 PAWS, INC. All Rights Reserved.
JIM DAVIS

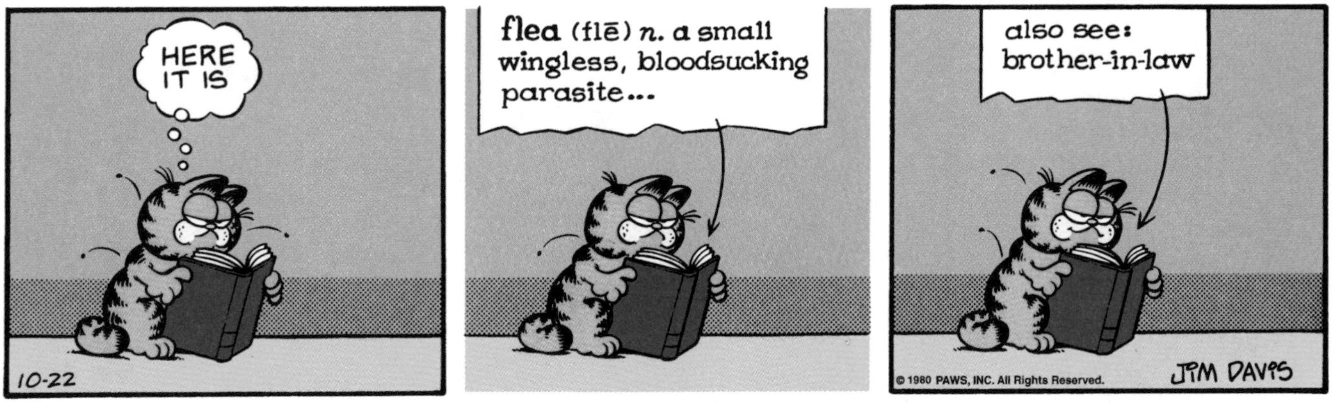
HERE IT IS
10-22
flea (flē) n. a small wingless, bloodsucking parasite...
also see: brother-in-law
© 1980 PAWS, INC. All Rights Reserved.
JIM DAVIS

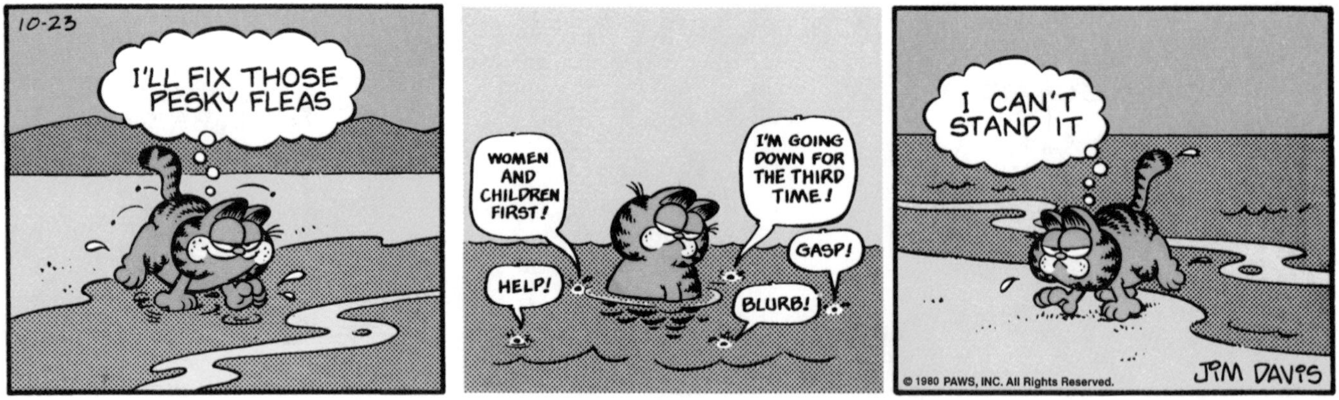
10-23
I'LL FIX THOSE PESKY FLEAS
WOMEN AND CHILDREN FIRST!
HELP!
I'M GOING DOWN FOR THE THIRD TIME!
GASP!
BLURB!
I CAN'T STAND IT
© 1980 PAWS, INC. All Rights Reserved.
JIM DAVIS

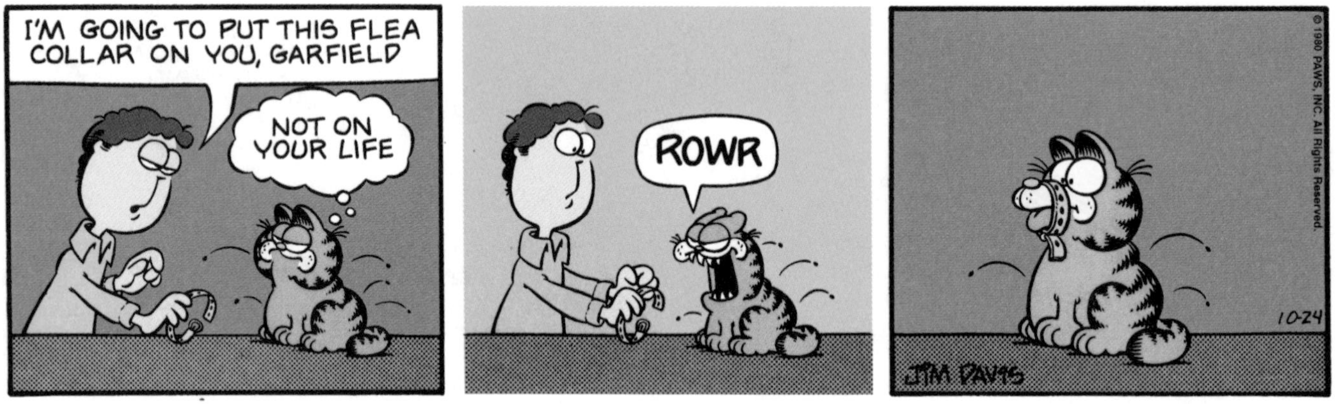
I'M GOING TO PUT THIS FLEA COLLAR ON YOU, GARFIELD
NOT ON YOUR LIFE
ROWR
© 1980 PAWS, INC. All Rights Reserved.
10-24
JIM DAVIS

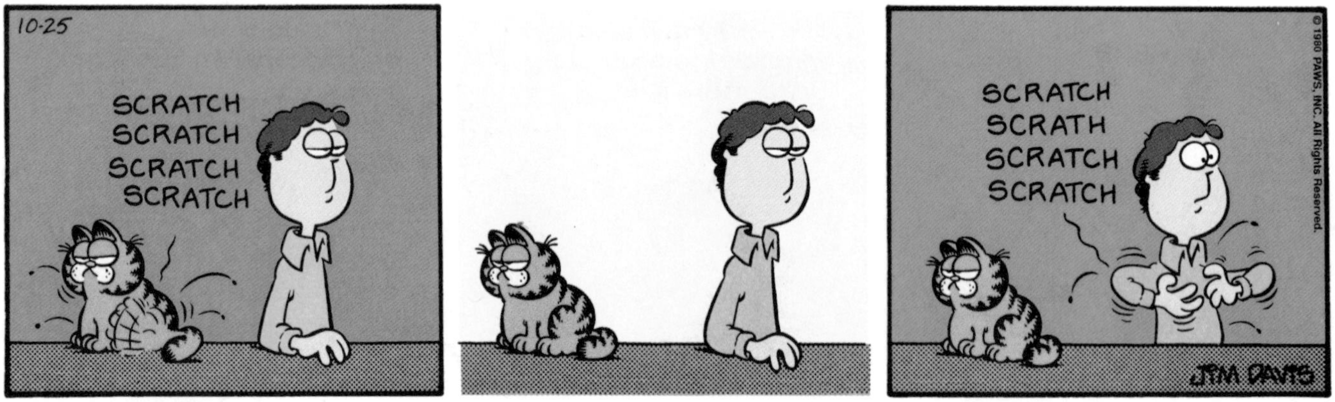
10-25
SCRATCH
SCRATCH
SCRATCH
SCRATCH
SCRATCH
SCRATH
SCRATCH
SCRATCH
© 1980 PAWS, INC. All Rights Reserved.
JIM DAVIS

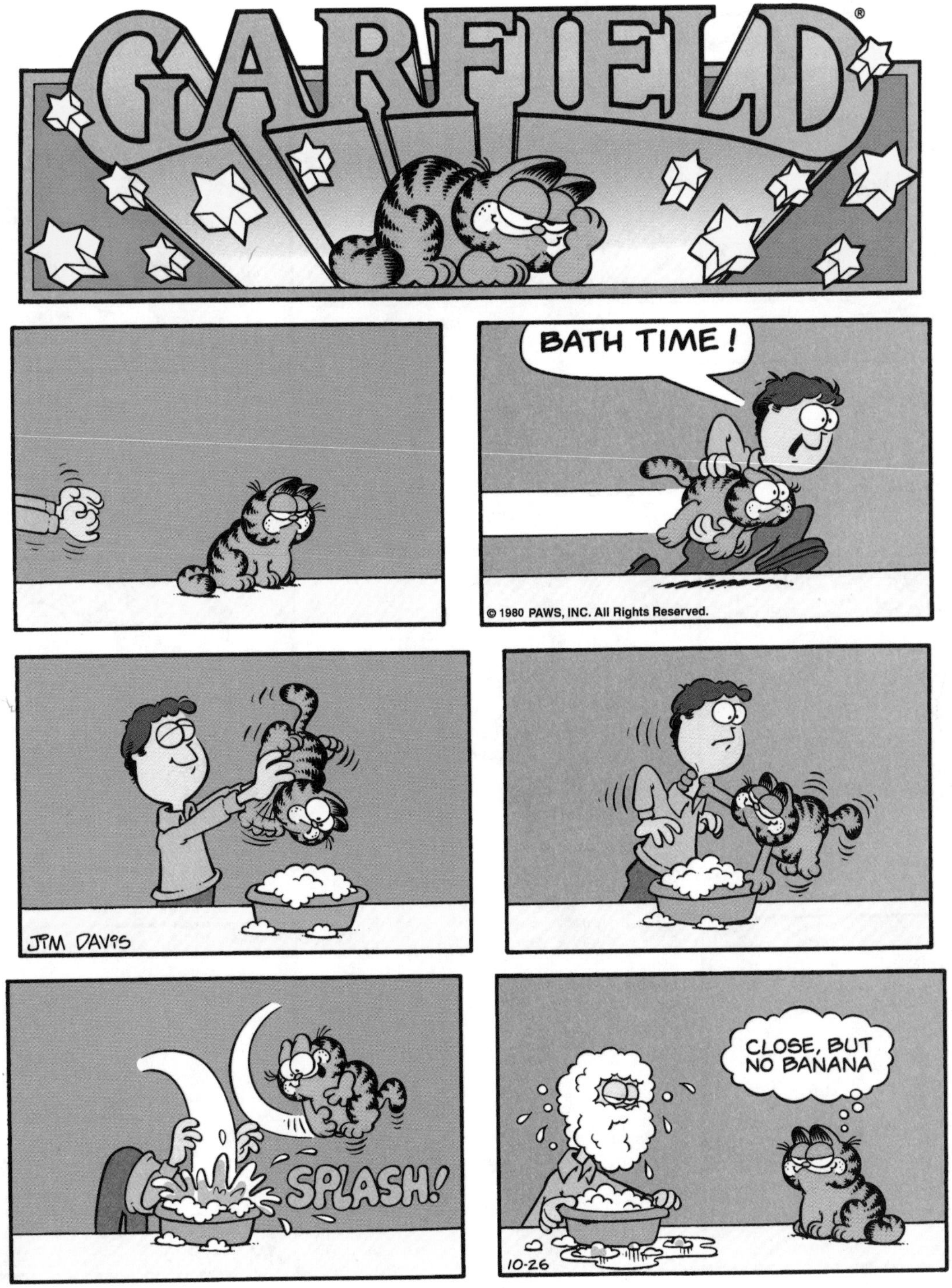
GARFIELD
BATH TIME!
© 1980 PAWS, INC. All Rights Reserved.
JIM DAVIS
SPLASH!
CLOSE, BUT NO BANANA
10-26

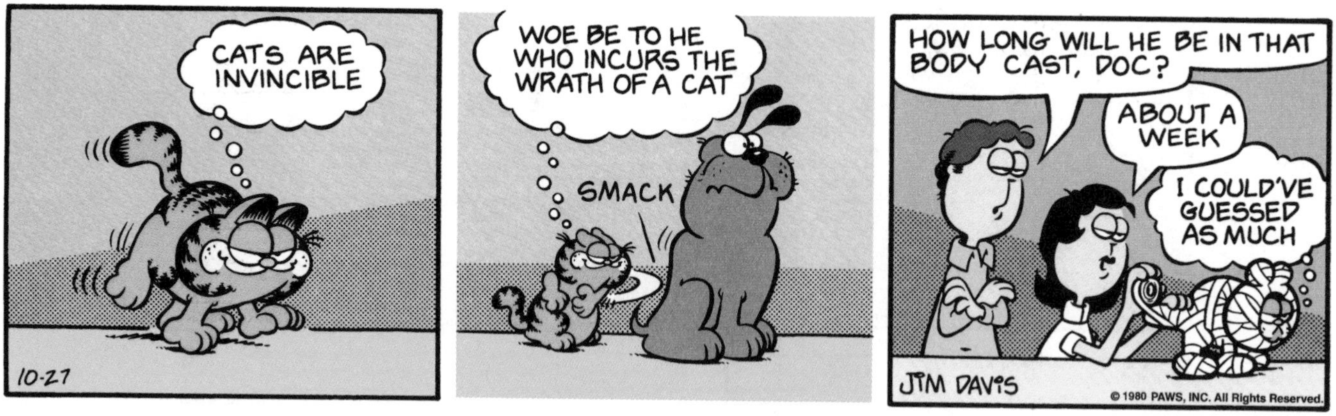
CATS ARE INVINCIBLE
10-27
WOE BE TO HE WHO INCURS THE WRATH OF A CAT
SMACK
HOW LONG WILL HE BE IN THAT BODY CAST, DOC?
ABOUT A WEEK
I COULD'VE GUESSED AS MUCH
JIM DAVIS
© 1980 PAWS, INC. All Rights Reserved.

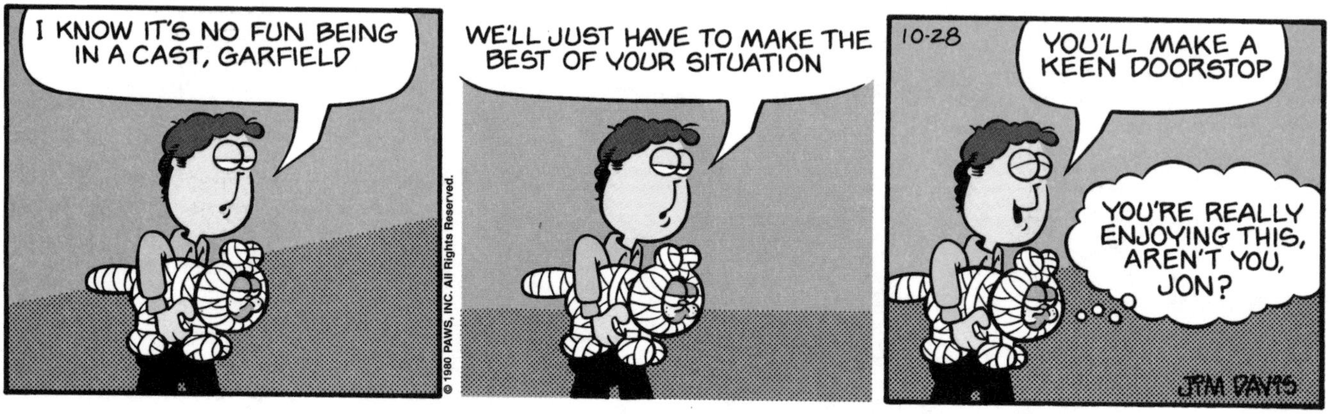
I KNOW IT'S NO FUN BEING IN A CAST, GARFIELD
© 1980 PAWS, INC. All Rights Reserved.
WE'LL JUST HAVE TO MAKE THE BEST OF YOUR SITUATION
10-28
YOU'LL MAKE A KEEN DOORSTOP
YOU'RE REALLY ENJOYING THIS, AREN'T YOU, JON?
JIM DAVIS

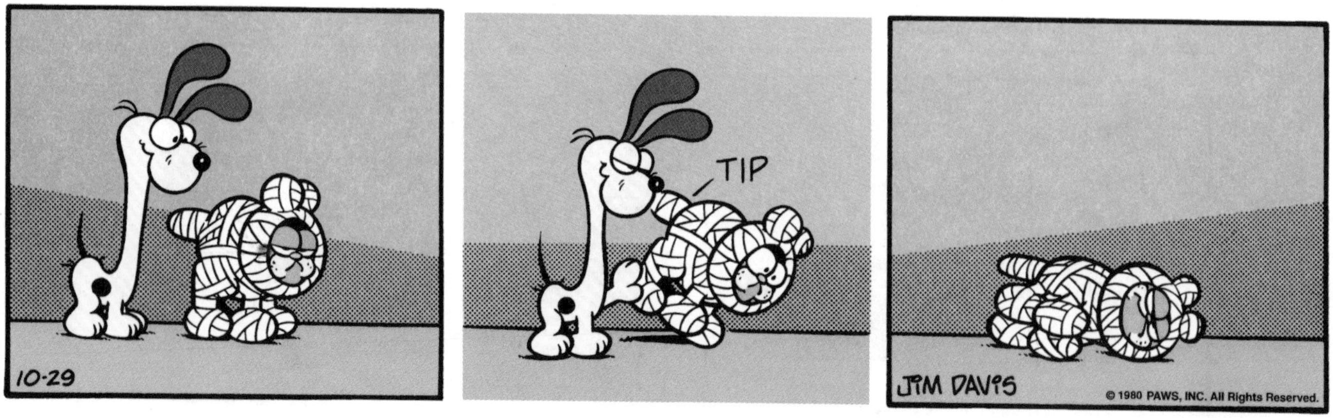
10-29
TIP
JIM DAVIS
© 1980 PAWS, INC. All Rights Reserved.

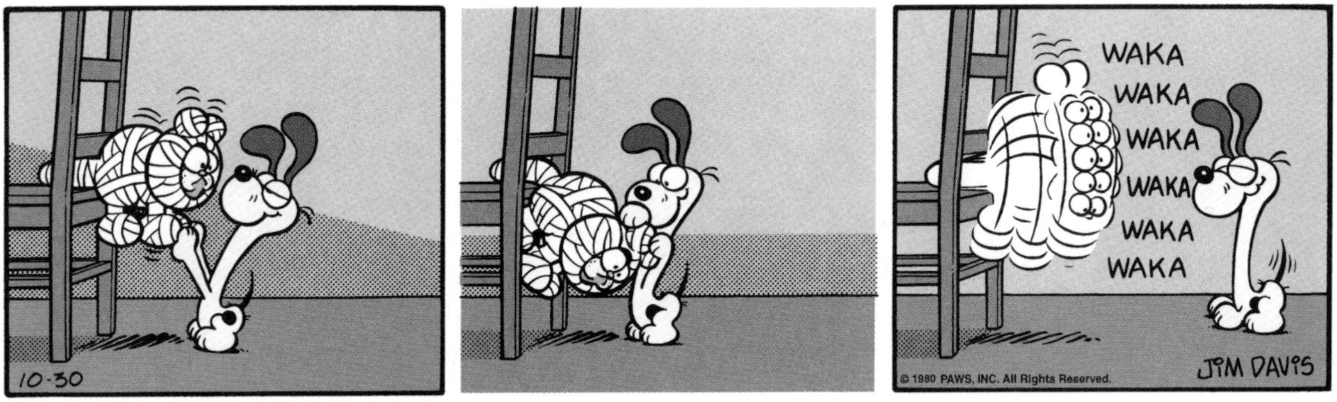
10-30
WAKA
WAKA
WAKA
WAKA
WAKA
WAKA
© 1980 PAWS, INC. All Rights Reserved.
JIM DAVIS

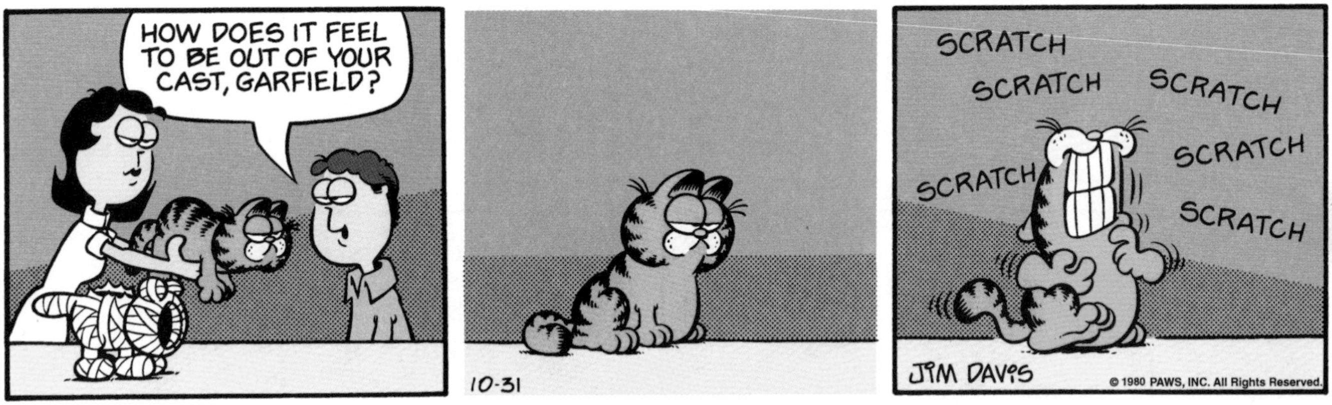
HOW DOES IT FEEL TO BE OUT OF YOUR CAST, GARFIELD?
10-31
SCRATCH
SCRATCH
SCRATCH
SCRATCH
SCRATCH
SCRATCH
JIM DAVIS
© 1980 PAWS, INC. All Rights Reserved.

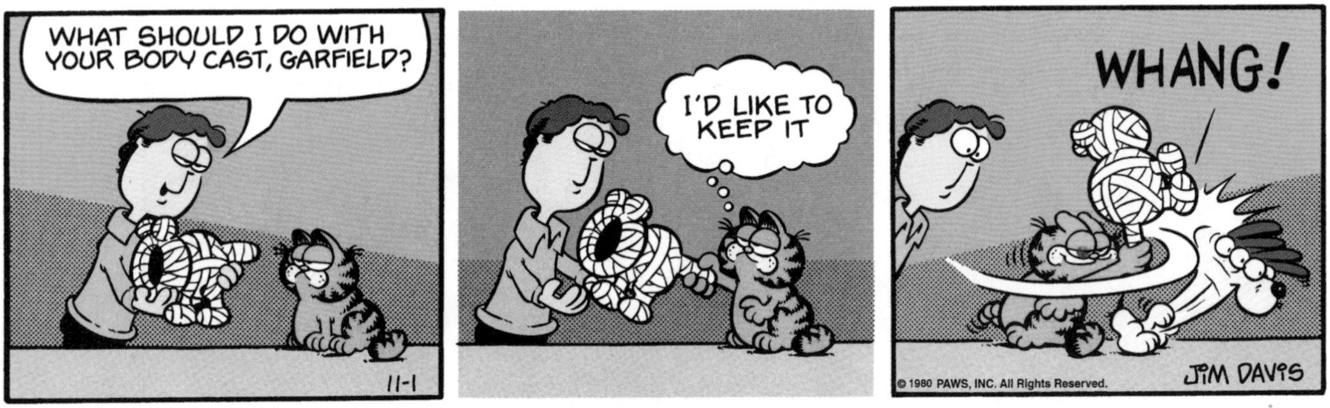
WHAT SHOULD I DO WITH YOUR BODY CAST, GARFIELD?
11-1
I'D LIKE TO KEEP IT
WHANG!
© 1980 PAWS, INC. All Rights Reserved.
JIM DAVIS

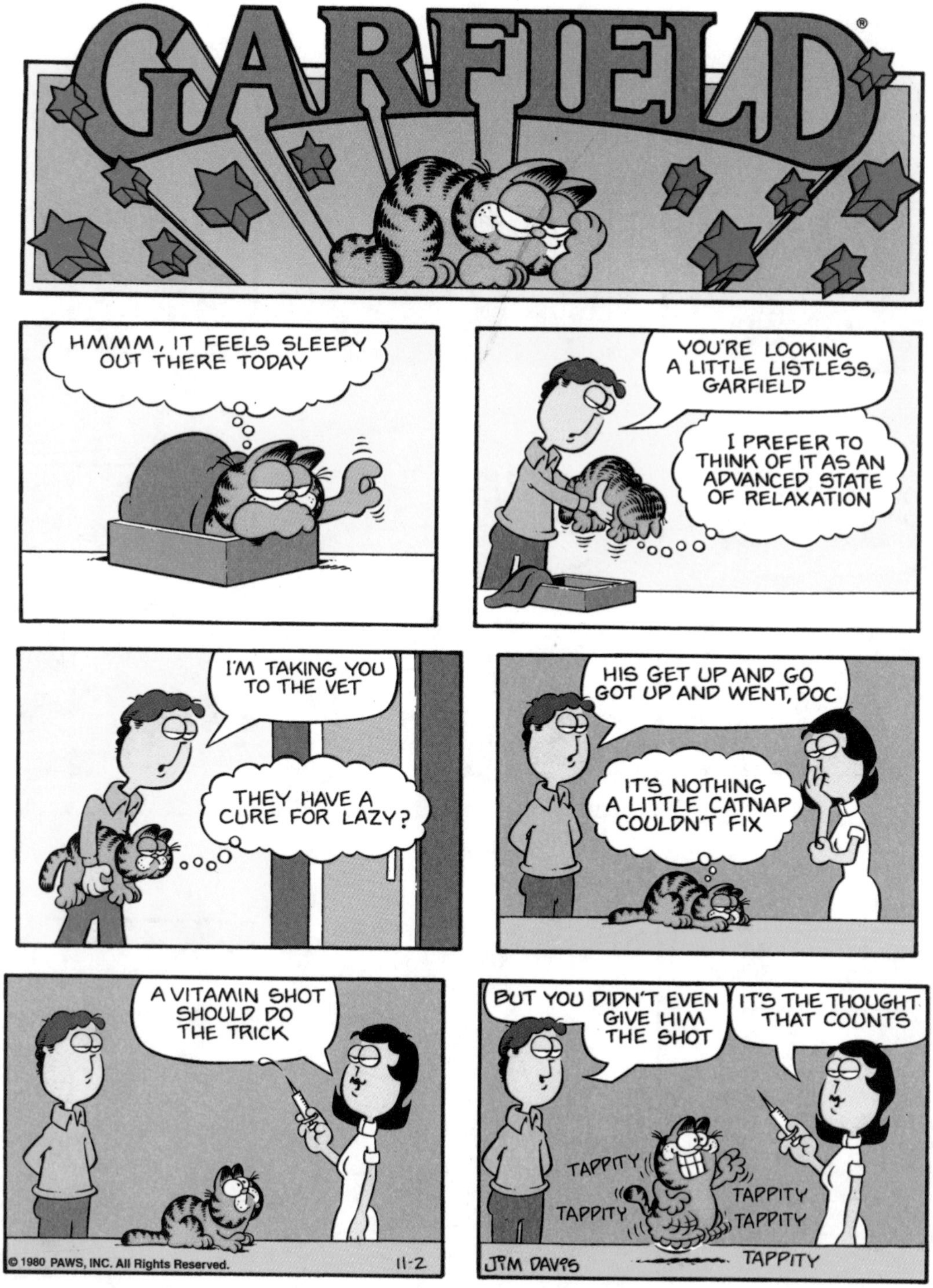
GARFIELD®
HMMM, IT FEELS SLEEPY OUT THERE TODAY
YOU'RE LOOKING A LITTLE LISTLESS, GARFIELD
I PREFER TO THINK OF IT AS AN ADVANCED STATE OF RELAXATION
I'M TAKING YOU TO THE VET
THEY HAVE A CURE FOR LAZY?
HIS GET UP AND GO GOT UP AND WENT, DOC
IT'S NOTHING A LITTLE CATNAP COULDN'T FIX
A VITAMIN SHOT SHOULD DO THE TRICK
© 1980 PAWS, INC. All Rights Reserved.
11-2
BUT YOU DIDN'T EVEN GIVE HIM THE SHOT
IT'S THE THOUGHT THAT COUNTS
TAPPITY
TAPPITY
TAPPITY
TAPPITY
TAPPITY
JIM DAVIS